Films That Spill

Films That Spill

••

Beyond the Cinema of Transgression

MARIE SOPHIE BECKMANN

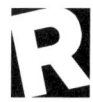

Rutgers University Press
New Brunswick, Camden, and Newark, New Jersey
London and Oxford

Rutgers University Press is a department of Rutgers, The State University of New Jersey, one of the leading public research universities in the nation. By publishing worldwide, it furthers the University's mission of dedication to excellence in teaching, scholarship, research, and clinical care.

Library of Congress Cataloging-in-Publication Data

Names: Beckmann, Marie Sophie, author.
Title: Films that spill : beyond the cinema of transgression / Marie Sophie Beckmann.
Description: New Brunswick, Camden, and Newark, New Jersey : Rutgers University Press, 2025. | Includes bibliographical references and index.
Identifiers: LCCN 2024040140 | ISBN 9781978839656 (paperback) | ISBN 9781978839663 (hardcover) | ISBN 9781978839670 (epub) | ISBN 9781978839687 (pdf)
Subjects: LCSH: Experimental films—History and criticism. | Experimental art—History and criticism. | Transgression (Ethics) in art. | Motion pictures—Aesthetics. | LCGFT: Film criticism. | Art criticism.
Classification: LCC PN1995.9.E96 B43 2025 | DDC 791.43/611—dc23/eng/20240912
LC record available at https://lccn.loc.gov/2024040140

A British Cataloging-in-Publication record for this book is available from the British Library.

Copyright © 2025 by Marie Sophie Beckman
All rights reserved
No part of this book may be reproduced or utilized in any form or by any means, electronic or mechanical, or by any information storage and retrieval system, without written permission from the publisher. Please contact Rutgers University Press, 106 Somerset Street, New Brunswick, NJ 08901. The only exception to this prohibition is "fair use" as defined by U.S. copyright law.

References to internet websites (URLs) were accurate at the time of writing. Neither the author nor Rutgers University Press is responsible for URLs that may have expired or changed since the manuscript was prepared.

∞ The paper used in this publication meets the requirements of the American National Standard for Information Sciences—Permanence of Paper for Printed Library Materials, ANSI Z39.48-1992.

rutgersuniversitypress.org

For B and B

Contents

	Introduction: Spilling/Containment	1
1	Forgetting the Cinema of Transgression	20
2	Downtown Images	41
3	Film Happens	68
4	Afterlife Formats	101
	Coda: Keep on Spilling	129
	Appendix	131
	Acknowledgments	133
	Notes	135
	Bibliography	163
	Index	175

Films That Spill

Introduction

Spilling/Containment

The Old Stories Are Getting Boring

In early 2012, I visited the exhibition *You Killed Me First: The Cinema of Transgression* at KW Institute for Contemporary Art in Berlin. The title sounded unfamiliar but had an exciting ring to it. Wandering through the darkened spaces of what used to be a margarine factory and is now a multilevel exhibition space in Berlin's central district, I spent a Saturday afternoon watching projections of short films that I found equally fascinating and repulsive. As a sensitive viewer who usually shies away from horror, splatter, or any kind of disturbing visual content, I remember having to force myself not to look away as wrists were slit open, blood was spilled, rats were dissected, gunshots were fired, and rape scenes seemed a little too real. Yet I was also drawn to the DIY spirit of these films, with their noisy post-punk soundtracks, shaky cinematography, flickering filmstrips, silly acting, and wacky narratives. Their overall messiness and rawness intrigued me. Despite their often gruesome content, these films looked like they had been fun to make, which made them fun to watch.

From the exhibition's information booklet, which itself looked like a punk zine, I learned that these films were made by a "group of filmmakers [that] emerged from the Lower East Side, New York, whose shared aims Nick Zedd later postulated in the Cinema of Transgression Manifesto." The booklet included an excerpt from that manifesto, which stated that the movement proposed "to go beyond all limits set or prescribed by taste, morality or any other traditional value system shackling the minds of men."[1] Although this seemed like an annoyingly polemic statement, one that I thought these films did not need, I left the exhibition buzzing, thrilled to have discovered something new, something I had never heard of, let alone seen. Needless to say, I wanted to know more.

Though the Cinema of Transgression (CoT) was a novelty to me (and apparently to the art world as well), I was surprised to find almost nothing in the way of scholarly research about it. Prior to the 2012 group exhibition, the only substantial documentation was the 1995 publication *Deathtripping: The Cinema of Transgression* (Jack Sargeant, Creation Books) and the 2007 documentary *Llik Your Idols* (Angélique Bosio). Both consist largely of interviews with participants in the New York Downtown scene from which the CoT emerged, providing a dense oral history but little critical historical contextualization and no theoretical reflection, though a few other accounts can be found in writings on underground or Downtown film culture. For instance, in his book *Subversion: The Definitive History of Underground Cinema*, Duncan Reekie describes the CoT as part of a "resurgence" of American underground cinema after it had lost its radical momentum in the 1970s and the avant-garde had institutionalized itself as the dominant form of experimental film.[2] The CoT is also often discussed in correlation with the more thoroughly historicized No Wave Cinema for their shared "blend of documentary realism (the result of location shooting) and fictional narrative," "significance of sexuality and violence," and "successful harmony of performances, music, and scripts," as Matthew Yokosbosky writes in a text republished in *Captured: A Film/Video History of the Lower East Side*, the edited collection compiled by Clayton Patterson, himself a filmmaker and Downtown scene participant.[3]

In that volume, three texts deal specifically with the CoT, its founding myth, and its speculative, anecdotal historiography. In "Nick Zedd" by Nick Zedd, the filmmaker and editor of the zine *Underground Film Bulletin* introduces himself as having "spearheaded the most controversial film movement of the 1980s, The Cinema of Transgression." The rest of his piece is a manifesto-like list of statements about the powers and potentials of film, such as "Laughter can be a useful tool in assaulting complacency" or "The idea that you have to tell a story is nonsense."[4] Even if these proclamations are not directly related to the CoT, their rigor inevitably draws a connection to the "controversial movement."

Casandra Stark Mele, on the other hand, shares her disillusionment with the CoT in her essay "Why I Left the 'Cinema of Transgression' Behind, or Why It Left Me." When she joined the scene—making films on the cheap, befriending other filmmakers, participating in screenings and festivals—she writes how she was thrilled to show her work alongside the "filmmakers who made up what I considered to be the New York underground film scene of the mid '80s." However, the vibrant and diverse scene "spiraled downward into a kind of conformity" and rigid definition, mainly through "self-gratifying and profit-driven demands of a few of the scene's over-dominating and controlling members." They demanded more violent, aggressive, and sexual content, rather than understanding transgression as Stark Mele did, that is, as going beyond the medium's form toward a "looser artistic expression of... underground film."[5]

Author Cricket Delembard then ponders the question "The Cinema of Transgression: Where Are They Now?" His recollection begins with a Nietzsche quote ("Who wishes to be creative, must first destroy and smash accepted values") and continues with a bold assertion: "The most radical movement of the 1980s was the Cinema of Transgression." The seeds, according to Delembard, were planted with the screening of Nick Zedd's Super 8 debut *They Eat Scum* on the Lower East Side in 1979. Delembard goes on to recount the wild ventures of the CoT's protagonists, who allegedly made films documenting days and nights filled with drugs and drink, sex and spectacle, camaraderie and breakups. He paints a picture of a movement that acted as much out of boredom as it did in response to censorship, police violence, or any presumed notions of morality. His text is followed by a note: "This story is apparently from the Cinema of Transgression Archives, ca. 1992. The veracity of the transgressions made in this story is left to the audience, as is with the other works of the Cinema of Transgression."[6] There is no further indication of what or whose archives hold this story. And even if the tone of the note is tongue in cheek, the fact that Delembard's anecdotal recollection appears alongside Zedd's self-promotion and Stark Mele's disillusioned text in a volume on the film and video history of the Lower East Side is significant. For the history of underground and avant-garde cinema, as Patricia Mellencamp has pointed out, often comes in the guise of "nostalgic documentations, circumscribed by intention, remembrance, and anecdote," which risks "an individualism of 'secret singularities' outside history, without politics, and thus without effect."[7] This is not to say that "slippery knowledge makers" like gossip, anecdotes, and rumors are dead ends in terms of criticality per se.[8] However, the borderline kitsch glorifications circulating around the CoT seem to be caught in a perpetual loop, rehashing and thus manifesting the tried and true tale of the aesthetic and formal transgressions of a male-dominated underground movement. It is not surprising, then, that the CoT's history—those old stories that are getting boring—reads as precisely that: a string of generally undisputed and vaguely contextualized statements by auteur-type filmmakers. The book by Sargeant, the documentary film by Bosio, the exhibition at KW, and all the other texts thus have one thing in common: they emphasize the supposedly transgressive character of the films, which in turn, following Zedd's manifesto, is interpreted as an era-specific political and moral revolt.

In the 1960s, there was already an appetite for multidisciplinary, multimedia experimentation. The integration of poetry, music, film, dance, and visual art into a single event was most famously and spectacularly realized in Andy Warhol's Exploding Plastic Inevitable. In the Downtown New York scene of the 1970s and 1980s, experimental theater, post-punk music, dance, performance, and Super 8 filmmaking continued to mix in nightclubs, private lofts, and performance venues, unraveling disciplinary boundaries. In the latter decade, however, the AIDS crisis and the increasing urban and "spiritual gentrification" of Lower Manhattan led to a significant shift in the cultural climate.[9] It was in this environment that those affiliated with the CoT collaboratively produced their low-budget Super 8 films. With a cast of scenesters, these films were screened at self-initiated festivals—often as part of performances or concerts—discussed in self-published zines, and often distributed informally on VHS tapes. The CoT's standard reception frames these films as documents of "a time when the fallout of a decrepit city manifested itself through the psyches of young and wild artists, musicians and filmmakers banging into each other in the scum drenched streets."[10] Though somewhat romanticized, such a statement is, of course, not entirely untrue. There is no question that the years of Ronald Reagan's administration and the burgeoning AIDS crisis were grim, that much of Downtown Manhattan had fallen into urban neglect, and that artists often responded to the resurgence of conservative morality and repressive politics with an art that sought first and foremost to shock and shake things up. Most accounts, however, say little about how these "young and wild artists, musicians and filmmakers" actually worked together and what kind of energy was generated by cross-disciplinary collaboration, while polemically recalling the subversive and transgressive agenda of this "movement"—clinging to the irritatingly hyperbolic words of the manifesto. Instead, the context of the scene and the dirty glamour of New York City, its bad-but-good old days only serve to imbue the films with a mystifying aura. The films have mostly been read as individual texts that feed into a larger narrative, with little attention paid to their various contexts of production, exhibition, and distribution or to the fact that, besides making films, those affiliated with the CoT and the larger scene around it were engaged in a messy intersection of artistic and social practices.

From these observations, questions developed that provide the starting point for *Films That Spill: Beyond the Cinema of Transgression*. How could something as entrenched as the concept of the Cinema of Transgression be set in motion again? What would happen if, for example, not only blood and sperm were to spill from the bodies on film but also, metaphorically speaking, the CoT itself were to spill over? At best, such a conceptual spillover could bring out the fascinating, even productive, messiness that has so far been contained by the tight framing of the movement's name, both in the sense of the many overlaps between artistic practices and scenes at the time and in how the films have always left their original context and circulated promiscuously ever since. It is precisely this dialectic of spilling and containment that will serve as the conceptual leitmotif and operational tool of this book.

Spilling: A Note on Method

To use the notion of spilling in a methodological sense, I am inspired by John Law's concept of messy methods. Rather than resorting to stabilizing, standardizing methods, Law suggests creating metaphors and images for what appears messy, that is, what appears unpredictable, complex, unspecific, manifold, or slippery and thus principally defies or destabilizes unifying definitions.[11] Law's proposal is based on a notion that comes from science and technology studies that states technologies and methods, as well as their applications, not only describe things but also help to produce them.[12] Applied to film and media studies, this means methods must be developed that do justice to the fact that films are by no means ahistorical, static objects, methods that acknowledge films' mutability, contextuality, and plurality. If these qualities are taken seriously, at least those approaches to film studies that imply that film begins and ends within its own frame are of limited use. (I will return to this point in more detail later.) Even terms such as multidisiciplinarity, interdisciplinarity, and transdisciplinarity (or multimediality, intermediality, and transmediality) predefine a certain mode of relation between disciplines and media. So why not make metaphors and images fruitful for film analysis by describing processes and movements rather than fixed states?

The notion of spilling lends itself perfectly to such an endeavor. It evokes associations with fluidity, transmission, disorder, and randomness. As such, it has little to do with the solid materiality that we usually ascribe to technical media in general and to film in particular, which is precisely why it can be used to conceive of film as a messy object that we encounter in temporary, often surprising formations and unexpected places, characterized, for instance, by its mobility and mutability. And since a spilling is both cause and effect of a certain disorder, it not only does not presuppose a predefined form or location but also deforms contours and destabilizes supposedly fixed categories. Objects, concepts, and meanings can spill over. A spilling, then, both lacks focus and intention and is also not bound to a single body. To put it another way, spilling is an articulation of shared agency.

Take the analogy of boiling milk. There is heat, a pot too small to contain the bubbling contents, and then the milk itself, which expands its body until it flows in all directions, leaving pale white patches of unpredictable shape. It follows that spilling, which is neither intentional nor completely random, requires the right conditions to occur. In most cases, this means accepting a loss of control, because "if you want to create a stain, then suitable conditions must be created so that it can arise automatically, autopoietically. The stain producer must allow the material to splash, smack, smear. Strong emotions . . . seem to be a suitable means of doing this."[13] Note how the art historian Friedrich Weltzien speaks here of allowing the material itself to act; the "stain producer" only provides the impetus. Perhaps a quick movement of the arm will cause the paint to fly from the brush, or an abrupt turn of the body will immediately knock over the entire paint bucket.

Of course, boiling milk or splashing paint are more obvious and literal visualizations of spilling. For a more abstract example of what can spill and how, we can turn to the writing process of André Breton and Philippe Soupault's *The Magnetic Fields* (*Les Champs Magnétiques*, 1919), considered the first piece of Surrealist literature. As described by Esther Leslie, the duo employed a mode of automatic writing to "navigate their own unconsciousness." She goes on to say that "the poetics that was inaugurated in these unconscious drillings might be well imagined as a kind of liquid, a dripping of words out of the mind onto the page. Dripping is an impersonal mode of poetic production, without the genius of a controlling, originating individual.... This poetic splurge streamed from a tap turned on until there was no more flow left."[14]

A second example from the field of writing is Alexis Pauline Gumbs's poetry collection *Spill: Scenes of Black Feminist Fugitivity*. In the preface, Gumbs explains that her "writing started to spill out one day" when she listened to Black feminist scholar Hortense Spillers at a workshop. Gumbs was inspired not only by what Spillers wrote but also by how her words "invited affect." Following this invitation, she began to pull sentences from Spillers's essays in *Black, White, and in Color* to place them in a new context, only to find that "context couldn't take them at all. Which is to say that when I turned these phrases, doors opened and everyone came through. All the black women writers Spillers wrote about and didn't write about.... The project took over and offered scene after scene out of time and invited voices and settings that I can't claim to have invented."[15]

The spill takes on multiple meanings here. The playful shortening of the name Hortense Spillers, to whom the book pays homage, becomes a poetic leitmotif and a literary operation. It is not only her own writing and Spillers's phrases that turn out to be uncontainable by any kind of context; it is also that the text itself has created space for "everyone to come through." The resulting collection of essays thus shows how to write not "about" but "with." As a reviewer for *Bitch* magazine put it: "Her writing blurs the lines between past, present, and future.... Gumbs' pages do more than speak, they spill, 'reveal,' 'induce falling,' 'flood.'"[16]

From all these examples, a certain scheme can be deduced. There is an interplay of objects, bodies, practices, and energy that creates a force that cannot be contained, leading to a spilling (of milk, of paint, of words) that not only transcends a definable vessel, form, or even time itself as it disperses but perhaps also becomes formless(ness) itself. Here formless is, according to Georges Bataille, "not only an adjective having a given meaning, but a term that serves to bring things down in the world, generally requiring that each thing have its form.... Affirming that the universe resembles nothing and is only formless amounts to saying that the universe is something like a ... spit."[17] The formless, then, has a purely operative existence; it does rather than is. Not only does it describe neither content nor preconceived form, but it is itself transition, transformation, or deformation, thus enabling declassification in the dual sense of productive degradation and taxonomic disorder.[18] The order-challenging power of the formless is comparable to the potential, I would argue, inherent in spilling. Like the formless spit that Johanna Schaffer so beautifully describes as an "agent of wetness," spilling could bring about a "ruinous softening"[19] of traditional forms and hierarchies. We can thus also think of such an overflow as a form of excess that, in signifying the unproductive, the nonsensical, and the residual, constitutes the rejected or impossible. After all, "where there is dirt there is a system."[20] The mess caused by a spilling (which is itself a kind of disorder) hence always and necessarily implies the possibility of being cleaned, removed, or contained so as to maintain order, both in a visual and structural sense.

Containment therefore has the opposite effect; it selects, organizes, preserves, and stabilizes. Unlike a spilling, containment is rarely accidental but more often "an active strategy for accomplishing goals" and thus a mode of power.[21] As Brooke Erin Duffy and Jeremy Packer write in their brilliant essay on Tupperware as container media, "Even in its most banal form, . . . containment preserves boundaries and preserves content as a means of addressing an imagined future. In its selection mode, it functions to determine what belongs and what does not. In its storage mode, it serves to maintain a fixed relation in time. . . . It modulates to maintain the boundary between outside and inside that is expected to occur in the temporal horizon."[22] Similarly, a containment operated by a concept like the CoT serves to delimit individual media and disciplines as well as to place films within a specific historical narrative.

With this in mind, it may appear tempting to frame spilling as a strategy of resistance, and of course this connection is not entirely implausible. After all, the disorder, deformation, and fluidity that spillings entail inherently resist what might provide orientation and stability but which is often restrictive: fastidious order, constricting form, arbitrary boundaries. I want to be careful, however, not to tie the notion of spilling to evaluative categories, that is, to claim that one process (an overflow) is always "good" and the other (a containment) is always "bad." Spilling is not inherently subversive. I am more interested in illuminating the respective interactions, contexts, and effects of containment and spilling in relation to the history of the CoT as a concept as well as to the films it seeks to describe—especially since, as I have already suggested, they are transgressive above all in the sense that they spill over in terms of their disciplinary classification and circulation, as well as on a visual, narrative, and formal level.

Excess, Expansion

The bodies shown in the films are usually pushed to their physical limits; they function both as objects and as agents of symbolic transgressions in the form of sexual and violent acts. In Bataille's terms, these bodies expend themselves and thereby necessarily extend themselves through destructive activities.[23] Bodies engage in orgiastic bodily excess, and grotesque, fantastic, and polysexual bodies spill over concepts of singularity and gender. In Nick Zedd's *The Bogus Man* (1980), for example, a fleshy figure with shiny pink lips, large breasts, and a round belly dances in front of the camera, alternately spreading their hairless labia or swinging their sparkling blue strap-on. This character, named Dee Dee Lux, was created by trans artist Greer Lankton, who wears a full-body costume in the film, as she occasionally did in everyday life as well.[24] Lankton (1958–1996) was a key figure in the East Village art scene of the 1980s, known for the dolls, ranging from miniature to life-size, that she constructed from coat hangers, scraps of fabric, glass eyes, and tights in the likeness of her friends, fictional characters, or celebrities.

Visually, the CoT films are usually dominated by flesh, bare skin, and bodily fluids; they present a "body spectacle," in Linda Williams's sense, that, interestingly, aims at both disgust and attraction.[25] A graphic example is Tessa Hughes-Freeland and Annabel Lee's *Dirty* (1993). Loosely based on the introductory chapter of *Le Bleu du Ciel*, the 1957 novel by Georges Bataille, the short film presents the viewer with the story of a young woman named Dirty who becomes increasingly drunk over the course of an evening at a hotel bar. Back in her room, her makeup runny, her hair disheveled, she continues to drink with the hotel staff until she urinates and defecates with indifference in front of them, much to their horror.

And while some films follow a kind of loose narrative, others remain fragmentary, resisting narrative continuity or revealing their constructed nature. For example, in *Bubble People* (1982) and *Totem of the Depraved* (1983), dialogues between filmmaker Ela Troyano and the actors become audible, and members of the crew enter the frame with spotlights, manuscripts, and props. One might even speak of a "generic overspill," as CoT films tend to spill over their vaguely defined genre categories of underground or experimental film into commercial niche genres such as exploitation, splatter, science fantasy, and porn.[26] Nick Zedd's episodic *War Is Menstrual Envy* (1990–1992), for example, can be understood as a postapocalyptic science fiction fantasy with its graphic depictions of bodily deformities and mutilations, and Richard Kern's films, for example *The Evil Cameraman* (1986–1990) or *Submit to Me* (1986), feature both an abundance of nudity and explicit BDSM scenes. Rendering the act of viewing disturbing and painful, many of these films are in the tradition of "unwatchable films" that stretches back to early modernist and experimental cinema—of which Luis Buñuel's famously horrifying *Un chien andalou* (1929) is perhaps the prime example—and continues into the present with transgressive representations of sex and violence in films by Michael Haneke, Gaspar Noé, and Lars von Trier.[27]

The term *spilling* can be used to acknowledge these excessive qualities while avoiding association with the more familiar descriptions of being taboo breaking or boundary crossing. For when transgressive film is discussed, the notion of transgression is often simplistically understood as a binary pattern of opposition and confrontation, either in the sense of an avant-garde that, as the "other" of dominant culture, confirms rather than challenges it or as a destructive transition into a space beyond socially accepted aesthetics, behaviors, and cultural expressions.[28] Yet the theoretical and philosophical history of the concept of transgression is far more complex. In Nietzsche, Bataille, and Foucault, transgression admittedly refers to sex and violence but also to forms of bodily excess and ecstasy that expose the arbitrariness of morality and the limits of productivity.[29] The crucial difference between this and the standard interpretation of transgression as opposition is that they understand it as a relational, processual, and correlative act, which in its compensatory function is constitutive for social and subject formation. Thus, instead of referring antithetically to a limit, transgression, in their sense, is necessarily tied to its continuation: "The limit and transgression depend on each other for whatever density of being they possess: a limit could not exist if it were absolutely uncrossable and, reciprocally, transgression would be pointless if it merely crossed a limit composed of illusions and shadows."[30]

This notion of transgression, however, is usually reduced to supposedly radical gestures of provocation and romanticized as a search for absolute truth, as exemplified by "The Cinema of Transgression Manifesto." Spilling, on the other hand, is free of associations with individual intentions to break taboos. Instead, it evokes a nonoppositional, often even unintentional excessiveness that the films not only show but also are themselves implicated in. Rather than being confirmed by an asserted transgression, spillings put forms and boundaries into flux, in this case, especially those that concern the historical, analytical, and disciplinary boundaries of film as medium and cultural object.

Reframing the notion of transgression in this way, however, requires considering the sociohistorical and cultural context of the CoT's emergence. In the following section, I would like to do this by briefly introducing the terms "indisciplinarity" and "scene," and by sketching out how the modus operandi of the New York Downtown scene of the 1980s not only transcended the rigidity of artistic disciplines but also embraced the unruliness and disorder of sexuality and the body, especially in that era of AIDS and political conservatism.

Indisciplinary Tendencies

Lower Manhattan, New York City, the 1980s. What can be said? In January 1981 Ronald Reagan is elected president and shot nonfatally two months later. Downtown experimental post-punk band 3 Teens Kill 4, who took their name from a news headline, record a cover of Rufus's "Tell Me Something Good" and include audio clips from the newscast that reported on the assassination attempt: "Mrs. Reagan rushed to the hospital and the president jokingly told her, 'Honey, I forgot to duck'" and "He was wheeled into surgery, and he said to his doctors, 'I hope you're all Republicans!'" In July of that year, the *New York Times* publishes the headline RARE CANCER SEEN IN 41 HOMOSEXUALS.[31] By July 1982, the syndrome is officially known as AIDS. In October, the seventh edition of the large-scale exhibition Documenta, a major art world event, opens in Kassel, Germany, and Downtown graffiti artists Keith Haring and Jean-Michel Basquiat are on the list, bringing international visibility to their East Village scene. The infamous Downtown art and music venue Club 57 on St. Mark's Place closes "around 1983," the same year Trump Tower is completed in Midtown Manhattan.[32] In 1985, Nick Zedd announces the birth of a movement, the Cinema of Transgression, in his zine *Underground Film Bulletin*. In October 1986, Haring, described by the *New York Times* as an "American artist, who first made a name for himself decorating vacant spaces of the New York City subway system with graffiti but who now earns up to $50,000 for one canvas," paints a mural on the wall that divides West from East Berlin, which will fall three years later.[33] In the summer of 1987, the *Times* also observes that the "Art Boom Slows in the East Village," with galleries closing or moving to SoHo and Tribeca, largely due to rising rents in the increasingly gentrified East Village.[34] Andy Warhol, who epitomized the constant slide between art and business, pop and underground, dies in February 1987.[35] In the same year, President Reagan openly addresses AIDS for the first time, and the AIDS Coalition to Unleash Power (ACT UP) is founded in New York City. Its float in the annual New York City Gay Pride March of 1987 is "trimmed with barbed wire and driven by a man in a Ronald Reagan mask [and] represented an AIDS quarantine camp" and is followed by activists on foot holding SILENCE = DEATH placards.[36] More than 5,000 new cases of HIV infection are reported that same year.[37]

I do not list these events, major and minor, in terms of causality; much more could be said about this decade, which on a larger scale was marked by subliminal anxiety and a questionable spirit of progress and optimism. Rather than being read as representative of the United States in the 1980s, the events mentioned above highlight moments of significance to New York's subcultures as well as the gentrification and political shifts happening on both local and national scales. As such, they serve as points of reference for the years in which the Downtown scene experienced the onset of its urban and, in Sarah Schulman's words, "spiritual gentrification." In her book *The Gentrification of the Mind: Witness to a Lost Imagination*, Schulman reads the outbreak of AIDS and the valorization of Lower Manhattan's real estate as interconnected cultural events. Both resulted in the elimination of diverse bodies and forms of expression, which were replaced by homogenized groups, institutionalized culture, and general containment.

The economic, cultural, and sociopolitical backdrop of the Reagan presidency is crucial in this context, as its impact reverberated deeply in the identity of the Downtown scene. Artists were united in seeing Reagan and the conservative values promoted by his administration as the ultimate enemy. Most importantly, his lack of leadership and transparency during the burgeoning years of the AIDS crisis affected the emotional and physical state of many members of the Downtown scene, for whom the outbreak of HIV resulted in a permanent state of outrage and fear. The government did not actively address the AIDS crisis in the United States until ten years after its outbreak, and by then it had already become an "epidemic of meanings or signification," a syndrome constructed mainly by the semantics of its medial and medical discourses.[38] Early discussions around AIDS classified it as a sexually transmitted disease, fueling notions of homosexual promiscuity (as opposed to respectable heterosexuality), threatening pleasures, and infectious desires that needed to be controlled and contained.[39] The pervasive fear of contagion, of a deadly, uncontrollable disease, evolved into a veritable panic that not only problematized bodily contact but specifically tabooed homosexuality.

Not surprisingly, this cultural climate of restriction, fear, and social exclusion led artists like those in the Downtown scene to push the boundaries of what was generally considered acceptable, both aesthetically and morally. The body became the arena of resistance in productions like Karen Finley's angry, food-smearing one-woman shows, in the enthusiastically rowdy choreography of Anne Iobst and Lucy Sexton's live duo Dancenoise, and in Richard Kern and Lydia Lunch's filmic depictions of sexual abysses. And then, of course, there is David Wojnarowicz, the multidisciplinary artist and activist who refused to have his desiring body policed or regulated, who expressed himself in writing, film, performance, installation, painting, photography, and various collaborative projects.

One such project is *Fear of Disclosure: Psycho-Social Implications of HIV Revelation* (1989) by Wojnarowicz and journalist, filmmaker, poet, and activist Phil Zwickler. In this video work, which was also part of the Cinema of Transgression group show in Berlin in 2012, a male-sounding voice-over describes the sexual economics and social components of being HIV positive. While the person talks, stroboscopic images of two men, dancing and kissing, dressed in tight shorts, alternate with spinning globes, a recurring motif in Wojnarowicz's work. The text one hears is based on a dialogue between Wojnarowicz and Zwickler. Reading the script, one cannot but feel a sense of urgency:

DW I'm living in a diseased and dying city and some of us spend all our time screaming that the house is on fire and the city officials pretend they can't hear us and the people of this city are too frightened or selfish or tired to demand real and sensitive changes. And in the midst of my anger I have to try and find something to displace some of my rage; something to give me even a momentary sense of peace in which to deal with this illness; in which to deal with my life.

PZ Sometimes out there in the wilderness I would ask myself—how did I get into this mess? [added in handwriting:] We didn't get this disease because we're homosexuals, we got it cause we had sex in New York in the 1970's–1980's. . . . [40]

Fear of Disclosure powerfully conveys how anger, fear, helplessness, and longing meet, multiply, and accumulate in the "diseased and dying city," with no prospect of relief. But it is also just one of many works in Wojnarowicz's extensive oeuvre in which he moves as effortlessly as he does frenetically between different forms of expression, between writing, photography, video, painting, and more. In this restlessness is also a desire to feel the boundaries of mind and body slowly dissolve. In "Losing the Form in Darkness," Wojnarowicz writes about the sensation of swallowing pills filled with a substance that "cancels out the lines of thought brought along with time and aging and serious understanding of the self" and of encountering bodies when cruising the dark ruins of the Lower East Side's abandoned waterfront: "I was losing myself in the language of his movements, the slow rise and fall of a cigarette as he lifted it to his lips and brought it back down again."[41] For Wojnarowicz, this palpable desire to feel oneself dissolving, even spilling over, through creative and erotic encounters has always been paired with an urgent need to find release for pent-up rage and to let it out into the world. Not without reason has Hal Foster identified the key motifs of the Western art world in the 1980s and 1990s as trauma and rejection, fueled by anger and anxiety over the ongoing AIDS crisis, the shattered welfare state, and a social contract that seemed broken with the rise of neoliberalism.[42] But rather than fall back on the oft-cited nihilism of this generation of artists, or on the arguably attractive but somewhat limiting notion of transgression, I would suggest that the modus operandi of boundary-pushing artists like Wojnarowicz is better understood in terms of another concept: indisciplinarity.

Since at least the mid-1970s, a desire to "undermine from within the traditional structures of artistic media and the culture that had grown up around them" has been at the center of artistic production in Downtown Manhattan, as Marvin J. Taylor, director of Fales Library's Downtown Collection at New York University, writes.[43] In a similar vein, Tim Lawrence, who wrote the nightlife chronicle *Life and Death on the New York Dance Floor, 1980–1983*, claims that the early 1980s in New York City mark an era that is intriguing "not in spite of its lack of generic clarity but because its itinerant leanings opened up so many social and sonic possibilities."[44] In his book, he collects memories and material recordings of DJ sets and band performances, as well as fashion shows, happenings, graffiti, and Xerox art. This eclectic mix aims to capture "the breadth of what happened and the spirit in which it happened," namely that of communities and scenes, and speaks to the author's decision to place "the era's indiscipline at the center rather than the margins."[45]

The idea of indiscipline indeed has potential. In an expanded understanding of the term, indisciplinarity could refer to the disorderliness of the body and the disregard for discipline in the sense of subjugation or taming. Disciplinarity, as defined by Foucault, is a technique of modern power that seeks to normalize, rationalize, and simplify in an effort to create legible and thus addressable bodies. The body is "directly involved in a political field; power relations have an immediate hold upon it: they invest it, train it, torture it, force it to carry out tasks, to perform ceremonies and to emit signs." And this political investment is bound up with its economic use, because "the body becomes a useful force only if it's both a productive body and a subjugated body."[46] An artist like Wojnarowicz, who refused to be either economically productive—in the traditional or at least accepted sense—or subjugated in terms of his sexuality, resisted the sociopolitical disciplining of the socially unacceptable gay male body by making his desires and rage the driving forces of his artistic and activist work.

Another understanding of indisciplinarity describes the impossibility of discussing the many practices and projects that emerged in the Downtown scenes solely in terms of individual artistic disciplines or singular intentions. As will become increasingly clear throughout this book, an experimental and collaborative practice was the key mode of operation in the Downtown scene. Collaboration in a general sense, as art historian Maria Lind points out, has served as an "open-ended concept" for various ways of coming and working together, whether in surrealist group experiments, constructivist theater projects, Fluxus games, Andy Warhol's Factory, or the participatory art practices of the 1990s.[47] Collaboration, then, could lead to what is often referred to as interdisciplinarity, a concept based on the idea that old boundaries can be crossed and formal fusions can be realized. According to Lind, however, this kind of subject and genre mixing is "as unusual as arranged marriages.... Instead of formal mergers, temporary collaborations within self-determined activities may frequently be observed, but these rarely entail the literal merging of categories."[48] The notion of indisciplinarity, on the other hand, productively and playfully ignores the very existence of such borders and in-between spaces. Indisciplinarity thus becomes particularly useful in the case of the Downtown scene where collaboration not only took on many shapes and forms but was also less a conscious concept or strategy than motivated by the artistic and social proximity that the scene itself provided. In this context, collaboration did not lead to a literal and permanent fusion, but rather to a temporary, almost casual spillover between disciplines that nevertheless had a destabilizing effect on both the traditional notion of the author and that of the "work" itself.

Such scene practice, moreover, can be viewed through the lens of what Erhard Schüttpelz calls "productive dilettantism." According to Schüttpelz, every discipline that has its specialists and its audience, whether in the humanities or the visual arts, the natural sciences or pop music, establishes a strict barrier between producer and recipient. According to this order, only "specialists" are allowed to produce and only "experts" are allowed to judge. This system automatically excludes nonspecialists, meaning dilettantes, from producing value and relevance, condemning them instead to create "nameless garbage."[49] However, since most disciplines value innovation but are skeptical of transformation, anything new is initially labeled as amateurish. As Schüttpelz emphasizes, this is not the usual narrative of avant-garde practice, being first devalued and only later recognized as progressive. Rather, the distinction between innovation and incompetence in dilettante practice is ambiguous to the extent that it creates a loophole or blind spot in which categories of reception and production merge. The binary dynamics of innovation and incompetence can thus be circumvented altogether if, as Schüttpelz says, one makes "oneself a dilettante, one works in a dilettantish manner, and one does this with other people, because otherwise this game is witless, it is no fun...."[50] Notions of failure and irony also resonate here. The combination of not striving for success, not seeking a place in history, and taking an ironic attitude toward art production results in a fundamental questioning of the critical apparatuses of judgment and validation: "One does not yet create the actual works, one does not create an 'actual work' at all, but a hole, trash, dirt."[51] Crucially, productive dilettantism "can only work in the context of a 'scene,' with some people ... who might want something different, but who participate in this game."[52]

What, then, is a scene? The concept of "scene" as I discuss it here is characterized by the "elusive slipperiness of scenes," by the fact that it keeps temporal and spatial boundaries flexible and describes activities and identities less narrowly than related sociological concepts such as "movement" or "subculture."[53] This suggests that spilling does not just happen within a scene. As Kate Eichhorn puts it: "However much we might like to confine scenes to a particular time and place, they are rarely so containable. Scenes spill over and migrate."[54] So when I speak of "Downtown scenes" in the following, I do so with the awareness that the term also implies a form of containment and that the geographical boundaries of these scenes are indeed permeable and their temporal allocation flexible. As an analytical tool, however, the notion of the scene allows us to map, though necessarily fragmentarily, "how social and cultural life are lived in space, in time and in relation with others."[55] It is precisely this conceptual generosity and the connotation of a decentralized interconnectedness of people, practices, and places that makes the term useful for this study.

Thinking about Film with and through the Cinema of Transgression

The ambition of this book is not to present a complete or even "authentic" history of the Cinema of Transgression. Instead, by thinking about film with and through the CoT, with the mechanisms of spilling and containment, its scene dynamics, and its indisciplinary tendencies at play, I hope to offer both a fresh perspective on an understudied generation of artistic film practice in New York and a meaningful contribution to an ongoing discussion within the discipline of film studies. This discussion revolves around the challenging question of what we conceive of as film and how we approach it methodologically in light of the oft-conjured postcinematic crisis. André Gaudreault and Philippe Marion preface their book *The End of Cinema? A Medium in Crisis in the Digital Age*, published in 2015, with the observation that while many mourn the death of cinema in its classical form, cinema as a medium is ubiquitous in the digital age and is thus experiencing something of an "identity crisis."[56] At first glance, exclamations found in the book such as "the shaking up of cinema's foundations" or "cinema is not what it used to be" suggest not only nostalgia but also the assumption of an original state of cinema that is now in fundamental crisis. However, the authors also make the necessary remark that "the emergence of digital media is not the first upheaval to rock the cinematic realm. It must be said and repeated over and over, tirelessly: cinema's entire history has been punctuated by moments when its media identity has been radically called into question. What people have called 'cinema' for over a century has seen a series of technological mutations throughout its history."[57]

If cinema is inherently and inevitably unstable, where does that leave the discipline of cinema and film studies? As early as 2003, Charles Acland got to the root of one of the discipline's ongoing challenges when he noted that "the problem with film studies has been film, that is, the use of a medium in order to designate the boundaries of the discipline. Such a designation assumes a certain stability in what is actually a mutable technological apparatus. A problem ensues when it is apparent that film is not film anymore."[58]

Following up on the necessity for film studies to admit its self-imposed limitations, Miriam De Rosa and Vinzenz Hediger discuss how the discipline might move from mourning the loss of cinema's specificity to acknowledging that cinema has always been an "unspecific medium, a medium of constantly changing and often transitory configurations of which 'cinema' is only one."[59] Rather than lamenting the crumbling of its supposed foundations, mourning bygone times that never really were, admitting that cinema has been complex all along (but in different ways) productively eschews its differentiation into a before and after of the purported digital (identity) crisis. In the same text, De Rosa, seemingly echoing Acland, states her assumption that "cinema is not only about film."[60]

Contrary to popular perception, the CoT is likewise not only about film, at least not if, in Acland's words, this "designation assumes a certain stability," both in terms of its technological apparatus and in its locations and formations. For again, the CoT emerged from a collaborative and indisciplinary scene where filmmaking was always inseparable from other disciplines and artistic, political, and social practices such as club culture, performance, zine making, curating, activism, and video and television production. The forms and contexts in which it appears today, from art museums and film collections to fan forums and private collections, both fossilize this initially diverse and uncontrollable phenomenon and allow for cracks to develop within this homogenizing narrative.

My exploration thus proposes a possible way of viewing film not as a fixed entity in and of itself, but as part of a shape-shifting configuration of activities, events, practices, texts, and sites. And if one takes the notion of film as a mutable object seriously, then traditional methods of film studies, such as textual and formal analysis, are only partially helpful, as they often assume that film begins and ends within its own—imagined—frames. As Rembert Hüser has said, "If you want to write about film, you have already lost if you look for 'film' alone. Film never comes on its own."[61] Here he suggests that film's inherent nexus of image and text, its requisite entanglement with other media, each with its own history and language, makes it impossible to grasp with any overarching method or theory. A project that acknowledges the changing dynamics of its objects thus calls for a set of methods that is just as flexible.

While written from the perspective of a film and media scholar, this book draws on observations from a variety of disciplines, including art history, social and cultural studies, and philosophy. This interdisciplinary framework helps to analyze the CoT's entanglement with performance art, video and television, and avant-garde, experimental, and underground cinema, while also approaching it in the context of scene structures, zine and festival cultures, and its methods of distribution and circulation. Queer and feminist perspectives on visual culture and politics will provide valuable insight into specific case studies and will also prove inspiring when it comes to the question of how to "mess with" seemingly linear, clear, straight narratives. As Heather Love writes in "Queer Messes," queer scholars have always been at the forefront of acknowledging and embracing "the messiness of their subject matter and have invented new modes of research, writing, and performance to deal with it."[62]

Returning to the notion of film existing beyond its own frame, a reading of film and media as proposed by Hüser also ultimately works against a hierarchy of the text, or rather, it argues for a redefinition of what constitutes a text in the first place and how that text is shaped by the configurations and contexts it enters. In this case, the films labeled "Cinema of Transgression" have now become part of university and film archives, museum collections, and art exhibitions, while some have remained in private collections or have been lost altogether. The latter also implies that CoT films are often unwatchable in more ways than one: both in the sense that they are "literally hard to watch," evoke visceral reactions, and sometimes even consciously enact a "refusal of pleasure as an aesthetic principle" and also because of their material unavailability.[63] So, when looking for and at the CoT, I look at film and performance documentation, but also paratexts such as club and festival programs, film posters, zines, VHS tapes, distribution catalogs, and exhibitions, which will often serve as the starting points for my investigations. What do they reveal not only about how and where the films that are now associated with the CoT were made, seen, and distributed but also about the conception, historicization, and changing meanings of the CoT? What understanding of film emerges from the analysis of these objects? Who is writing whose (film) history and by what means? These questions will guide me as I also contrast and interweave different narratives, drawing on personal interviews, writings produced from within and about the scene, and archival material, which I will contextualize, historicize, and reflect upon theoretically.

In turning my attention to the conditions, sites, and contexts of film production, presentation, distribution, exhibition, preservation, and materiality, I thus join what Erika Balsom has called "a contextual turn" in film studies. She observes that this turn "entails an important methodological shift away from a focus on the supposed autonomy of the text and toward an examination of the networks ... through which these texts travel, the sites at which they are encountered, and the material and discursive practices that frame them."[64] This methodological shift accounts for the realization that film can take place independently of the spatial conditions of the cinematic dispositif and in fact occurs in "nontheatrical settings" such as the home, the classroom, and the museum, as well as in public and digital space and sometimes even without any screen at all.[65] In calling for an offscreen film and television studies, Jonathan Gray, for example, discusses the proliferation of filmic and televisual texts, in the form of what is commonly considered their "paratexts."[66] Trailers, fan fiction, merchandise, soundtracks, DVD bonus material, which have recently attracted increased attention from film and media scholars,[67] are, Gray writes, "not simply add-ons, spin-offs, and also-rans: they create texts, they manage them, and they fill them with many of the meanings that we associate with them."[68] Such realizations, in turn, have resulted in the emergence of new fields of research dedicated to amateur, educational, or industrial film, as well as to an increased interest in the changing locations, forms, and uses of film.

With respect to research that considers the "new old" configurations of film and media, this book looks at film through the lens of the past and present networks, contexts, and practices that frame and shape it. Following the CoT's spills into the present supports the argument that it is an ongoing phenomenon rather than a closed chapter of (film) history and thus reinforces the claim that film needs to be studied within its shifting contexts. Taken together, these observations indicate that following film or media objects into their various locations and settings, tracing their histories nonchronologically via their recontextualizations and shifting meanings, ultimately leads to the realization that these are by no means "abstracted totalities" with timeless, "fixed hermeneutic, intrinsic properties," nor are their ontologies self-evident.[69] From this perspective, films appear complex, mutable, and shape-shifting, as a fluid rather than stable concept. If films "seem to appear everywhere," they are indeed messy, even spilling objects.[70] This book takes seriously the notion that film is somewhat all over the place, not least by considering film in terms of metaphors of fluidity, contingency, and uncontrollability.

Chapter Summaries

Although each of the four main chapters in *Films That Spill* will make repeated excursions into the present and generally proceed in a nonchronological fashion, the temporal focus of my explorations is the mid-1980s. The year 1985 marks the moment when Nick Zedd launched the CoT as a film movement unified by his manifesto. However, due to its multiple configurations, the CoT has, from the beginning, spilled over its own boundaries. The spilling and containment of the CoT is therefore not a singular event, but a process that begins in the mid-1980s and continues into the present moment.

The first chapter, "Forgetting the Cinema of Transgression," asks whose perspectives shape the CoT's historical narrative, who publishes and documents that narrative, where this documentation is located, and to whom it is accessible. It returns to the site of the Kunstwerke in Berlin for a thorough analysis of the exhibition in light of both the original "Cinema of Transgression Manifesto" that Nick Zedd printed in 1985 in his self-published zine *Underground Film Bulletin* and its reception. I juxtapose the art world's historical reframing with Zedd's own attempts to institutionalize his 1980s underground origin story, particularly through the housing of his papers and ephemera in the archives of New York University's Fales Library.

Chapter 2, "Downtown Images," elaborates on the historical context and distinctive structures of the Downtown scene, asking who or what constitutes a scene and how a scene is imagined and made visible. First, I describe how the idea of the East Village became both an internationally recognized scene and an art genre, the hype around it fueling both individual careers and the urban gentrification that led to the scene's slow decline in the mid-1980s, precisely the moment when Nick Zedd launched the Cinema of Transgression. Next, the zine *Underground Film Bulletin* receives closer scrutiny in terms of its visual aesthetics, format, editorial guidelines and content, and distribution channels. The zine played an important role in building and promoting the CoT, even after it ceased publication: Zedd used it to publish his manifesto in order to draw attention to himself and like-minded filmmakers and to position his concept of the CoT within a specific history of underground cinema. While acknowledging the zine's function as a promotional tool and instrument of historiography, I also show how the zine can be understood as a means of undoing the dominant concept of the CoT, for it reveals that film practice was rooted in an indisciplinary scene and that the CoT was therefore as much about drawing cartoons, publishing zines, and writing reviews as it was about making films. I conclude the chapter with a discussion of the New York Film Festival Downtown (NYFFD), initiated by filmmakers Ela Troyano and Tessa Hughes-Freeland and held annually from 1984 through 1989. By analyzing the festival's local programming as well as its travels to Europe, I argue that while the NYFFD functioned as a crucial platform for Downtown filmmaking and performance practices, it also helped to disembed the films from that very context, containing their spillover and reducing them to auratically charged visions of New York City.

The third chapter, "Film Happens," focuses on three specific film and performance events within the indisciplinary scene discussed in the second chapter. Here I juxtapose a detailed analysis of Anthony Chase and John Kelly's *The Dagmar Onassis Story* (1984), Nick Zedd's *Me Minus You* (1985), and Ela Troyano's *Bubble People* (1982) with a history of the theories and concepts that contains each artistic form. I argue that these cases not only demonstrate the indisciplinary nature of the Downtown scene, and the CoT in particular, by presenting film and performance as intertwined, but also complicate the ontological distinction between film and performance by asking us to think of the two in terms of spilling over into each other, in terms of a messy but fascinating intersection of forms.

Finally, the fourth chapter, "Afterlife Formats," is devoted to the circulation of the films on VHS tapes, on television, and in the digital realm. In 1985, Nick Zedd released the videocassette compilation *Cinema of Transgression, Vol. 1*, distributing it through his one-person company Weirdo Video and promoting it in the *Underground Film Bulletin*. This final chapter takes the tape as a point of departure to probe engagements with video and television, from ventures in home video distribution to productions for public access cable television that the CoT label usually conceals, such as Nick Zedd's own *The Adventures of Electra Elf* (Manhattan Neighborhood Network, 2005–2008). By focusing here on the distribution and reformatting of films, this chapter not only connects the study to current research on distribution channels and the messiness of (digital) circulation, it also, crucially, broadens the media-historical perspective on the CoT.

1
Forgetting the Cinema
of Transgression
■ ■

Resurrected in the Exhibition

As if the graffiti had just dried, as if someone had hurriedly scrawled the big, bold letters on the wall, little drops of black spray paint run down from them: X IS Y, Baby Doll, FEAR OF DISCLOSURE. Pink-purple neon lights and red wall paint give the room the feel of a basement nightclub, where the warm light tends to make everything feel a little more intimate. Lying on black square cushions scattered around the room, one can watch three different short, digitalized clips projected on painted black rectangles with smeared edges. In the clips, women play with machine guns; two topless dancers prepare for their night of work while talking about self-empowerment; strobe light flashes on two men dancing in shorts while a male voice talks about his sex life in the days of HIV. Leaving this room and following the staircase down to the second and first floors, a flickering light irritates the eye. It is as if someone forgot or did not care to change an old light bulb. Another setting: neon lights bathe the room in a dim, cold, bluish light; the floor is covered with bare tiles; thin drips of black paint run down the walls. In this rather inhospitable atmosphere, projections on the wall show a family dinner that ends in a massacre, or a hairless body dancing in a thong in front of an American flag, showing off its protruding belly, buttocks, and heavy breasts while licking its shiny lips. Descending another flight of stairs, the viewer is greeted by a naked woman setting herself on fire, her image projected onto a wall painted neon green in sloppy brush strokes. Three arrows made from

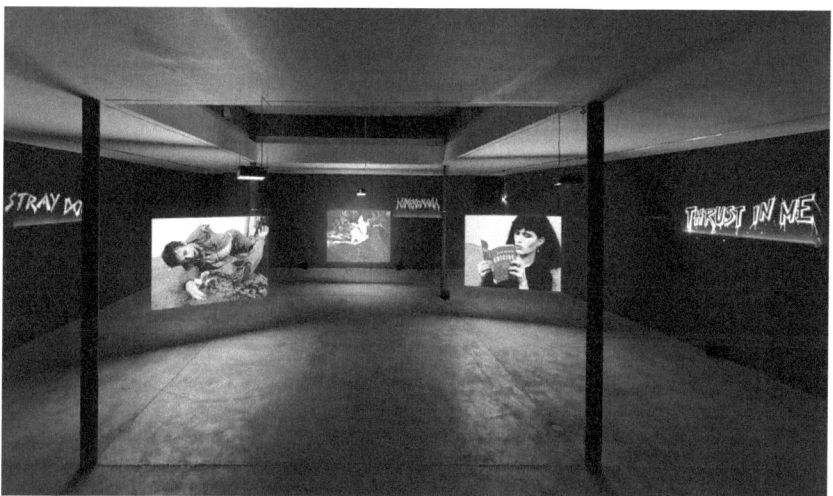

FIGURE 1 Ghostly performances

torn pieces of tape point to entrances between heavy black curtains, inviting you to peer through and onto a wall-as-screen to watch a woman's labia being sewn together. Dissonant guitar riffs, moaning vocals, and industrial sounds echo through the austere space. The onslaught of unexpected images continues in the basement of this former margarine factory, where three death scenarios hang from the ceiling. A zombie-like man magically loses his arm, spurting blood. Next to him, a nymph dances in a meadow to Claude Debussy's *Prelude to the Afternoon of a Faun*, only to be violently raped by a satyr. The third screen shows the story of a suicidal woman and her necrophiliac boyfriend, both embodied by the same performer. Pitch-black walls, on which the titles of the films are written in fluorescent, dripping letters, surround these ghostly performances. Accentuated by purple neon light, the typography is reminiscent of the illuminated advertisements of a haunted house or the cover design of R. L. Stine's *Goosebumps* series of teen horror novels (see Figure 1). It is this combination of horror and juvenile fantasy, genre convention and provocation, commercial expectation and conscious DIY aesthetic that makes the staging of these images so irritatingly appealing.

You Killed Me First: The Cinema of Transgression at the KW Institute for Contemporary Art in Berlin (which was curated by Susanne Pfeffer and ran from February 19 to April 8, 2012) was a group exhibition of eighteen films by and with various filmmakers from New York's Downtown film, music, art, and performance scenes. The title is borrowed from one of the films in the exhibition, in which a rebellious teenager (Lung Leg) kills her religious-conservative parents and sister, shouting directly into the camera, "You killed me first!" After the closing credits, the panting, slightly distraught daughter stands in a nondescript red room, looking nervously from left to right, then back to the viewer as the image slowly fades to black. KW used a still from the film, showing Lung Leg holding a gun, as the press image and cover of the information brochure. The press release states that the filmmakers who are presented here as part of the Cinema of Transgression (CoT) were on a "collision course with the conventions of American society," suggesting that these very conventions are not only responsible for keeping the movement "largely unknown" but perhaps also figuratively killed it. Given KW's emphasis on the fact that *You Killed Me First* was the first exhibition of its kind, that is, the first to bring these filmmakers together under this particular label in the context of an institutional group show, one might as well think of the show as an attempt to bring the CoT back from the dead.[1]

Fittingly, wandering through the exhibition's "theme park-like recreation of the once sketchy, run-down Lower East Side," where one never knows what scary scenario might be waiting around the next dark corner, is like visiting an R-rated haunted house.[2] Like teen horror novels, theme parks, and haunted houses, *You Killed Me First* gives its visitors goosebumps. In doing so, it shifts the dynamics from exhibition viewing to entertainment. Arthur C. Danto distinguishes between art of "disturbation," which breaches the boundaries between art and life by incorporating an element of reality, and works that are disturbing "in that what they show is disturbing, as is the way it is shown." Of the latter he writes that these works are usually encountered in the polished environment of a gallery space, where "the fact that these ghastly visions can be contained carries a compensatory comfort."[3] Similarly, at KW, the sense of a somewhat pleasurable discomfort derives from the staging being intriguing despite (or maybe precisely because of) its theatricality. The disturbance is contained; it does not spill over the projection frame. Walking through these perfectly gritty, carefully disheveled scenarios matches the thrill of seeing the splatter of fake blood, the cheap special effects, and all the flirtations with violence, sex, and death that the films on display have to offer: they're scary yet entertaining, a little messy but also neat enough not to make you forget that you are visiting a prestigious art institution. The seemingly still wet spray paint and the flickering lights are calculatedly careless, the result of a carefully planned curatorial strategy. This setting evokes the mystified image of a radical, sexy, and violent East Village of the 1980s, which may have been frightening. But in 2012 you can always step out into the courtyard and take a break in KW's Café Bravo, a sleek and shiny stainless-steel construction by artist Dan Graham.

Originally shot on Super 8 and 16 mm, the films on view date from the late 1970s to the early 1990s. Tim Lawrence argues that in the early 1980s, despite, or perhaps because of, the bleak state of New York City (when it reached a peak in recorded criminality, landlords were burning down buildings for insurance money, and the urban landscape was deteriorating due to city budget cuts), the city experienced a "community driven cultural-renaissance."[4] How the Downtown scene formed and how this relates to a consideration of the CoT will be explored further in the following chapter, "Downtown Images." For now, let me just note that within this scene, artists worked collaboratively and across various media, with Downtown nightclubs functioning as key sites for working, socializing, hanging out, performing, and showing films. At the time of their production, the films exhibited at KW were being screened in these nightclubs and at concerts and festivals; in other words, mostly outside of traditional movie theaters. Some filmmakers transferred their films to video for distribution through small-scale or self-organized VHS mail-order systems, which will be discussed in chapter 4. However, compatibility problems often arose, and conversion was expensive. Many films were also rejected by distribution companies, faced censorship, or both.[5] Now some can be viewed on informal streaming platforms or purchased as DVD collections. In recent years, some films have been restored by film institutions, distributed through galleries and nonprofit organizations, or acquired for museum collections.[6]

Until the 2012 exhibition, however, the CoT had attracted little interest in either the academic or art world. All the more so, the exhibition at KW and its specific framing of the CoT represents a meaningful contribution to its historiography. "Culture scenes survive to become history . . . only if they are publicized or documented in some way."[7] But who publicizes and documents these scenes? Whose perspectives shape their historical representation? Where is their documentation located and who has access to it? In this chapter, I trace the historiography of the CoT by looking at three cases that significantly shaped it. I begin with KW's exhibition in 2012, continue with Nick Zedd's 1985 "Cinema of Transgression Manifesto," and conclude by reflecting on what has remained of the CoT today in institutional and private archives. This nonchronological retracing describes my own paths of research, from the first encounter in the Berlin art world to subsequent investigations that led me to archival research and interviews in New York City. By juxtaposing different framings and institutionalizations of the CoT, I ultimately argue for forgetting the CoT as we have come to know it.

In his seminal work *The Queer Art of Failure*, Jack Halberstam proposes "failing, losing, forgetting, unmaking, undoing, unbecoming, not knowing" as modes of being that not only resist ideas about productivity shaped by heteronormative and neoliberal agendas but also express suspicion against memorialization, even memory itself: "Memory is itself a disciplinary mechanism . . . , it reads a continuous narrative into one full of ruptures and contradictions."[8] Along these lines, forgetting contains a generative and future-oriented moment. In this case, it serves to disrupt entrenched narratives that aim to reshape the concept of CoT as it was created through the exhibition at KW, among other things. The exhibition's framing obscures the fact that these films were not primarily made under the banner of Cinema of Transgression but emerged from the fertile ground of indisciplinary practice, where performance, visual art, film, and music making spilled into one another. The presentation at KW situates the CoT within the mystifying narrative of a deviant countercultural film movement. This framing, however, is not unique to KW's presentation but exemplary of the discourse that has formed around the CoT and an art world that tends to turn complex artistic practices into single objects for easy consumption and insertion into circuits of value production.

The exhibition *You Killed Me First* can be viewed within the scope of a continuing fascination with, or even longing for, what art critic Dan Fox has called New York City's "bad old days," meaning the 1970s and 1980s, when the city was "bankrupt, on fire and ravaged by heroin" and the HIV crisis but the artistic scenes flourished nevertheless. In the last few years, large-scale exhibitions presented by major art institutions in New York City such as *East Village USA* (New Museum, 2004–2005), *The Downtown Show* (Grey Art Gallery, 2006), *Greater New York* (MoMA PS1, 2015–2016), *Club 57: Film, Performance, and Art in the East Village, 1978–1983* (MoMA, 2017), *New York, New Music 1980–1986* (Museum of the City of New York, ongoing) and, most recently, as part of MoMA's new collection presentation in spring 2021, a room dedicated to *Downtown New York*, have renarrated the artistic scenes of the city's own recent past.[9] Renarrations like these are, of course, not only found in exhibitions, but also books, films, and autobiographies. And, as Fox observes, they make one wonder if "in truth, it's not the work that we crave; it's the time and place in which it was made."[10] Do these exhibitions mostly just make us wish that we had been there? Film and media scholar Lucas Hilderbrand visited *East Village USA* and *The Downtown Show*, which presented, respectively, artworks that were shown initially in East Village galleries between 1981 and 1987, plus video, film, and performance documentation, as well as artworks and archive material from the Downtown Collection of the Fales Library.[11] Reflecting on his visits, Hilderbrand states that "the primary feeling I got was that the work was about its energy, its moment, and its context. I had missed all of these, and the exhibits reinforced this feeling: I was not there."[12] Richard Kern, a filmmaker who *had* been there, remembers his visit to the exhibition *You Killed Me First* at KW as follows: "I walked through it, thinking that this is as close as you can get to a perfect overview [of the Cinema of Transgression]. Seeing them [the films] all like that in that space really felt like being in the '80s in New York.... It reminded me of these clubs that were around, like Danceteria... which was this multilevel club, you know, every floor had something weird going on.... And it didn't just have the vibe of here; it had the vibe of old Berlin, too."[13]

While the first statement suggests that one had to be there, to be part of a particular community to appreciate the output of the Downtown scene in general, and perhaps the CoT in particular, the second statement connotes that for those who were there, *You Killed Me First*'s artificially messy environment, with its trickles of paint, sparse lighting, dark rooms, and scrawly graffiti, was "as close as you can get" and hence evoked the feeling of being there. Those who had not been there might have felt like they were walking through a "theme park-like recreation" of the East Village.[14]

Revivals, reinterpretations, and re-creations come into play here, which in the end either recall a particular place and its temporal specificity or reinforce the feeling of never having experienced it. What is at stake is a rather complex notion of presence, which can be further explored by thinking of *You Killed Me First* as a reenactment. Reenactment allows for the reperformance and reexperience and ultimately the revision of a past event that is thus made "visually imaginable and sensually tangible" in the present.[15] However, let us note that any event to which reenactment refers is itself always already mediated—and that this aspect is not obscured but emphasized by the new representational staging of the reenactment.[16] This is especially true for the CoT, as will become increasingly evident throughout this chapter. Any exhibition can be understood as an "articulation of a particular physical space through which relations ... between objects, viewers, and their specific exhibition context are staged."[17] Similarly, a reenactment deploys practices of locating, embodying, and visualizing. As a reenactment, *You Killed Me First* makes the CoT present as a staged event taking place in a specific place. (I will elaborate later on how KW itself embodies a glorified period of Berlin's own history.) Most importantly, the CoT is made present through the bodies of the visitors who watch the films, walk through the rooms, and perceive the changes in light, smell, and sound in the present moment and for whom these sensations might evoke nostalgia, regret, or discomfort. More generally, framing the exhibition as a reenactment shows how the CoT becomes quotable and repeatable and thus available for divergent future approaches and reappearances in perhaps unexpected places.

By selecting and arranging objects in a spatial setting, any exhibition naturally presents a narrative about its subject matter. However, discussing how "real" or "authentic" these narratives might be is not the point. Instead, it is crucial to consider who is creating them and in what context. Returning to a question raised earlier, we can ask who is mobilizing whose past for whom, which requires a reflection on the specifics and politics of place. Interestingly, KW's institutional and programmatic history is closely linked to two institutions in New York City, namely MoMA and MoMA PS1. A brief parallel with the development and agendas of these institutions sheds light on the circumstances under which the CoT was resurrected in Berlin in 2012.

Seventeen minutes' walk south from the Berlin Wall Memorial site and seventeen minutes' walk west from Alexanderplatz, it is safe to say that KW Institute for Contemporary Art is located in the heart of Berlin. Its building, a former factory, is now protected as a historical monument on Auguststrasse of Berlin's Spandauer Vorstadt, an area whose small alleys, streets, and historic buildings suffered comparatively little damage during World War II. In the years following the fall of the Berlin Wall, artists' collectives, squatters, and later galleries took up residence in the vacant buildings of Auguststrasse, and in 1991, "a group of young art enthusiasts" settled in number 69 and turned it into an exhibition and studio space that would soon become KW.[18] Quickly after its founding, KW established an ongoing exhibition program under the direction of one of the "young art enthusiasts," Klaus Biesenbach. Its existence was secured by the foundation Deutsche Klassenlotterie Berlin, which purchased the building for KW's use. One of the first major projects was *37 Räume* (*37 Rooms*), which took place parallel to Documenta in Kassel in 1992. Here, artworks were displayed in the vacant apartments and business premises of Auguststrasse. Ironically, the exhibition was intended as a critical commentary on the rapid gentrification of Berlin's Mitte district, a process in which KW and Biesenbach played no minor role.[19] Today, KW is the epicenter of a cluster of galleries, art institutions, and private collections.

Since KW operates on the model of a *Kunsthalle*, meaning a nonprofit art institution that organizes events and exhibitions without a collection of its own, it is run by a registered association. With the help of several foundations and the city's urban monument protection, the building was renovated and reopened in 1999. In that same year, KW became the permanent host of the Berlin Biennale of Contemporary Art. As the biennale format is historically and inextricably linked to the negotiation of local political interests, urban infrastructures, and tourism, accumulating both economic and symbolic capital, it also implicitly aims to put its institution, and especially its city, (back) on the map of an increasingly global art world, a process that was already well underway in Berlin.[20] The first edition of the Berlin Biennale, titled *BERLIN/BERLIN*, claimed to critically reflect precisely the economic and political driving forces inherent to its format.[21] It is worth noting that the Berlin Biennale of Contemporary Art was launched during what Charlotte Bydler describes as the proliferation of an increasingly flexible, experience-orientated Biennial format.[22] According to Caroline A. Jones, this format has itself stimulated an aesthetic shift toward more experiential forms of art, such as site-specific and time-based works, media art, and live performance: "Biennials are the event structures where this taste has been cultivated, and its aesthetic codified and defined."[23] This shift is particularly evident in Biesenbach's curatorial work at MoMA and MoMA PS1.

In the mid-1990s, Biesenbach began working as a part-time curator at New York City's P.S. 1 Contemporary Art Center. Founded in 1971 as the Institute for Art and Urban Resources (IAUR), it was originally a nonprofit organization that hosted exhibitions, performances, and artist studios in abandoned spaces across the city. It was renamed P.S. 1 Contemporary Art Center in 1976 and, in the same year, moved to its permanent location, a school building first opened in Long Island in 1892, where it still resides. Since 2000, it has been formally affiliated with MoMA. Thus, both MoMA PS1 and KW were founded as somewhat underground initiatives that can be seen as both products and driving forces of the gentrification of 1970s New York and 1990s Berlin, respectively. The close collaboration between MoMA, MoMA PS1, and KW also reflects in their frequently overlapping programming. In recent years, numerous exhibitions have been mounted that feature work created between 1971 and 1991 by New York avant-garde and underground artists, work that emerged from those now mythical and marketable decades that lie between the founding years of PS1 and KW. To name a few artists that have been featured: painter and performance artist Joe Coleman (*Internal Digging*, KW, 2007), cross-disciplinary artist David Wojnarowicz (*David Wojnarowicz Photography and Film 1978–1992*, KW, 2019), theater director Reza Abdoh (*Reza Abdoh*, MoMA PS1, 2018 and KW, 2019), and underground filmmakers Kenneth Anger (*Kenneth Anger*, MoMA PS1, 2009) and Jack Smith (*Jack Smith: Normal Love*, MoMA PS1, 2012).[24]

Which leads back to the question: who is mobilizing whose past? And also: what past? In the case of KW and MoMA PS1, they are mobilizing and mystifying their own city's past while burnishing the glamour of the other city's past as well. After all, *You Killed Me First*, as Richard Kern put it, "didn't just have the vibe of here [New York's East Village], it had the vibe of old Berlin, too."[25] Of course, it is important for institutions to show the works of the artists just mentioned and thus make it available to a wider audience, and I am not arguing against that. What I intend to point out is that these works are framed in a way that highlights the dirty glamour of this supposedly pregentrified time but in fact presents a sanitized version. In addition, they seek to take on the pioneering quality they ascribe to the avant-garde and its subcultures. Like *You Killed Me First*, the exhibitions of these formerly underground artists are often marketed as "the first" to recognize the value of the respective artist's work: "the first ever to encompass all aspects of [artist's] work," "the first major survey of the filmmaker's body of work at a U.S. museum in over a decade," "the first large-scale retrospective of [artist's] work."[26] This rhetoric, often employed in press releases, follows the liberal capitalist logic of the value of novelty.

Consequently, what brought the CoT to Berlin in 2012 is a transatlantic nexus of people and institutions that show a notable interest in the work of New York's underground and avant-garde scenes and strive to present it to a wider audience, while at the same time capitalizing on its appeal within the logic of urban gentrification. The result is threefold. First, by rediscovering or resurrecting the work of these artists, prestigious art institutions valorize, institutionalize, and initialize their canonization. Second, the works become museum objects. Although the films of the CoT have been shown before and since in museums and art institutions, *You Killed Me First* decisively presented them installed in an exhibition, effectively redefining them as what Haidee Wasson calls "discrete cinematic object[s]," stripped of the traces of the cross-disciplinary environment in which they were once produced and presented.[27] Finally, these artists and scenes are presented within a readily marketable narrative. While it is difficult to disentangle the overlapping scenes and practices that gave rise to the films shown, *You Killed Me First* attempted to weave these many fluid interactions into the narrative of a transgressive film movement. However, this encapsulating concept was, at least to some extent, already proposed by the artists themselves, and in particular by Nick Zedd. It was Zedd, after all, who published "The Cinema of Transgression

Manifesto" with the intention of turning a loosely knit, cross-disciplinary group into a somewhat cohesive movement and thereby inserting it into film history. In any case, the notion of containment is as central to CoT's history as that of transgression.

Born in the Manifesto

When I entered KW in March 2012 and bought a ticket for *You Killed Me First*, I received an information booklet. Photocopied in black and white on cheap grayish paper, the booklet was stapled and folded into a standardized A5 format. With its mix of handwriting and typesetting and its collage of text and image, it seemed to simulate a self-made zine like Nick Zedd's *Underground Film Bulletin* (1984–1990) (see Figure 2). Just as KW's rooms present an atmospheric mixture of an intimate nightclub and bleak urban space, the information booklet (as well as the exhibition catalog, which appears in the same design) simulates the cheap, fast Xerox aesthetic "that came to mark the [Downtown] scene" especially in the 1970s and 1980s. These were the years when, as Kate Eichhorn writes, "walls of xeroxed posters and street art distinguished the Downtown scene from other neighborhoods by creating constantly changing and highly textured facades for the neighborhood's crumbling architecture," and Xeroxed zines, scores, postcards, and flyers circulated in and beyond the scene.[28]

While flipping through the booklet at KW, I saw that the inside cover included a double-sided photograph of the filmmaker and cast posing for a behind-the-scenes shot on the set of Richard Kern's *Fingered* (1986). Like the centerfold of a teen magazine, it can be removed and pinned to the wall. The rest of the booklet consists of floor plans that guide the visitor through the four exhibition spaces, the credits of each film presented, and two texts. The first is a quote from filmmaker Nick Zedd ("'Basically, in one sentence, give us the definition of the Cinema of Transgression.' Nick Zedd: 'Fuck You.'") that is followed by an introduction to the CoT. It is described as a "group of filmmakers [that] emerged from the Lower East Side, New York, whose common goals Zedd later postulated in the 'The Cinema of Transgression Manifesto.'" A quote from said manifesto appears as well, and it begins as follows: "We propose . . . that any film which doesn't shock isn't worth looking at. We propose to go beyond all limits set or prescribed by taste, morality or any other traditional value system shackling the minds of men."[29] The full text can be found on the last pages of the booklet, along with film stills and portraits of selected filmmakers. On the back page, there is a list of ten names in capital letters, as if handwritten with a thick black marker. This list tells visitors to the exhibition that these are the artists participating in the exhibition, but the list also says that these are the filmmakers belonging to the Cinema of Transgression. But what is the actual genesis of this concept? Where did it originate, how did it circulate, and how was it adapted in public discourse? And what does this mean for the perception of the films

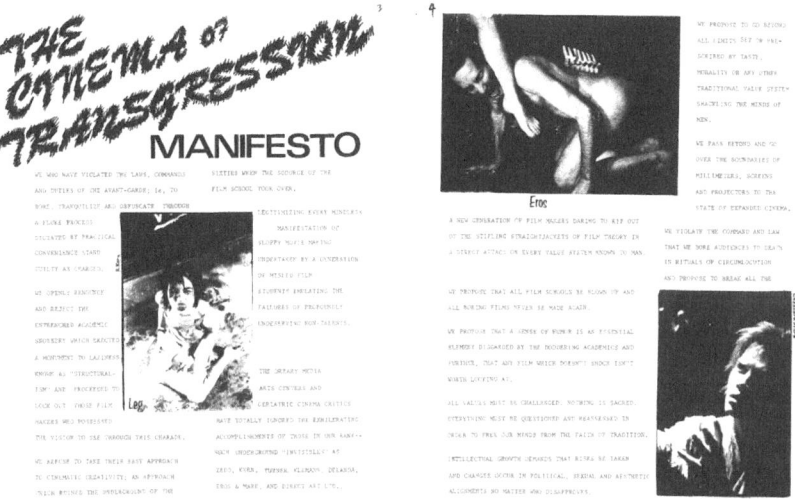

FIGURE 2 Exhibition brochure as zine

referred to as Cinema of Transgression? In the following, I will explore these questions with particular attention to the manifesto quoted in the exhibition.

In 1979, Nick Zedd released his first film, *They Eat Scum*. Featuring giant cockroaches and punk zombies destroying New York City, the seventy-nine-minute-long Super 8 film screened at nightclubs and other venues like Max's Kansas City, Club 57, and at O-P Screen. Film critic Amy Taubin attended the latter venue and wrote a review entitled "The Other Cinema" for the *Soho Weekly News*: "The esthetic [sic] operative here is transgression, both in terms of the events of the narrative, and in formal filmmaking terms. If it gets shot, use it.... And if your subject is the world of garbage, why not make a film that looks like garbage?—the form is the content and so forth."[30] Six years later, Zedd adopted both the term "transgression" and the label "The Other Cinema" to first announce the existence of the Cinema of Transgression. In 1985, he published two texts in the *Underground Film Bulletin*, which he had begun editing under the name Orion Jeriko in 1984. The third issue includes the piece "Long Live the Cinema of Transgression," in which Zedd declares:

> A new movement is born and it is my destiny to make the world aware of its existence. It is an Invisible Movement, unseen by the narrow-minded old timers who write for the Voice, Film Comment, American Film, East Village Eye and virtually every other film journal in the world but it exists nonetheless. It has been rendered invisible by critical indifference and an inexcusable ignorance which runs in terror from acts of 'transgression' committed by the

bold new minds of the post punk super-8 underground.... This Other Cinema is making its mark.³¹

Zedd goes on to cite the 1979 article by "the now-discredited" Taubin, one of the "old timer" critics, and declares *They Eat Scum* to be "the first spiritual forebear" of the Cinema of Transgression, "whose strongest sin is to shock in as direct a manner as possible."³² In his 1996 autobiography, he writes of this period: "Nobody seemed to realize we were just as important as the Dadaists."³³ The reference to this group is significant because the Dadaists are among those "aesthetic coteries of the historical avant-garde" who, as Jane Lyon writes, "adapted the manifesto's revolutionary discourse to signal their own radical departures from bourgeois artistic forms and practices."³⁴ At that time, the manifesto, which straddled the boundary between the aesthetic and the political, between subjectivity and collectivity, became the "signature genre for avant-garde groups announcing the birth of artistic movements."³⁵ It is this historical lineage, then, that Zedd takes up when he publishes his "Cinema of Transgression Manifesto" in 1985. And it is also the formal and rhetorical strategies of earlier manifesto writings that echo in the following demands:

> Any film which doesn't shock isn't worth looking at. All values must be challenged. Nothing is sacred.... We propose to go beyond all limits set or prescribed by taste, morality or any other traditional value system shackling the minds of men.... We violate the command and law that we bore audiences to death in rituals of circumlocution and propose to break all the taboos of our age by sinning as much as possible. There will be blood, shame, pain and ecstasy, the likes of which no one has yet imagined. None shall emerge unscathed. Since there is no afterlife, the only hell is the hell of praying, obeying laws, and debasing yourself before authority figures, the only heaven is the heaven of sin, being rebellious, having fun, fucking, learning new things and breaking as many rules as you can. This act of courage is known as transgression. We propose transformation through transgression—to convert, transfigure and transmute into a higher plane of existence in order to approach freedom in a world full of unknowing slaves.³⁶

The manifesto's tone is proclamatory and fiercely oppositional, asserting its claims collectively. Although Zedd wrote and signed the text himself, or rather as his alter ego Orion Jeriko, the recurring "we" purports to speak for other "underground invisibles," specifically Richard Kern, Tommy Turner, Richard Klemann, Manuel DeLanda, Bradley Eros and Aline Mare, and Direct Art Ltd. Given that Zedd printed it in his zine, there is no evidence that the manifesto was ever distributed as a flyer or poster, or read to an audience, as was often the case with other artists' or political manifestos. Nevertheless, as a performative utterance in the Austinian sense, it proclaims something that is thereby made manifest.³⁷ To say that "a new movement is born and it is my destiny to make the world aware that it exists" really means that this movement is only generated in, by, and through the text.

In the following years, Zedd frequently added or excluded members. In 1985, for example, he released a video compilation entitled *Cinema of Transgression Vol.1*, which comprised films by the filmmakers mentioned in the manifesto and three others. The text on the backside confidently promotes the CoT as "the single most exciting thing to have happened in the creative community in the last years." A poster advertising a screening of Zedd's films *Police State*, *Kiss Me Goodbye*, and *The Wild World of Lydia Lunch* in 1987 announces them as "The Cinema of Nick Zedd." Below, written in a smaller font, "The Cinema of Transgression" lists yet another group of names. Thus, the manifesto and the concept of a movement served not as the self-description of a unified group but as deliberately constructed tools for (self-)promotion. This is a fact that most historical accounts fail to mention. Zedd himself, however, was quite open about it. In a 1993 interview for *Cyber-Psycho's A.O.D.*, he responded to the question of how the Cinema of Transgression project came about as follows:

> I formulated this plan to get the attention of journalists, by creating a movement and calling it the Cinema of Transgression, but that wouldn't work unless there were other film-makers doing films similar to mine. So I had to wait five years for some other people to be influenced by me.... These people also lived in New York, and they started making films around 1984. Then I put out a magazine with other people, called *Underground Film Bulletin*, and wrote some manifestos and editorials describing the emergence of this movement, the Cinema of Transgression.[38]

For a slightly different perspective on how the CoT came to exist, consider also the accounts given by Zedd's peers, filmmakers Tessa Hughes-Freeland and Ela Troyano. Hughes-Freeland notes that "the films had already existed before Nick decided to coin the term and write the manifesto. It's not like he wrote the manifesto and then everybody went and made these films; they pre-existed."[39] And Troyano agrees that "it had to be a movement to be paid attention to," adding that "that doesn't mean he [Zedd] didn't seriously believe in his ideas, but I think there is a broad way to use transgression and then there's the Cinema of Transgression, and what is it? ... It was a very conscious creation."[40]

Janet Lyon remarks that "to write a manifesto is to announce one's participation, however discursive, in a history of struggle against oppressive forces."[41] This means that the formal and stylistic features of the manifesto matter; hyperbole and immediacy give form to, even embody, urgency and political dissent. In the case of "The Cinema of Transgression Manifesto," the rhetoric of refusal mainly works to construct a dualistic order of self and other: Zedd positions the rhetorical "we" not only in opposition to more general categories of religious morality and political and legal authority but also specifically in opposition to earlier (avant-garde) styles of filmmaking, contemporary film criticism, and curation. In this regard, a comparison with the manifesto of an earlier generation of New York filmmakers proves to be instructive.

In 1961, Jonas Mekas, Alfred Leslie, Robert Frank, Shirley Clarke, and others called themselves the New American Cinema Group and issued their "First Statement." In their manifesto, they allied with "a new generation of film makers" and international "young movements" against the impersonal slickness, censorship, and distribution policies of the "official cinema." The New American Cinema wanted films in the color of blood; Zedd demanded the blood to be real.[42] And while the former defined itself primarily in opposition to classic mainstream filmmaking, the enemy in Zedd's manifesto is not just the dominant culture. Instead, he rejects in its entirety the legacy of the 1960s avant-garde, more specifically the "academic snobbery," the "laziness known as structuralism," "dreary media arts centers," and "geriatric cinema critics."[43] In the text "Long Live the Cinema of Transgression," which reads like an early version of the 1985 manifesto, Zedd claims that the group has been widely ignored by the film critics at the *Voice*, *Film Comment*, *American Film*, and *East Village Eye*. These journals and magazines, however, did not solely promote mainstream film but also featured avant-garde film, art, and New York City's local film culture. In his 1996 autobiography, Zedd also declares war, somewhat retroactively, on artist spaces and film venues such as Collective, ABC No Rio, Bleecker St. Cinema, the Kitchen, P.S.1, and Millennium, many of which were actually supportive of underground film and performance art.[44]

In all these statements, Zedd performs an act of othering in which his own (however loose-knit) group is the other, placed at the very fringes of (film) culture. The common opposition of avant-garde against dominant/mainstream culture might thereby be shifted and complicated—since Zedd, in the name of the "bold new minds of the post punk super-8 underground," calls out to oppose both the mainstream and the old avant-garde system—but a binarism remains. Such oppositions are not only problematic but also ineffective, as Lauren Rabinovitz reminds us. The words "avant garde" themselves, "connoting a militant, even macho purpose, . . . signify that the avant-garde has a fundamental charge to oppose or even overthrow existing art practices."[45] However, if we define the avant-garde in the way that Scott MacKenzie defines manifestos, namely as "ruptures" that intend to challenge "the steady flow of politics, aesthetics, or history," we run the risk of continuing to valorize the status quo, for everything else is consequently defined by its relation to the culturally dominant, to which it can only ever offer a momentary alternative.[46]

The present manifesto may be radically subversive in its claim. Its effect, however, is another. The above quotes from Hughes-Freeland and Zedd himself already suggest this: the manifesto gave a more definitive—and indeed marketable—shape to what already existed in a much more vague and slippery mode. For while Zedd explicitly refers to movements like Dadaism and Futurism that actively promoted interdisciplinarity, his manifesto accommodates his movement in a single medium, limiting and taming the spirit of messy interdisciplinarity in the scene of which he was a part. In this sense, he cleaned up the CoT to market and promote it, quite like KW Institute for Contemporary Art did years later.

Zedd's efforts, however, proved effective. The manifesto circulated, and the term Cinema of Transgression caught on. In 1985, New York–based *ZAT magazine* ran a story on the CoT, praising it as "the single most exciting thing to have happened in the creative community in the last six years," while Bryan Bruce took up five pages of the Spring 1986 issue of Canadian *CineAction!* for eloquently "Pissing on the Cinema of Transgression."[47] At most subsequent screenings announcing Cinema of Transgression films, whether in New York City, Chicago, Munich, Gothenburg, San Francisco, Amsterdam, Stuttgart, or Bremen, Zedd's films were included, sometimes along with those of other filmmakers, but often not. Zedd himself was often present at these screenings, introduced as the movement's "pioneer" (in Munich) or as the "master of transgression" (in Stuttgart).[48] He also made sure to keep his name firmly attached to the movement that his manifesto conjured into existence. To this day, however, the text also clings tightly to the films it claims to represent, while often neglecting those filmmakers who fell out of favor with Zedd.[49] This is not surprising per se, as the manifesto's fierce exclamations lend themselves to being quoted in press releases, screening announcement, article headlines, and so on. In this way, Zedd's manifesto is indicative of how an artist becomes a historian for his own work. Both Lauren Rabinovitz and Patricia Mellencamp have written about how U.S. avant-garde filmmakers often acted as both curators and critics: because the filmmakers' presence was integral to the screenings, their words took on considerable textual significance, often becoming the primary source of historical interpretation.[50] While this is by no means an uncommon practice in art history, it is important to see how it contributes to the construction of meaning.[51] "The Cinema of Transgression Manifesto" exemplifies how intention and interpretation readily intersect and how, when historians, curators, and critics adopt that narrative, "the discourse about the object becomes (is the same thing) as the discourse of the object."[52]

Take as an example the VHS compilation released by the British Film Institute (BFI) in 2000. It is simply titled *Cinema of Transgression* and, according to its synopsis, includes ten "films made by avant-garde filmmakers and artists based in the New York City's Lower East Side between 1979 to 1993. In 1984 the manifesto for the 'Cinema of Transgression' was announced, a movement looking to transform values by breaking all taboos of cinematic expression, conservative religion, politics and aesthetics."[53] The VHS, which I will discuss further in the fourth chapter, was released as part of the BFI's *History of the Avant-Garde* home video series. Through this compilation, the BFI placed the CoT within a specific film historical context, while also reiterating the claims made in Zedd's manifesto. By being included in this institutionally constructed "history of the avant-garde," the CoT is not only historically linked to other filmmakers featured in the series (such as Hans Richter and Kenneth Anger) but also validated by one of the world's largest organizations for the promotion and preservation of moving image culture.[54] One also encounters the manifesto on the CoT's entry in UbuWeb's digital library, where twelve films by various filmmakers are listed along with the full-length version of the manifesto.[55] KW's catalog likewise uses Zedd's manifesto as an introduction to the exhibition. It is precisely this adherence to the manifesto that has led not only to a streamlined framing but also to a discursive impasse. I am aware that the processes I associate with the consolidation of the CoT, first and foremost the manifesto but also all the other selective canonizations and acts of exclusion that will concern me in the next chapters, are not unusual for most self-declared artistic movements. What interests me about these processes, however, is not so much their mere fact but the way in which they affect the reception and historization of the respective "movement." Because, in the case of the CoT, as long as the manifesto, with its reduction of a complex, cross-disciplinary artistic and social scene into a film movement, functions as the primary source of reference and interpretive template for these films, their spillover into other activities, practices, media, places, and scenes remains contained. So once again: to unlock this impasse, I propose to forget the dominant notion of the Cinema of Transgression. And for this gesture, turning to its place of preservation—the archive—is of particular relevance.

Buried in the Archive?

Searching for documentary traces of the CoT, I traveled to New York City in 2018 and 2019. There I was fortunate to speak with participants in the Downtown scene of the 1970s and 1980s and to visit the archive dedicated to documenting that scene, the Downtown Collection at New York University's Fales Library and Special Collections. The visits to this institutional archive, as well as the brief glimpses into private collections I was granted, served as a starting point for my thinking on the archival historiography of the CoT: Where are the material documents of the Downtown scene located and how are they organized? Who has access to them and under what conditions? And how can something as ephemeral and messy as the work(ing)s of a scene be documented in the first place?

A brief note on terminology at the outset: the word "archive" is truly a "loose signifier for a disparate set of concepts" that has undergone various theorizations. However, there is widespread agreement that no archive is a neutral repository, that they operate through interpretation, selection, and usually also classification, making a statement about what is worthy of preservation and future reception.[56] With this premise in mind, I use the term to refer both to the Fales

Library, a physical and public archive that processes and preserves paper-based and audiovisual materials, and to materials held by individuals, specifically Jürgen Brüning, Anthony Chase, Manuel DeLanda, Bradley Eros, Karen Finley, Tessa Hughes-Freeland, John Kelly, Richard Kern, Michael Overn, JG Thirlwell, and Ela Troyano, which I consider private archives.[57] In these private archives, club program flyers, zines, photos, and films were presented to me in an often casual way ("Here's something you might be interested in") that was diametrically opposed to the targeted search and schematic viewing of the public archive. What is more, it seemed as if this material was kept over the years, stacked on shelves in living rooms or work spaces, because of its emotional value, or because it is seen as memorabilia that will eventually acquire commercial value (being "worth what someone will pay for them," as Richard Kern said about his zine collection), not necessarily because historical relevance is ascribed to it by an institution like New York University.[58]

Accessing the archive that houses the Downtown Collection means entering the "flagship" Elmer Bobst Library. Completed in 1973, the twelve-floor building was conceived, along with Tisch Hall and the Hagop Kerkovian Center for Near Eastern Studies, by architects Philipp Johnson and Richard T. Foster as the keystone of a large-scale rebuilding program of the NYU campus, which appears disproportionally large compared to the other, mostly small-scale houses around Washington Square Park. "The status and the power of the archive derive from its entanglement of building and documents. The archive has neither ... without an architectural dimension," writes Achille Mbembe.[59] The deliberately overwhelming architectural scale of the Bobst building underlines this, as does what Foucault describes as the library's implicit "idea of accumulating everything, of establishing a sort of general archive."[60]

Fales Library's Downtown Collection has indeed grown to become the largest of its kind pertaining to the Downtown New York scene, and it includes the personal papers of artists, filmmakers, writers, and performers such as David Wojnarowicz, Dennis Cooper, Richard Hell, Jack Smith, and Kathy Acker, as well as the archives of art collectives and galleries, AIDS activists and theater groups, and nightclubs that had been active from the 1970s to the early 1990s. Crucially, the collection was founded in 1994, when much of the Downtown scene had already succumbed to the disintegration that began in the mid-1980s, thanks most notably to increasing gentrification and the effects of the AIDS crisis. Artist and critic Toby Haslett even argues that New York University, and by extension Fales Library, had played a role in the scene's demise. He writes that the Downtown Collection is

> a tribute to the bohemia that NYU had happily destroyed. For years, the university ... had hacked away at the tangle of establishments and apartment buildings in Greenwich Village and beyond. By the early 90s, it was far from alone. Developers everywhere joined forces with police to take revenge on a

city they felt they'd lost to perverts and the poor.... The mood grew foul. It was clear that *something*—something called Downtown—had been stamped out. So a loose clique of painters, novelists, performers, filmmakers, punks—pallbearers of the avant-garde—began to root around their lofts, snatching up whatever seemed significant. Personal effects took on the zombie flow of the archive.... Boxes stuffed with ephemera, flotsam of a life lived on the so-called fringe, were packed up and sold to NYU, to be rather spookily enshrined as one's "papers."[61]

This statement is interesting in that it makes clear, if rather heatedly, the double-edged nature of the Downtown Collection. Can something living be archived? Does it have to end first? Or does the process of archiving bring it to a definitive end? Does the Downtown scene become history with the launch of the Downtown Collection? Haslett would say yes. And yet it is never quite that simple, for there are other questions that follow. What remains of a phenomenon as fleeting as a scene? What is left behind, for whom, and for what purpose?

Nearly two decades after the Collection's inception, and shortly before he left New York for Mexico City in 2011, Nick Zedd sold an extensive amount of personal material to Fales Library, where it is organized into twelve categories: Writing, Projects, Correspondence, Dad's Pornography Collection, Photography, Illustrations and Artwork, Objects, Film, Video, Audio, Data Storage, and Accretions. For the most part, the collection represents Zedd's work as a cartoon artist, writer, filmmaker, and distributor. However, interspersed with these professional documents are biographical references to his childhood and adolescence ("Dad's Pornography Collection" being the most striking one) as well as his eventual move to Mexico. The Film category contains "Harding family movies" (Harding being Zedd's birth name); the Writing category contains "Juvenilia" and an "assortment of student materials" that rests alongside manuscripts, poetry, and screenplays; and stored near the film props and self-designed clothing is something called "The Mexican Kit," which includes an assortment of souvenirs.[62]

Out of all the participants who were most closely associated with the CoT, Nick Zedd was the only one to give his papers to Fales during his lifetime. This gesture is not necessarily surprising, given Zedd's previous efforts at self-historicization. Indeed, the content and structure of his papers are further evidence of how closely his name remains associated with the CoT, or rather, how his personal history is inextricably linked to that of the alleged movement. The summary of the collection itself introduces Zedd as "the leading figure of the Cinema of Transgression Movement (1984–1990)," and if one types "Cinema of Transgression" into the library's search engine, most results also lead to the Nick Zedd Papers, to folders or items such as "Cinema of Transgression International Press," "Cinema of Transgression Event Flyers," or even "Red T-Shirt with 'Cinema of Transgression, Volume 1' Patch."

On the one hand, one could certainly say that by giving selected material to Fales Library, Nick Zedd wanted to retain control over his own artistic legacy and, by extension, that of the CoT, while also ensuring its historical validity. After all, as Achille Mbembe asserts, it is the institutional archive that gives its documents and the person or groups they represent "a foundational status of existence," confirming that something or someone truly existed.[63] At the same time, however, this archive also opens up a space in which a critical revision of precisely this supposedly secure narrative becomes possible. Not only do many documents from Zedd's papers—and the fact that I, as a researcher, have access to them—provide the basis for the analyses in this book but their sheer scope and content also offer a more complex picture of Zedd's highly indisciplinary practice and of how that practice was embedded in an equally diverse, complex, and incredibly fertile period of cultural production whose ephemeral and immaterial nature challenges the very logic of archiving.

The guide to the Downtown Collection states that its purpose is "to comprehensively collect the full range of artistic practices and output of the Downtown scene, regardless of format."[64] There seems to be an awareness in this aspirational statement of how, in Derrida's words, "archivization produces as much as it records the event," in the sense that the technical structures of the archiving process determine the form of the archivable content itself, or, rather, make its existence as such possible in the first place.[65] Thus, the archive is "not simply a recording of the past, but also . . . a selective power."[66] It is this regulating, indeed often limiting and containing power of selection, followed by processing and classification, that director Marvin J. Taylor critically reflects on when describing the beginnings of the Downtown Collection:

> As I began to process the books, manuscripts, and other materials we were acquiring . . . , I began to experience problems. Downtown works, by their very nature, did not fit into the neatly defined categories the library had established, . . . did not even come from acknowledged publishers or suppliers of materials with whom our accounting office was comfortable dealing. I began to see that the same kinds of disruptions Downtown works effected outside the library were occurring as I brought these materials into a major research collection.[67]

And by "disruptions," he means not only the often sexual or transgressive content but also the transgression of boundaries defined by authorship, genre, or artistic disciplines that characterizes most output from that scene. Moved to Fales Library for the sake of preservation and documentation, these works could productively challenge the archive's "classification schemes, processing rituals, and economic modes for assessing historical or literary value," what José Esteban Muñoz might call the institution's "protocols of rigor."[68] Nevertheless, since the Downtown works are subject to these conditions in one way or another, they run the risk of being limited in their defining unwieldiness. The only solution seems to be to apply the strategy described above and to collect as comprehensively and in as much detail as possible, both in terms of the suppliers of the material and the material itself."[69]

This generous approach can already be felt when browsing through the online catalog and becomes even more tangible when viewing the folders on site, some of which, precisely because they appear to overflow with the abundance of papers stored in them, invite you to linger with them. That is to say, the detail and diversity of the material is almost pleasantly overwhelming. The David Wojnarowicz Papers alone comprise "211 Linear Feet in 117 record cartons," containing original drawings and film copies as well as numerous personal items, one of the most notable being the series "Phone Logs, circa 1970s–early 1990s." It chronicles, in twenty-nine folders, "Wojnarowicz's phone calls, and includes notebooks, loose paper, and scrap sheets upon which Wojnarowicz noted pertinent phone call information."[70] There is something deeply moving about the meticulousness and efficiency with which this part of Wojnarowicz's life and work has been handled. For it shows that this archive takes seriously the ephemeral, the interpersonal, and the intimate; it acknowledges that phone calls to friends, lovers, and collaborators mattered. And while these relationships, naturally, cannot be archived, the slips of paper with information about the phone calls can. In this sense, Wojnarowicz's "Phone Logs" are exemplary of the archive's approach to documenting the Downtown scene's affective tissue. The papers are "ephemera" not so much in the descriptive sense but rather in the way José Esteban Muñoz defines them, namely as containing "traces of lived experiences" and "maintaining experiential politics and urgencies long after these structures of feeling have been lived."[71]

Melissa Adler writes of the library as an "erotically charged space" that invites a mode of cruising, that is, the "pleasurable experience of browsing and losing and finding oneself in the stacks," but which is regularly undermined by the disciplinary divisions and regulatory techniques of the library.[72] Much the same can be said of Fales. While sifting through the boxes of material is quite pleasurable, a part of the experience also always feels somewhat contained. As with most archives, specific folders must be requested in advance, which makes independent or random browsing of shelves impossible. And in the case of Zedd's papers, when one finds something of particular interest, one is asked to fill out a form requesting a scan of the document in question, since "the donor has mandated that self-shot photography by researchers is not permitted for this collection."[73] Although this is not an uncommon procedure, at Fales, Zedd's are amongst the few papers subject to this restriction, which makes the research process particularly laborious.

This is not to say that I did not occasionally stumble upon material I otherwise did not expect to find. In fact, some documents struck me as intriguingly and productively ambiguous. Take, for instance, an item entitled "Nick Zedd Appreciation Society (Materials), ca. 1988."[74] It includes, among other things, membership cards guaranteeing lifetime membership, a template for a "confidential letter" to each new member, and a list of purchasable "sacred objects relating to Our Master NICK ZEDD which are unavailable anywhere else on this planet," like "ZEDD IN DRAG (with coffee mug, looking sad next to a bizarre smiling bust of a man. color, 2–6$)" or "PISSING ON THE CINEMA OF TRANSGRESSION (by Bryan Bruce from *CineAction!* Spring 1986, an article attacking Zedd and everything he stands for, 3$)." In this text, the author (who would later be known as filmmaker Bruce La Bruce) not only accuses Zedd of misogyny for excluding and publicly denouncing filmmaker Ela Troyano from his movement but also exposes the construction of the CoT as a means to generate publicity for Zedd's own films.

This find is an example of how the archive can help rewrite or reinterpret a history that is already considered consolidated. At first glance, the Appreciation Society appears to be one self-mythologizing project among many others. Then again, the fact that Zedd included this scathing attack on the CoT as part of his Appreciation, and then added these materials to his papers, appears to me to be a somewhat defiant, but no less humorous and self-deprecating, gesture of disclosure. It is almost as if Nick Zedd is giving up the primacy of historical representation of the CoT, as if to say, go ahead and paint your own picture. Donating his papers to the Downtown Collection, then, goes beyond a strategic self-inscription into the archival historiography of the scene, for it also carries with it a sense of dispossession, even loss.

This is not least because of the intimate relationship between archiving and forgetting. Following Aleida Assmann's distinction between the archive and the canon, understood as performed cultural repertoire, Abigail De Kosnik argues that forgetting and archiving are correlated. Any text that is no longer actively used by a culture, she writes, "exits the canon and enters the archive ... [and] archived texts sit unaccessed most of the time, unread most of the time, unperformed most of the time."[75] In *Archive Fever*, Derrida not only explains how the contents of the archive, precisely because they are preserved in a singular place, are in constant danger of being lost or forgotten but he also argues that the authority to preserve is fundamentally bound up with the power to destroy.[76] In this vein, Verne Harris offers a deconstructive reading of the link between archive and memory. Rather than assuming a linear progression from memory to archive, it is a process of folding one into the other. Citing Derrida, Harris writes that: "For deconstruction, ... memory and archives are best understood as genres of the trace, subject to what Derrida calls 'the law of the law of genre,' namely, 'a principle of contamination, a law of impurity, a parasitical economy.' ... The boundary between memory and archives should be seen as a process and, more specifically, as a process of invagination."[77]

What follows from this is also a complication of the opposition of memory and forgetting: "The logic of the trace is an enabling to forget. Every movement to record memory, to keep it safe, is a movement to forget, whether it is the movement... from consciousness to unconsciousness, from memory to archives."[78] Considering this complication of the archive, memory, and forgetting, my proposal to forget the CoT takes on another layer of meaning. This archive does not so much work toward remembering the CoT as it aids in my forgetting it. Forgetting—in the sense of a generative moment that brings to light all the contradictory memories, unruly objects, ephemeral aesthetics, messy trajectories of circulation, and indisciplinary tendencies—ultimately underscores the possibilities and also the limits of archiving a scene's history.

2
Downtown Images
■■■■■■■■■■■■■■■■■■■■■

After visiting Club 8BC shortly before it closed in 1985, cultural critic C. Carr, who regularly reported on experimental art and performance for the *Village Voice*, noted that club culture in the East Village was in upheaval. Due to a lack of licenses, rising rents, or both, many small nightclubs were forced to close. Those that remained open seemed less daring and experimental in their programming, attracting "a whole new audience..., some of it with less interest in the work than in Making the Scene."[1] In her commentary, Carr uses the theatrical metaphor of the word "scene" to emphasize its function as a stage for self-expression and presentation, thus, probably unknowingly, creating a link to John Irwin's conception of the scene as a specific social world that offers collective expression. In his 1977 study of urban scenes, Irwin writes that people take to the "public stage" to "find action, . . . enter the drama or 'make the scene.'"[2] In this chapter, which delves deeper into the artistic scenes of 1980s Downtown Manhattan, I will use Irwin's formulation as an opportunity to reflect on how these scenes were made, that is, how they were visualized, imagined, and performed.[3]

The making of a cultural scene never happens solely from the "inside" but stands in reciprocal relation to its urban setting and the images and imaginations it produces that are then reproduced by the press, books, and exhibitions. "Scenes make the city visible in particular kinds of ways," writes Janine Marchessault, referring both to how films and novels depict cities and how visually oriented cultural scenes draw visibility to its cities.[4] This interrelatedness plays a role for the scene(s) at stake here in two ways. First, the participants in the 1980s scene were drawn to New York's Lower East Side because of its image: since the 1960s, various cultural scenes had already emerged there in part because, at least until the early 1980s, rents were still fairly cheap. Second, the films labeled as Cinema of Transgression and Downtown, respectively, created images of New York City's Lower East Side themselves. Many of the films were shot in the East Village's abandoned buildings, deserted streets, and private apartments or on makeshift sets at home and featured performers otherwise known for their involvement in the Downtown art, music, and performance scenes. As information about these films began to circulate via zines like *Underground Film Bulletin* and the films themselves were screened in Canada and Europe, most importantly via the New York Film Festival Downtown (which was initiated in Downtown Manhattan in 1984 but would soon leave its local context), they also conveyed a certain image of Downtown New York City. This chapter thus also investigates how the scenes themselves contributed to the creation of the East Village and Downtown as both monikers and cultural labels. Much like the Cinema of Transgression (CoT), these labels worked to somewhat manage the spilling of artistic practices during this period.

Making (and Breaking) a Scene: The Case of the East Village

Geographically, Downtown Manhattan begins south of 14th Street and encompasses both the East Village (the area between Bowery and Franklin D. Roosevelt East River Drive [FDR Drive]) and the Lower East Side (the area between East 1st Street to East 14th Street).[5] Socioculturally and economically, the Lower East Side has been the antithesis of Uptown Manhattan since the nineteenth century, when it gained its reputation as a poor, industrial, working-class and immigrant area. In the 1950s and 1960s, "Loisaida" formed as a Puerto Rican enclave, overlapping with what would be known as the East Village or Alphabet City in the 1970s and 1980s. The name game can get confusing, especially since the Lower East Side, Loisaida, Alphabet City, and East Village all partially refer to the same area. However, the significance of the East Village goes beyond its geography. In her eclectic treatise on "Getting the Alphabet Right," Kathy Acker writes that "in the beginning, the beginning of the East Village, there was, almost, no such place."[6] It makes one wonder, when did the East Village begin? And how does a place become one "such place"? I am less interested in providing definitive answers to these questions than in examining how specific sites, agents, and events were involved in the emergence of Downtown Manhattan/the East Village as a local scene, genre, cultural phenomenon, and concept and how the CoT emerged in relation to them.

Artists and filmmakers whose work was often associated with the CoT entered the Downtown scene in the late 1970s and early 1980s. Filmmakers Manuel DeLanda and M. Henry Jones and the painter and performance artist Joe Coleman came to New York City to study at the School of Visual Arts (SVA), where they met in classes led by film critic Amy Taubin and filmmaker P. Adams

Sitney.[7] For Richard Kern, the city's unique allure came from its cultural history. He remembers that "in college, all the art books I read, everything was happening in New York. There was nothing happening in Philadelphia so I decided to live out my dream and go live in New York."[8] Once in New York, he moved from making zines to working on films, first assisting filmmaker Beth B, then making his own. Kern's first Super 8 film *Goodbye 42nd Street* (1983) is not exactly an homage to the kind of art he would have seen in his college textbooks but instead an appreciation of the exploitation movie theaters on Midtown Manhattan's 42nd Street. The five-minute film documents a stroll past the street's flashing neon signs promoting Adult Hits, PEEP SHOWS, and XXX Movies, peeking into the window displays of venues that "struggled along a diet of gristly grindhouse," meaning low-budget, independently distributed movies dealing with "forbidden topics" like sex, vice, drug use, and nudity.[9] That such topics would become the key characteristics of Kern's own films only emphasizes the "grindhouse nostalgia" that the title *Goodbye 42nd Street* already suggests.[10] At the time, however, New York City was known not only as a haven for exploitation cinema but also as home to the communities and institutions that provided essential support for experimental and underground film practices. By the late 1960s, with the formation of the film society Cinema 16 (1946), the creation of publications such as *Film Journal* and the *Village Voice* (1955), and the launch of initiatives such as the Film-Maker's Cooperative (1962), the Film-Makers' Cinematheque (1964), and Millennium Film Workshop Inc. (1965), independent film culture was firmly established in the city.[11] Soon after, many of these structures expanded or gained recognition or support from larger art institutions; for example, MoMA began an avant-garde and independent film series in 1969, while the Whitney Museum began its New American Filmmakers series in 1971. But while these film venues were important for creating an awareness of and infrastructure for new film practices, their crossover between disciplines was limited. In contrast, the Downtown nightclubs that emerged from the mid-1960s onward fostered more of a spillover between disciplines and practices that would later be echoed in the activities of the art scenes of the 1980s. At places such as Max's Kansas City (1965–1981), CBGB (est. 1973), or the Mudd Club (1978–1983), music, performance, and filmmaking cross-fertilized, sparking a moment of filmmaking most often referred to as "No Wave" or "New Cinema" (named either after the music scene with which it shared many participants or the short-lived screening room at St. Mark's Place).[12]

Within this newly forming scene, musicians became performers in films, films were made that documented or accompanied live music performances, and local bands delivered soundtracks for the films. An experimental, "highly theatrical, performance-based approach to music, characterized by rough and often dissonant sounds," met with a style of filmmaking that crudely combined documentary footage and fictional, genre-bending narratives in these often cheap Super 8 productions.[13] The city, its nightlife, and its scenes are at the core of these films, both textually and structurally. Amos Poe's *The Blank Generation* (1976), for example, is a montage of concert footage of Richard Hell, Talking Heads, Television, and Patti Smith at CBGB or Max's Kansas City. Vivienne Dick's films star female players from the No Wave music and art scene, such as Lydia Lunch of Teenage Jesus and the Jerks and Pat Place of James Chance and the Contortions and Bush Tetras. These films both documented and constructed the scenes from which they emerged. Fittingly, as Mark Benedetti describes, they screened at "the New Cinema [where Super 8 films were transferred to video, an exhibition style which differed strongly from other alternative screening venues] and bars and clubs where No Wave audiences socialized, but also at other venues like Millennium Film Workshop, the Collective for Living Cinema, and the Film Forum."[14] While institutions associated with avant-garde film of the 1960s and 1970s were still relevant for this new generation of filmmakers, venues linked to post-punk music and club culture were just as, if not more, vital.

This scene fluidly transitioned when new participants emerged in the late 1970s and early 1980s. Similar to those who came out of the No Wave moment, these new players arrived via music, performance, filmmaking, or visual art and were actively involved in the fast-growing East Village club scene. For instance, Ela Troyano worked as a projectionist at the Pyramid Club where she met Tessa Hughes-Freeland, with whom she later collaborated on projection performances, organized screenings, and the initiation of the New York Film Festival Downtown (which I will discuss in the last section of this chapter). Troyano also ran Chandelier Club with Uzi Parnes, where they hosted performances and experimental theater works. Richard Kern showed his first film at Danceteria and met his collaborators Tommy Turner and David Wojnarowicz at the Peppermint Lounge, where all three worked as busboys. Venues like Danceteria (1979–1986), Club 57 (1980–1983), and Pyramid (est. 1981), as well as Limbo Lounge, Darinka, and 8BC, all of which opened in 1983 or 1984, took an even more ambitious or, rather, lavish approach to crossover programming than their predecessors CBGB and Max's Kansas City, which were still mostly music-based. For instance, Danceteria established a multifloor program with live bands, DJs, and video presentations, offering "revelers with a novel element of choice, not because of the range of entertainment but because all of the options were available at once."[15] Even at Pyramid, which was much smaller than Danceteria, all week long there were scheduled (or unscheduled) concerts, film screenings, drag shows, readings, slide projections, and all kinds of dance parties that blended into one another. As one of its weekly programs shows, the drag scene (Ethyl Eichelberger), the performance scene (Holly Hughes), the spoken word scene (Lydia Lunch), and the comedy scene (Rockets Redglare), as well as the Sunday party folk (Soiree Piquante and Café Iguana), all met at the Pyramid (see Figure 3).

Ela Troyano remembers that even though all of that "wasn't . . . happening at the same time, but on the same night and at the same place, . . . it had this sense of continuity. You wouldn't be going to see this one thing, but the ongoing, the

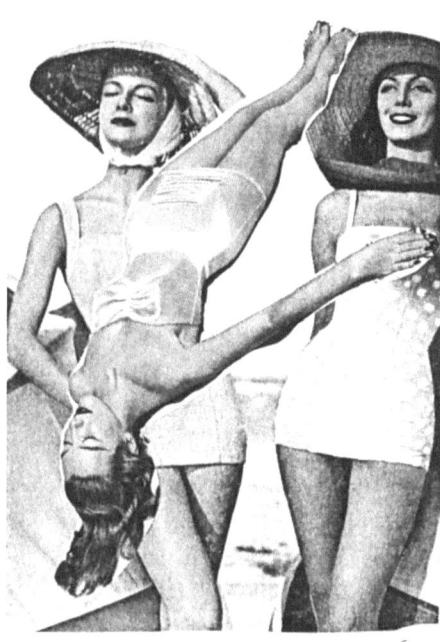

FIGURE 3 Weekly flyer for the Pyramid Club

whole surrounding."[16] Thanks to their approach to programming, clubs like Pyramid were key facilitators of what I earlier called the key operational mode of the Downtown scene, namely indisciplinarity. And even though film institutions like Millennium or Anthology Film Archives did not altogether reject films that carried the CoT label, it was the small, short-lived, cross-disciplinary clubs that embraced them most. As important sites for "socializing, for entertainment, for doing things," clubs operated "as both a scene unto itself and also as a scene generator."[17] The fact that films were screened at these clubs is thus crucial in this context for two reasons. First, by being embedded in a multipart program that involved other Downtown scene participants, the screenings automatically rendered their context of production more visible. Second, by being shown in clubs, they became part of the ongoingness that Troyano described, where the transitions between films, performances, and concerts, and also between entire scenes themselves, were often fluid, as one medial form or space spilled over into the next. This also invites us to consider the particularities of the club setting and how it influences the viewing conditions of the films. As Joan Hawkins put it: "In instances where the films were projected behind bands, the story was not the point—and people rarely stopped dancing in order to gaze at the movie. When the film was shown in a backroom, people did watch the film in pretty much a traditional way—but there was more coming and going . . . and the audience was vocal—yelling out opinions and questions and cheering whenever someone they recognized came on-screen."[18] Short attention spans and competing programs might have led to the film being seen not from start to finish but in fragments. This circumstance then shapes the film itself: instead of being perceived as a complete and isolated work, it becomes something that happens as well and, in happening, opens onto everything else that happens around it.

The experience of a continuous flow of events was further enhanced by the clubs' spatial proximity, which made club hopping easy and turned venues into "neighborhood places" for those who lived around the corner.[19] One could just as easily learn about the events by word of mouth, by picking up a Xeroxed flyer featuring the weekly program, or by flicking through the ads in the latest copy of the *East Village Eye* (*EYE*) (1979–1987). Organized by departments (News, Art, Books, Fashion, Film, Music, Performance, Photos, Theater, Video), the *EYE* had participants of the scene(s) cover the scene(s): musician Richard Hell wrote about inventing punk, actress Cookie Mueller gave health advice to readers, and filmmaker Tessa Hughes-Freeland introduced the latest movies. Local clubs and galleries placed ads for their programs and upcoming shows. By presenting specific agents and places as belonging to the East Village, the *EYE* made and mapped its scene in significant ways. For instance, the October 1985 issue featured an East Village map and gallery guide that indicated its hot spots and geographical demarcations as well as the inaugural edition of David Wojnarowicz's column "Sidewalk Begging." This short text begins with Wojnarowicz riding in a car through the East Village. He describes the sounds (Puerto Rican music blasting from another car) and sights of the still dirty but increasingly gentrified neighborhood. After wandering the streets, high on drugs, and observing the bustle around him, Wojnarowicz visits a "post-show acid party thrown by Carlo McCormick," curator and art editor of the *EYE*. There he meets Richard Kern, "director of those already classic Super 8's," and watches a recently finished music video for Sonic Youth, starring Lung Leg, an actress whom Wojnarowicz had met at Ex Voto Gallery and had seen perform at Darinka. While staying at Kern's apartment, after being "thrown out of my apartment of four years by a plague of gentrifying artists," Wojnarowicz writes he has been "privy to all sorts of strange psychotronic rituals." The column ends with a reflection on watching a video copy of the Super 8 film *Desperate Teenage Love Dolls* with Kern while tripping on acid and slowly "turning into an enormous jelly donut."[20]

Giving readers a feel for floating from one East Village party to the next, Wojnarowicz addresses gentrification issues just as casually as he drops names of people and places that may or may not be familiar. His column gives a highly personal insight into the scene's workings, ultimately revealing the self-referentiality of the magazine, and, by extension, of the scene(s) it simultaneously represents and constructs. And although, or maybe precisely because, the magazine had the sensibility of an in-joke, the fact that readers from other U.S.

states and Canada subscribed to it suggests that beyond the East Village's seemingly tight limits, there was an eagerness to get in on that joke.

The wish to be in the know about the East Village comes as little surprise considering that its scenes started to draw attention to the neighborhood. Maybe as both symptom and result, by the mid-1980s, "East Village" had become a label commonly used in national and international media reports, just as Downtown Manhattan was increasingly sought after by the real estate industry. It might have been, as Joan Hawkins writes, the "neighborhood itself that provided a sense of artistic cohesion, and it is perhaps for that very reason that both the artists and the work they produced were labelled with geographic epithets."[21] Nevertheless, the creation of these labels requires a closer look.

In the 1980s, the terms East Village and Downtown, respectively, were perceived as aesthetics, styles, and cultural genres. And these genres were in the process of becoming increasingly consumable—via the art market and real-estate development—and visible through press coverage and self-referential exhibitions. As Christopher Mele summarizes it, "the Downtown scene was transformed by media, spectators and participants from the marginal and rebellious to an urban genre well suited for urban revitalization. Both real estate developers and the city government employed representations of the Downtown scene to legitimize neighborhood restructuring practices and policies, to exculpate the social costs of community displacement, and to challenge the validity of resistance efforts mounted by threatened resident."[22]

The mentioned wave of new clubs in the early to mid-1980s correlated with the introduction of the art world to the East Village and vice versa. On the one hand, a very quickly emerging gallery scene, with eleven galleries opening within three years, let the already thin "division that separated the art world and the party scene dissolve."[23] Even though most of these gallery shows deliberately evoked the spirit of a club night rather than the pristine feel of the White Cube, they still brought, quite literally, creations from the street, the studio, and the club into the gallery space, making it unambiguously recognizable as art. On the other hand, various gallery and institutional exhibitions with an East Village theme helped formalize the neighborhood not only as a scene but also as a style and genre. What is more, since scene participants themselves often curated these shows, they can be considered a means through which the East Village imagined and performed itself, thus also turning its own scene into a more identifiable and containable concept.

In 1981, for example, *NEW YORK/NEW WAVE* brought East Village graffiti, music, and writing to the walls of P.S.1 (now MoMA PS1) in Queens. Diego Cortez, cofounder of the Mudd Club, curated the show, which featured work by the club's regulars. In its Tribeca space, the Hal Bromm Gallery took stock in 1984, bringing together twenty-five artists under the title *Climbing: The East Village*, not as "a definitive search of what's happening but a search for the most promising of the lot."[24] Shortly after the show, the gallery opened a second space in the East Village. Downtown-themed exhibitions were not limited to New York galleries and institutions, however, but were popping up all over the United States and in Europe.[25]

Naturally, the entry of the East Village into the international art world was accompanied by corresponding media coverage. American lifestyle and art magazines as well as local and international newspapers deemed its art and agents either adolescent and silly or exciting and groundbreaking, praised its energy or criticized its commercialization, and gleefully predicted or polemically mourned its decline into insignificance. The year 1985 seems to have marked a pivot point in the East Village's ongoing oscillation between the underground and commerce. Carlo McCormick, in a semi-ironic obituary of the scene published in the 1985 October issue of the *EYE*, declared that "East Village art is dead."[26] The *New York Times* noted that "the party seems to be over" when it reported on the closing of the East Village's 8BC, Darinka, and Limbo Lounge.[27] Fun Gallery, which had spearheaded the influx of galleries in the East Village, closed its doors that same year with a group show metaphorically titled *Sink or Swim*.

Strikingly, it was around this pivot point that Nick Zedd declared the birth of the CoT in his manifesto and through his zine *Underground Film Bulletin*. It seems that as the East Village concept failed to maintain its appeal and lost its momentum, the adoption of other labels became all the more necessary. In the following sections of this chapter, I will address "underground" and "Downtown" as two key terms that influenced the understanding of the artistic practices at issue in this book and, to some extent, contained their messiness. I will do this by discussing two initiatives that emerged in 1984, precisely at the moment of the deflation of the East Village and the beginning of the proliferation of the Cinema of Transgression label: *Underground Film Bulletin* and the New York Film Festival Downtown. In what follows, I want to explore what the zine and the festival can tell us not only about the making of a scene but also about the spillings and containments that they attempt to manage.

Underground Superstars

A stubborn face stares back at me from the cover of the zine. The disheveled hair and dark circled eyes are filled with a pattern reminiscent of the Ben-Day dots of Roy Lichtenstein's pop paintings. Black print on white paper, only the lips are painted red with a felt-tip pen, the color smearing over the contours of the mouth. Six names float underneath; above, the words "The Underground Film Bulletin 6" hover in thick black capital letters. This assemblage of images and letters makes up the cover of the sixth issue of Nick Zedd's Xeroxed zine. He edited and published nine issues at irregular intervals between 1984 and 1990 under the pseudonym Orion Jeriko. It was a cheaply produced bulletin, but one that, as I will argue, had a definite purpose. Even then, the *Underground Film Bulletin* (UFB) played with, or rather anticipated, its borderline status between ephemeral throwaway and valuable object. In issue 8, a page where readers could order back issues proclaimed that the zines were "excellent for swatting flies" but that they were also "Super-Scarce Collectors Issues." Since then, UFB issues have indeed become scarce. They can be found in institutions like Fales Library, in private archives, and through specialized dealers like Printed Matter Inc. in New York City, where I spent an afternoon flipping through several copies. As I opened the pages, I was mesmerized by the jumble of words and images that unfolded before my eyes. Tiny type, like an afterthought or a whispered secret, alternated with bold, flashing letters; the pages were crowded with messy collages of photographs and other snippets of writing and images. This zine seemed to open up a bubbling and exciting space, one filled with names and faces both familiar and unfamiliar, activities, gossip, and in-jokes: the space of a scene.[28]

Most text and images in the UFB were produced by Nick Zedd (or his alter ego Orion Jeriko) and other Downtown scene participants such as Tessa Hughes-Freeland, Richard Kern, Casandra Stark, and Lydia Lunch. There are lengthy, chatty, and often intimate interviews with artists and filmmakers, announcements for film screenings or VHS releases, snarky or admiring film commentary, as well as political, autobiographical, lyrical (and not so lyrical) texts. (An article in issue 2 from 1984 is headlined "Richard Kern's Farts—An Analysis by R. Jacoby.") The texts are interspersed with cartoons, drawings, and photographs, either appropriated from other sources or produced by the filmmakers whose work the UFB featured, all collaged in a manner typical of handmade zines. Many issues reprinted texts by or about figures known for their transgressive art and writing, like theater director Antonin Artaud, philosopher Georges Bataille, and Austrian *Aktionskünstler* Otto Mühl. Other issues addressed gentrification politics, specifically greedy landlords and the commercialization of the Lower East Side, and informed readers about upcoming rent strikes and the legal aspects of squatting. With this editorial approach, the UFB seems to assume that both writers and readers "get it" (or want to get it), that is, that they share an aesthetic sensibility, a sense of humor, and perhaps even a philosophical and political stance. Whether or not they know each other personally or frequent the same East Village clubs is not necessarily important. What matters is that a reproducible, circulating organ like the UFB has the potential to build a community in and around its pages. As Daniel Kane points out in his discussion of the 1960s Downtown Manhattan literary scene, the fact that a group is drawn together in the space of a magazine "does not necessarily mean that there is a community *prior* to the publication. Rather, it is the gathering of names, and the conscious decision to repeat those names throughout the various issues, that generates the sense of community."[29] Lucy Mulroney makes a similar observation when stating that the so-called little magazines of the Downtown poets were "scenes of neither identification nor disidentification" that "document the momentary coalescence of a group of individuals—a series of idiosyncratic endeavors collated, stapled, and sent out into the world with the hope of finding an audience."[30] In the case of the UFB, its audience was by no means limited to the Downtown scene.

In the beginning, the zine was sold at places like Sohozat, a comic and zine shop in SoHo, and Rafik, a film, video, and audiotape store in the East Village.[31] Zedd also mailed the UFB to subscribers across the country or gave away copies at screenings and festivals outside New York. Other U.S. zines, such as *Sex and Guts* from Brooklyn and *Film Threat* from Royal Oak, Michigan, also featured ads to order the UFB. In this way, it grew a relatively small but nonetheless international readership: for example, in the Junk Mail section of issue 7, published in 1988, letters from readers in Fairfield County, Connecticut; Washington, D.C.; and Rochester, New York, express concerns ranging from friendly subscription requests to death threats against Zedd/Jeriko. In an interview with "The Most Hated Filmmaker in the World: John Spencer" (issue 6, 1987), interviewer (Jeriko) and interviewee circle around the question of why Spencer's films *Ponzos Masterwork*, *Shithaus*, and *PUS*, which include scenes of slaughterhouses, Hitler speeches, and "the filmmaker's asshole dripping shit," received such bad feedback. Together, they ponder why people didn't get that they were jokes and whether his films could therefore be considered a "kind of failure." When asked why he had not shown his films more often, Spencer answers, "I guess in 84 or 85, I showed 'em around in like five places in New York City. I was real excited because I had come to New York after finishing a semester and seen a show and I read Underground Film Bulletin, so I got really excited and I really wanted to show the stuff and I did and nobody really came." Spencer might have made his films during his studies at Brown University in Providence, Rhode Island, but it was coming to New York City and reading the UFB that made him want to "show the stuff" in the city. For Spencer, the UFB promoted the idea of an existing network for films like his, a scene in which to participate. That this scene, however, did not "get" the films, led him to consider them failures.[32]

By growing a domestic and even international readership, the UFB became part of an alternative distribution network for communication and exchange, which also involved the informal distribution of other zines and videotapes. The correspondence housed in the Nick Zedd Papers at Fales Library includes letters from readers of the UFB who ask to buy or trade VHS tapes, and some say the UFB inspired them to make their own zines. These letters come from all over the world and sometimes reached Zedd years after the last issue of the UFB was published.[33] The zine's distribution and circulation thus not only helped to construct a scene locally but also loosened the scene's geographic boundaries. As Kate Eichhorn points out, copy machines "not only helped to establish the scene and define its unique aesthetic but also eventually facilitated the scene's migration well beyond 14th Street."[34] The notion that "scenes become scenes because they are publicized and [that] publicity requires a medium" therefore not only foregrounds the relevance of zines like the UFB in the making of scenes but also shifts our attention to the key role that media and technology played in their creation.[35]

Let me now return to the cover of the UFB described above. Who is looking back at the reader from this Xeroxed page? The masthead of the sixth issue from 1987 reveals that the cover features "the very beautiful and talented Underground Superstar LUNG LEG humbly rendered by her great admirer Nick Zedd." Elisabeth Carr, aka Lung Leg, directed the Super 8 short *Worm Movie* (1985) and also made appearances in Richard Kern's Super 8 films *You Killed Me First* (1985), *Submit to Me* (1985), *Fingered* (1986), and *Submit to Me Now* (1987). She also appears on the cover of Sonic Youth's third studio album *EVOL* (1986). Each cover page of the UFB prominently featured a star, or "Underground Superstar," most of whom sooner or later acted in one of Zedd's films. Thus Lung Leg joined the ranks of musicians, performance artists, and filmmakers Donna Death, Lydia Lunch, Phoebe Legere, Richard Hell, John Spacely, Rockets Redglare, Kembra Pfahler, and Casandra Stark, all of whom were rendered by Zedd in black and white hand-drawn cartoon portraits embellished with a single splash of color: a green tongue, yellow cigarette smoke, orange eye shadow.[36]

The UFB's cover style, editorial policy, and visual and material aesthetics situate it at a curious juncture between artists' magazine and subcultural fanzine. On the one hand, its focus on the personal and its DIY production and small circulation are very much in line with what Stephen Duncombe describes as typical (fan)zine characteristics. The fanzine format emerged in the United States in the 1930s in science fiction fan communities and reached a peak in music subcultures of the 1970s and 1980s, but its history leads further back to amateur publishing in the nineteenth century.[37] The UFB's design and layout are reminiscent of the messy, collaged, Xeroxed punk zines and also shares a focus on reviews, editorials, and interviews with filmmakers, musicians, and performers. However, by placing the artist at the center, the UFB also encourages comparison with artist books and art/lifestyle magazines like *Rolling Stone* (founded in 1967), *Interview* (first issue published in 1969 as *INTER/View*), and *Avalanche* (1970–1976).

Although very different in orientation, *Interview* and *Avalanche* magazines shared two defining features, namely an emphasis on artists' writings or interviews and the portrait cover shot. For instance, Gwen Allen writes about *Avalanche* that while its "stated goal . . . was to empower the artist, its format echoed the cult of celebrity then sweeping American popular culture."[38] Most representative of this merging of art world, celebrity cult, and pop culture was Andy Warhol's *Interview*, particularly with its mixed-media cover portraits by Richard Bernstein. Bob Colacello, who was the magazine's editor from 1970 to 1982, talks about how the choice of cover image reflected the magazine's promise to "letting them [the readers] into the party": "Late one afternoon in early 1975, Andy [Warhol], Fred [Hughes], and I tried to figure out who to put on the next few covers. Looking over the sales figures for the previous year, we realized that our best sellers were also our best friends.... It was a breakthrough and it confirmed our instinct to make *Interview* a reflection of Andy's celebrity-studded world."[39]

By calling Lung Leg an "Underground Star," Zedd followed Warhol's strategy of making his friends the (cover) stars and the stars his friends. *New Yorker* magazine fittingly called *Interview* "the ultimate fanzine: friends writing about friends in articles that looked like the ads."[40] This somewhat dry observation attests to the fact that fanzines and artist magazines are akin in the respect that their editors, writers, and cover stars, not to mention interviewers and interviewees, likely all belong to the same scene. Thus, in Warhol's *Interview*—and to a lesser degree in the UFB as well—the entanglement of social world and art world, of friendship and collaboration, constitutive of any scene, is not only unveiled but marketed. What the UFB thus shares with both fanzines and artists' magazines is the promise of getting to know the artist (or filmmaker or musician) and becoming part, or at least getting a glimpse, of their scene. Just like *Interview* conveys the feeling of "hanging out in the back room of Max's Kansas City," the UFB, through the highly subjective lens and language of the scene participants themselves, grants access to what is presented as the world of "Underground Film."[41] What is, then, the function of this metaphorically and conceptually charged term "underground" that is so prominently placed in the title of the zine? And how do this term and the potential of the UFB as a means of building community among a small but international readership relate to the idea of a Cinema of Transgression?

Before it was used in the context of film, the term "underground," as Duncan Reekie notes, "was first deployed by beat and early counter-cultural agents to designate their subculture of resistance beneath the square world: it was a metaphoric invocation of the resistance groups of World War Two who secretly sabotaged the Fascist occupation of Europe."[42] The concept of underground film, as will be explained in the following, retained this sense of resistance and work against the "square world" from below, where "below" refers to aesthetic and formal aspects as well as to conditions and possibilities of filmic production and distribution.

When the notion of underground film was introduced in the 1960s, it offered an alternative to avant-garde or experimental film but was soon used synonymously with those designations.[43] For instance, when filmmaker Stan Vanderbeek listed "Films from the Underground" in his 1961 manifesto "The Cinema Delimina," he referred to 16 mm works by Robert Frank, Jonas Mekas, Shirley Clarke, and other members of an avant-garde that extended back to the 1940s.[44] At the end of the decade, two authors attempted to deliver a more comprehensive definition as well as a historical lineage of the category; Parker Tyler was one of them.[45] In *Underground Film: A Critical History*, first published in 1969, he recognizes common subjects and techniques in the films of Andy Warhol and Stan Brakhage and puts them in a historical perspective by drawing on the works of Luis Buñuel, Man Ray, and Marcel Duchamp. In general, however, Tyler's study reads more as a polemic, ascribing infantility, regression, self-centeredness, and spectacle to underground film, while criticizing both the popularization of underground themes that was already underway in Hollywood, animated, and art films at the time as well as those who used the term "underground" for self-promotional purposes. Specifically, he levels criticism at the screening practices of Jonas Mekas, denouncing his self-presentation and accusing him of institutionalizing underground film. In the early 1960s, Mekas organized the series Underground Midnights at the Charles Theater and Bleecker Street Cinema. By showing films in the cinema and labeling them underground, Mekas's "uncritical permissiveness," says Tyler, worked against the potential of the term and led to its becoming yet another tool for (self-)promotion.[46]

Issuing a swift response, Mekas published "Underground Film After Parker Tyler" in December 1969, in his *Village Voice* column "Movie Journal": "At the end of the decade, we should settle for good the question of underground film. What kind of film is it? What does it do? How would you define it?" After asking this, Mekas goes on to deliver an extensive list of attributes, collected from the pages of Tyler's book: "Underground films are 'peepholes,' 'peepshows,' 'infantile gimmicks,' 'fetish footage,'" exhibiting "formlessness, triviality, messiness, and amateurishness."[47] While Tyler criticizes Mekas for his supposed self-promotion, Mekas seems to be bothered by Tyler's desire for definition. Tyler does, however, credit underground film with a strong potential for subversion, particularly through its questioning of old stereotypes and its emphasis on daring, unconventional, provocative visions. Note also how Tyler's text already hints at what Jan-Frederik Bandel aptly describes as the "constitutive contradictoriness" of the underground. Bound to an almost utopian vision of independence, opposition, and change, the underground is ultimately fragile and may not be able to survive the tension between the visibility and growth brought about by networking on the one hand and institutionalization, appropriation, and consolidation on the other.[48]

Despite, or perhaps because of, this contradiction, Tyler's text has been followed by many others that have addressed the question of what is at stake in underground filmmaking. While these accounts all offer their own conceptions and periodization, there is a general understanding that the historical underground in the United States is a 1960s phenomenon characterized by an anti-commercial, anti-academic, and overall radical attitude toward filmmaking. British filmmaker Malcolm Le Grice, cofounder of the London Film-Makers' Co-op workshop in the late 1960s, even declared that "the classic Underground cinema was transgressive." By classic, he means a film like Jack Smith's *Flaming Creatures* (1963), whose transgressive character lies in its presentation of unrepressed, queer sexuality, which in turn led to the film becoming subject to censorship and police raids.[49] For similar reasons, J. Hoberman and Jonathan

Rosenbaum rank *Flaming Creatures* as the "most notorious underground film." Writing in 1983, they are more explicit in distinguishing underground film as a historically specific configuration of styles, protagonists, events, and locations. Thus, while Tyler's early examination of underground film is rather broad, reaching back to European and U.S.-American cinema of the 1920s, Hoberman and Rosenbaum suggest narrowing the notion of underground film to "filmmakers who emerged in NYC during the early sixties whose work was distinguished from commercial movies and the earlier avant-garde by a combination of willful primitivism, taboo-breaking sexuality, and obsessive ambivalence toward American popular culture."[50]

Nick Zedd consciously linked his publication to the conceptual history just described and not just by calling his zine a bulletin for underground film. The discourse (and incipient canonization) of underground film is also one of the key reference points for the articles he edited and wrote, in which both the demand for a break with the "old" avant-garde and the presentation of the CoT as a sort of neo-underground often resonate. For instance, while underground filmmakers such as Jack Smith or Kenneth Anger often appear as idols in the UFB, people and institutions associated with the established avant-garde are scorned, unmistakably so: in the editorial of issue 7 (1988), Nick Zedd-as-Orion Jeriko describes Mekas and his New American Cinema as "dinosaurs buried in their own rubble" and *Village Voice* film critic J. Hoberman as the "cliquish and worst of all superfluous . . . J. Ostrich Hoberman." He also demands the "dreary and crumbling mausoleum known as Collective [for Living Cinema]" and the "perpetually irrelevant Millennium [Film Workshop]" to be blown up. By neglecting or refusing to review or show CoT films, goes the accusation, Hoberman and others have caused an "enormous setback" for "underground and independent films in general."[51] Consequently, issue 8 (1989) is entirely "Dedicated to the Destruction of the New American Cinema."

"The Ten Greatest Underground Films of All Time by Orion Jeriko" (issue 6, 1987) on the other hand, is a list of films that fall into the category of 1960s New York underground film as outlined by Hoberman and Rosenbaum in their book *Midnight Movies* (although the authors are not directly mentioned). The list includes *Flaming Creatures*, Kenneth Anger's *Inauguration of the Pleasure Dome* (1954), Barbara Rubin's *Christmas on Earth* (1963), George Kuchar's *A Town Called Tempest* (1963), and Andy Warhol's *Chelsea Girls* (1966). Zedd as Jeriko, however, expands this group of underground classics to include his own works as well as those of Richard Kern and Manuel DeLanda, whom Zedd had named as members of the CoT in his manifesto two years earlier.[52]

But even though Zedd, especially in the pages of the UFB, repeatedly emphasized his desire to supersede the "old" avant-garde, the structures initiated by the previous generation were by no means irrelevant to the younger Downtown film scene, or even to Zedd himself. They not only provided the infrastructure that made New York City a hotbed for filmmaking but also actively supported

1980s scene participants by screening, distributing, and restoring their work.[53] Also, and somewhat paradoxically, Zedd followed in the footsteps of one of the most active supporters of underground film, Jonas Mekas himself. Both Mekas and Zedd took on the multiple roles of filmmaker, programmer, critic, and editor. Both founded a magazine with the agenda of publishing and promoting a new movement and the work of the filmmakers associated with it. Yet, while Mekas's efforts were aimed at professionalizing the infrastructure surrounding the avant-garde and thus legitimizing its existence, Zedd took the opposite approach. By employing tactics in line with the do-it-yourself ethos of punk culture, he set out to reclaim the underground's initially subversive connotations and use its appeal to launch his own concept.

In this sense, one could argue that Tyler's accusation that Mekas misused the term "underground" as a promotional tool is also true for Zedd. His CoT makes its first appearance in issue 3 (1985). "Long Live the Cinema of Transgression," written by Orion Jeriko, announces that "a new movement is born," which remained "unseen by the narrow-minded old timers who write for the *Voice, Film Comment, American Film, East Village Eye* and virtually every other film journal in the world." In the following issue, "The Cinema of Transgression Manifesto" states that this movement proposes "to go beyond all limits set or prescribed by taste, morality or any other traditional value system shackling the minds of men," which reads like a pledge to take the 1960s underground's interest in "willful primitivism and taboo-breaking sexuality" to the extreme.[54]

A 1997 interview in the *Sex and Guts* zine titled "Beyond the Myth of Nick Zedd" offers insight into how Zedd conceived of the UFB as a kind of extended promotional and historiographical tool. When asked to what extent the zine presented his desired public image of the CoT, he replied that "it was very successful, because even now . . . the repercussions have been the book *Deathtripping* that Jack Sargeant put out, most of the material was inspired or paraphrased from the magazine."[55] It may seem like a rather vain claim that Sargeant's book, first published in 1995, merely paraphrased the content of his zine. But it is true that *Deathtripping: The Cinema of Transgression* consolidates the narrative of the CoT that Zedd constructed with the help of the UFB. In this regard, let us look at the first sentence of the introductory chapter of Sargeant's book: "The Cinema of Transgression may have been the first underground film 'movement' to expressly articulate an aesthetic of transgression/confrontation via the pages of *Underground Film Bulletin*, but various other directors had created similarly transgressive films. East Coast American underground cinema produced several filmmakers whose work must be viewed as paving the way, as demarcating the terrain, which the Cinema of Transgression filmmakers would themselves later explore."[56]

Sargeant goes on to point out aspects of the films of Jack Smith, Andy Warhol, George and Mike Kuchar, and John Waters that he feels have recurred in the CoT: Smith's inimitable anarchism, Warhol's underground star system, the

Kuchar brothers' parody of Hollywood tropes, and Waters's "aesthetic of bad taste."[57] While Sargeant is careful to call the CoT a movement, he does two things to reinforce Zedd's conception of the CoT: First, Sargeant supports the UFB historiography of underground film by presenting the CoT as the heirs to those "East Coast American Underground" protagonists who also number among the makers of "The Ten Greatest Underground Films of All Time" according to Jeriko-as-Zedd. Second, Sargeant claims that the zine presents the CoT's "official" history. He explicitly states that the CoT articulated its aesthetic "via the pages of *Underground Film Bulletin*" and explains that the influence of filmmakers like Smith and Waters is demonstrated by the fact that they were "featured in, interviewed in, or contributed to, Orion Jeriko's *Underground Film Bulletin*, while some of them engaged, and even worked, with various filmmakers associated with the Cinema of Transgression."[58] Sargeant's book thus presents the UFB not only as the CoT's mouthpiece but also treats it as its unambiguous chronicle, rather than critically reflecting on its content and editorial policy. In doing so, he has chosen to decline an offer that, in my eyes, the zine makes: to become an accomplice in a reexamination of the CoT that questions the myth of its origin.

In this chapter, I am first concerned with the broader social and artistic context out of which the CoT was constructed, namely the cultural scenes of Lower Manhattan in the 1980s. Specifically, I am interested in exploring how these scenes were performed and made visible and how concepts such as "East Village" or "Downtown" managed to simultaneously contain and bring into circulation certain artistic practices, and to what effect. A consideration of a zine like the UFB belongs here for several reasons. It played an important role in building and promoting the CoT concept, not least since its fourth issue in 1985 featured "The Cinema of Transgression Manifesto." The zine's function as a promotional tool also meant that Zedd, whose birth name was James Harding, adopted not one but two aliases. This "polyonymy" allowed him to experiment with the roles of snarky editor/critic and manifesto-writing underground filmmaker, switching back and forth between them without compromising their respective images.[59] In other words, these alternating names allowed him to keep his filmmaking, zine making, writing, and illustrating separate, at least superficially, when in fact these practices were crucially entangled. His own zine perhaps shows this indisciplinarity in the most exemplary way. The inclusion of the nonfilmic output of filmmakers and performers, such as poems by Lung Leg and Casandra Stark, photographs by Richard Kern and Annie Sprinkle, drawings by Manuel DeLanda and Nick Zedd, and reports on performances by Kembra Pfahler and Joe Coleman, implies that the films of the UFB scene were produced alongside and in exchange with a rich repertoire of other artistic practices. In other words, the fact that these contributions were gathered under the heading "Underground Film" underscores not only Zedd's aspiration to be part of a history and canon of transgressive film but also, and perhaps more importantly, the fact that filmmaking necessarily spilled over into performance, poetry, photography, visual arts, and vice versa. Reading Zedd against himself, so to speak, we see that behind his conception of a movement stands a group of people who, alone but more often together, are engaged not only in filmmaking but also in zine making. All of this makes the UFB neither a mere supplement to the CoT and its associated films nor a document that represents its definitive history. Rather, the UFB is part of the CoT in the sense that it was and is instrumental in creating, shaping, and framing it. This is not necessarily the CoT that the manifesto proclaimed but the one that spills over the boundaries established by its very concept of containment.

In the next section, as I turn to one of its most important initiatives, we will see another moment in which the Downtown scene of the mid-1980s—and, by extension, the CoT—is seen and imagined both within and beyond its local context.

Club to Kino: The New York Film Festival Downtown

New York Film Festival New York Film Festival New York Film Festival New York Film Festival New York Film Festival New York Film Festival. The four words in black letters repeat six times, shrinking like an echo from top to bottom on the neon pink paper, until they make room for DOWN TOWN, in capital letters, as if someone were shouting it out. Above it all is the statement "The Film Society of Limbo Center Presents." At the bottom, wiggly letters, seeming to dance out of the lines of their triangular border, form the name LIMBO. Turning the page over, the back reveals the dates (October 21–23), the names of the festival's organizers ("Ela Troyano and Tessa Hughes-Freeland in conjunction with LIMBO ARTS INC."), the venue ("Limbo Lounge, 647 East Ninth Street NYC"), the fact that awards will be presented, and the ticket price ("$5.00 at the door"). What at first glance appears to be a regular film festival may turn out to be an event of a slightly different kind, because you are not told exactly what you are going to see at this festival. The flyer simply states that on Sunday, Monday, and Tuesday, starting at 9 P.M., there will be "films, performances, and slides by" a list of thirty-six names that may or may not sound familiar. There are no further details about titles, formats, lengths, or running order, but there is a phone number to call for more information (see Figure 4).

In 1984, these pink Xerox flyers promoting the New York Film Festival Downtown (NYFFD) were placed in clubs, cafés, bars, and film supply stores, as well as at the New York Film Festival in midtown, which closed that year on October 14 with Wim Wenders's *Paris, Texas*, just one week before the start of the Downtown event. For the New York Film Festival's regulars, the pink flyer must have evoked familiarity. It used the midtown festival's font and simply added DOWN TOWN, and mockingly adopted its air of institutional formality by exchanging "Lincoln" with "Limbo." Founded in 1963, the New York Film

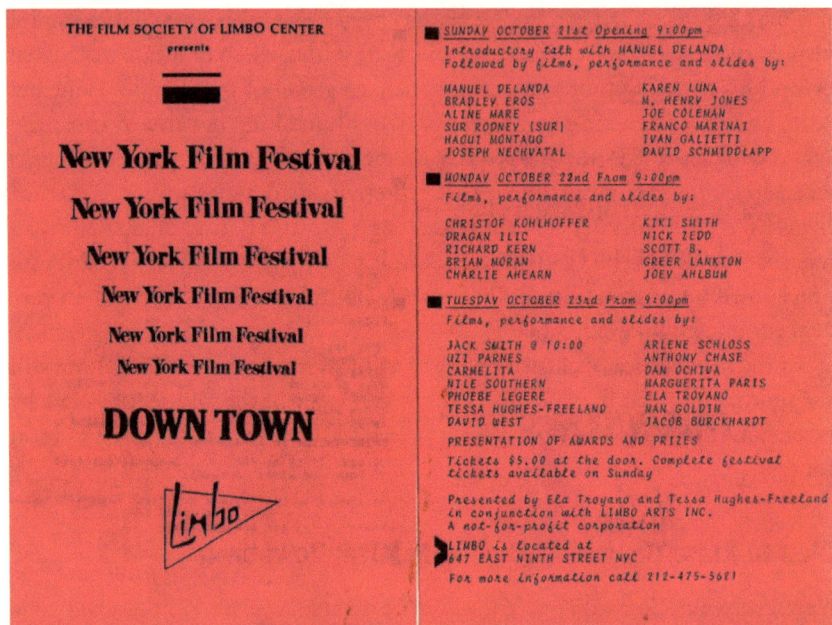

FIGURE 4 Flyer for the New York Film Festival Downtown, 1984

Festival had been presented and hosted by the Film Society of Lincoln Center since 1969. The institution supports various other film festivals and theaters and publishes *Film Comment* magazine as well. Together with the Metropolitan Opera and the New York City Ballet, it is one branch of the prestigious Lincoln Center for Performing Arts. The Limbo Lounge, on the other hand, was a small East Village gallery and performance space with no associated society whatsoever. Indeed, the very notion of "society" seems to belong more to "Lincoln" than to "Limbo" Center.

Tessa Hughes-Freeland and Ela Troyano founded the NYFFD as a continuation and formalization of their previous irregular screenings in East Village clubs such as Danceteria, Club 57, and Chandelier as well as their Celluloid Cantina series at Limbo Lounge. With an annual multiday festival, they hoped to establish a more concentrated and dense presentation of filmmaking practices as specific to the Downtown scene, one that could complement and contrast the New York Film Festival and its focus on U.S. and European avant-garde film. The fact that the first NYFFD took place immediately after the midtown festival, "in the vain hope that someone from there would come down to see it," suggests that the goal went beyond piggybacking off the influx of visitors generated by the more established festival.[60] The desire to attract international critics or programmers also suggests that the Downtown scene, through the NYFFD, was seeking attention and validation for its activities beyond its local scope. Nevertheless, the fact that the audience had to "come down to see it" confirms the festival's structural embeddedness in the Downtown scene. Not only did it primarily present works by participants of the local scene but, in its early years, the festival also took place in East Village nightclubs and was hosted by Downtown performance artists. Like most club nights, it aimed to create the sense of an ongoing experience, with one performance or screening blending into the next. In the words of the two founders, programming NYFFD's first edition meant making a long list of "all these things that wouldn't fit into the more established art culture," putting them together "in such an order that always kept it moving," in an environment that "wasn't pristine" on any level.[61]

Given that it adopted the atmosphere and circumstances of a rowdy club night, the festival was certainly not "pristine," what with its easily distracted audiences chatting and ducking out of screenings for more drinks. The NYFFD's imperfect, even messy, quality applied to its programming as well. Films were often shown unfinished, as works in progress, excerpts, or slides. If a film was not completed in time, its maker was encouraged to show it anyway.[62] In the 1986 program, for example, the listing of David Schmidlapp's *A Place to Beware* comes with the following comment: "This is a title I came up with last night. I don't really work towards a finished product. There could be a lot of excuses for this: but the truth of the matter is the more I work, the less I finish." In the case of Andy Somma's *White Rabbit*, however, the fact that the film was not finished in time meant that no film was shown at all. Instead, by standing on stage and describing the images that would have appeared on the screen had his film been ready to be picked up from the lab in time for the third edition of the NYFFD in October 1986, Somma turned the film into a performance in situ.

Improvisation and spontaneity were often born of necessity. At other times, unpredictability was an inherent element of the film (as) performance, not least since films often alternated or shared the stage with performance, theater, and dance pieces involving projections or experimental live happenings. One example of this method is Jo Andres, who frequently performed her film/light/dance shows at the NYFFD.[63] In 1985, C. Carr wrote about Andres's contribution to the festival:

> I'd gone to the Downtown Film Festival at the now-defunct 8BC—liquorless and leased out for the occasion—and found the place to be packed to the bricks.... Took me ten minutes to squeeze within view of the stage. Jo Andres appeared midway through the evening's dozen films and slide shows for an "expanded cinema" performance. This is dance for people who hate dance.... At the Film Fest, she worked with slide projections on four layers of tulle-like fabric, fat human outlines in red yellow green blue, stretching and playing with the figures, lifting the veils to show that only one color was visible on each layer of "alternative screen." ... The piece ended with Andres, Steve Buscemi, and C. Meyers squiggling over their black clothes with phosphorescent liquid as

they danced, splattering phosphorescence over the stage and out into the audience, covering the first rows in glowing spots.[64]

Carr describes her visit to the film festival as an intensely physical experience: cramped in the crowded space, she watches the bodies in Andres's performance "squiggling with phosphorescent liquid," literally spilling phosphorescence into the audience area. By inviting Andres—an artist who projected moving images onto "alternative screens" such as moving bodies and flimsy fabrics and who blended film projection with live action on stage—to participate in the festival, the NYFFD not only presented itself as a platform for "any kind of moving image," it also proposed an understanding of film that went beyond the conventional definition of projected image on screen.[65] In this way, film was instead conceived of as a dynamic category that encompassed a variety of practices. In other words, it was presented as part of an indisciplinary practice.

In her review, Carr also lets us see how the festival's clinging to small spaces like the "now-defunct 8BC" made the East Village's waning club culture all the more tangible. Fittingly, Carr dedicates her text to "Art Crimes" and "Illegal Performances," namely those that took place in venues that were either already shut down or on the verge of losing their licenses. "It's as if the city had just discovered its fringe art," she writes, "hanging from a ghastly little thread from the real estate brocade."[66] Limbo Lounge and 8BC hosted the first two editions of the NYFFD, but both venues were closed by 1985 in a wave of shutdowns that signaled the beginning of the end of the East Village's significance to the scene. The festival remained in the neighborhood for its 1986 edition, but with more clubs closed and a larger audience attending the NYFFD, it moved to a larger venue, the Charas New Assembly Theater. That year also marked the first time the festival obtained public funding.[67]

The NYFFD, which remained under the curatorship of Troyano and Hughes-Freeland, received significantly more coverage in the local press during its fourth and fifth editions. Ranging from brief announcements to in-depth interviews with the two organizers, these write-ups show that, at least since its third year and certainly within its own scene, the festival had established a reputation as a "unified showcase for the increasingly diverse experimental community."[68] As the next profile shows, the CoT had become not only a familiar feature but also one that provided the festival's literally messy spillover:

> The next night, that first row was in danger of more indelible spots, when a naked and shrieking Brian Moran poured a bucket of blood over his head. It was Cinema of Transgression night, a real droolfest of current underground gore, plus two performances. Filmmaker Nick Zedd, wearing a black dress, Cleopatra wig, and the gaze of a dying starlet, drifted across the stage, accompanied by a schmaltzy soundtrack that might ordinarily signal the entrance of a mutant B-movie crab. Richard Hell narrated.... The next week, Zedd had

moved this female victim/victimizer nonsense down to the Collective for Living Cinema, appearing once more as "Nichole." This play ended in a bloodbath, Zedd shooting a couple of "plants" in the audience who collapsed at their seats, bursting little blood bags. Smoke from the cap pistol hung in the air throughout the screening of Zedd's *Geek Maggot Bingo*.[69]

Carr's review may need some context. What she describes as Zedd drifting across the stage with the "gaze of a dying starlet ... accompanied by a schmaltzy soundtrack" is his performance piece *She*. Based on a script initially titled *The Perfect Woman*, the performance was announced in the festival program as an "ordeal he co-wrote with Lydia Lunch." Brian Moran frequently collaborated as Blood Boy with Richard Kern. As Kern's first Super 8 film *Goodbye 42nd Street* was only four minutes long and thus too short for the twenty-minute time slot offered by most clubs, he began working with Moran on live events to fill the slot.[70] These live events were often incorporated into Kern's films, such as *Zombie Hunger 1* and *Zombie Hunger 2* (1984), which screened while he and Moran were "on stage shooting up and fainting, or dying, whatever."[71] In one of their performances, the naked Moran recited Amnesty International statistics on torture, poured blood over himself, and was interrogated, tortured, and finally "killed by Kern for refusing to kiss the American flag."[72]

Moran as Blood Boy also appears in Kern's *Submit to Me* (1985/86), excerpts of which were shown at the NYFFD in 1985. In it, the slender bodies of young women are seen moving and undressing to the sounds of the rock band Butthole Surfers. They gaze straight into the camera as it circles around them. As the film progresses, scenes of increasing violence unfold: a couple chokes each other with tightropes until blood gushes out, another person appears to be overdosing, and a male body, nude but for a latex mask on his head, is held on a leash. In the final scene, Moran, naked and covered in blood, screams silently. The festival program lists Kern's contribution as follows: "RICHARD KERN. *Submit to Me* or *From Sex to Death*, new film in progress. Performance with Brian Moran. *Manhattan Love Suicides*."[73] The short description of *Manhattan Love Suicides* is in quotation marks, indicating that the filmmaker wrote the text himself: "New York City 1985—A churring world where the realities of poverty and sex among the desperate musicians, artists and scene makers dictate a mutated parody of normal lifestyles. Consumed with bitterness and hatred, the characters of *M.L.S.* stalk their objects of attention through the depths of the Lower East Side. ... This film contains four vignettes featuring NYC cult stars Nick Zedd, Bill Rice, Adrienne Altenhaus, David Wojnarowicz, Tom Turner and Amy Turner."

While other descriptions adopt a more sober tone (Manuel DeLanda's *ISM ISM* simply "documents graffiti from 1975–1978"), Kern distinctly frames his films as products of the Lower East Side and its "scene makers," supplying a narrative of their "realities of poverty and sex." Fittingly, the text is accompanied by a still from *Submit to Me Now*, depicting a half-naked Tommy Turner tied to the floor as if crucified, sharp wooden sticks goring his flesh. Kern also introduces the performers in his film as "NYC cult stars," half-mockingly alluding to the fact that their stardom (except perhaps for Wojnarowicz's) is very much confined to the Downtown scene, which is still capable of producing its own cult or underground stars.

Richard Kern's and Nick Zedd's *Thrust in Me* is announced with similar semi-ironic hyperbole as a film that "perfectly embodies all the esthetic [*sic*] imperatives manifested by the Cinema of Transgression, the secret underground movement which is currently on everyone's lips." As a matter of fact, it had only been a month since Zedd had published said manifesto in his zine. It must have pleased Zedd that a *Village Voice* critic picked up on the term, even if she was unimpressed by his performance. If anything, he would have used the fact that Carr dismissed their performances as "a juvenile spectacle" to bolster his claim that critics consistently underestimated his work. In the NYFFD program, Zedd gives himself the prefix "underground legend," ironically creating the illusion, as Kern did with his "cult stars," of having achieved a generally accepted level of fame.

What the glimpses into the festival's genesis and venues, its programming and reception, further reveal is how the NYFFD consolidated the loose structures of the scene into a condensed format. Given that Carr even described it as "Cinema of Transgression Night," this platform all but introduced certain films and performances as belonging to the Cinema of Transgression. The festival regularly featured those who were perceived to be at the core of the "movement," such as Kern and Zedd, as well as those more loosely associated with it through collaborations, joint screenings, or shared aesthetics and themes (including Manuel DeLanda, Erotic Psyche, David Wojnarowicz, Cassandra Stark, Lung Leg, Tommy Turner, DirectArt Ltd., Kembra Pfahler, Richard Kleman, and Jon Moritsugu, as well as Ela Troyano and Tessa Hughes-Freeland themselves). At the NYFFD, the work of these filmmakers was shown alongside that of artists from other scenes and generations, like multidisciplinary artists Kiki Smith and Jack Smith, sculptor Greer Lankton, dancer Ellen Fisher, and painter Dragan Ilic, to name only a few. Crucially, it did so by describing it all as "Downtown."

The "recursive self-reference by which [this] festival (re-)produces the place in which it occurs" prompts us to consider it in terms of Derrida's notion of an event, a "disjunctive singularity." Such an event cannot be derived from its social context alone, precisely because its occurrence affects that very context. Thus, even if the NYFFD is understood as a recurring, singular "moment of self-celebration of a community," it does not exist apart from its spatial and social context but rather is implicated in its very emergence.[74] This is especially significant if we recall the performative notion of a scene as being continuously made by various interacting agents and sites. At the same time that the East Village's art and party scenes were dying, the NYFFD grew into an established event, leaving behind, albeit involuntarily, the spaces of the club scene in which it was rooted. Hence, the festival's inauguration in 1984 marks a moment in which the filmmaking and performance scenes—and Nick Zedd's CoT concept in particular—became increasingly formalized. This development also has to do with the fact that the NYFFD, while largely retaining its nonpristine quality, adopted many of the functions, structures, and rituals of larger film festivals, thus adopting a format that looks back on a decades-long history that had gone through several stages of development since its emergence in postwar Europe.

Like art biennials, the first European film festivals in Cannes, Locarno, Venice, and Berlin had distinctly political agendas, influenced by national diplomatic strategies. These festivals were also the first to recognize and even generate national new waves and auteur directors, which explains how festivals contribute to the establishment of historical film canons.[75] The 1960s and 1970s saw the rise of festival subcircuits for social movements and minor genres, such as events geared toward feminist, gay and lesbian, or Black/African American communities. In the 1980s, the proliferation of the format shifted away from the traditional centers, transforming the festival into a form of event culture and the circuit into a global one.[76] While they had always interacted with the film industry, it was during this decade, as Skadi Loist notes, that film festivals "moved from being passive platforms and facilitators for the film industry to becoming intermediaries and increasingly active players in all aspects of the film industry themselves."[77]

Thus, by the time the NYFFD was launched, film festivals already constituted a complex but ubiquitous and, above all, global reality, providing, in Bill Nichols's words, a "continuous, international pattern of circulation and exchange for image-culture."[78] Moreover, regardless of their scale and orientation, film festivals also "categorize, classify, sort and sift the world's annual film-production . . . by supporting, selecting, celebrating and rewarding—in short, by adding value and cultural capital."[79] Regarding their function as taste makers and sites of cultural legitimation, Marijke de Valck suggests approaching film festivals with a Bordieuan frame in mind; for, in organizing competitions and awards but also generating writing, "niche" festivals in particular create symbolic rather than economic capital for filmmakers.[80]

Albeit on a smaller scale, the NYFFD did fulfill most of the functions ascribed to traditional film festivals. Each year it had a growing impact on the production and circulation of films from the Downtown scene, increasing their visibility considerably. While the first year's festival showed preexisting films dating back to the 1970s and early 1980s, Hughes-Freeland said that "after that people started to make films using the festival as a deadline," meaning that films were completed in time for or even made explicitly to be shown at the NYFFD.[81] In terms of selecting and awarding films, Hughes-Freeland and Troyano pursued an open and inclusive agenda. Troyano recalls, "We only said no to one entrance. I don't even know the name of it anymore . . . but it was flowers . . . for a long time."[82]

Being inclusive, however, did not only mean having a relaxed curatorial agenda but also explicitly aiming for a more diverse program in terms of race, sexuality, and gender. This is where Ela Troyano's ties to WOW Café Theatre came into play. Founded as a theatrical festival in 1980 by Holly Hughes and other collaborators, WOW developed into a collective theater space for women, women of color, and queer and trans artists such as Ela Troyano's sister Alina Troyano, also known as the performer Carmelita Tropicana. This particular crossover of theater and film within the Downtown scene is crucial. For here another limitation of the CoT concept becomes clear, namely, that the interpretation of radicality and transgression was mostly reserved for White, heterosexual men, while women of color like Troyano were actively excluded. In her own words: "Nick Zedd throws me out of the Cinema of Transgression? Fuck it, I go to WOW."[83] It was thus also an experience of marginalization within the Downtown scene that sparked a desire to curate their own programming, whether it was through Troyano's Club Chandelier or NYFFD's idiosyncratic agenda.

Part of that agenda included the fact that the Downtown festival's awards ceremony had no specific categories or jury and was based purely on personal judgment. The founders awarded selected filmmakers with a cheap "Oscar" candle figurine, a tongue-in-cheek reference to the overprestigious golden "Academy Award of Merit."[84] Most important, in terms of the festival's ability to add value and accumulate cultural or symbolic capital, however, is the fact that the festival facilitated the circulation of films beyond its local realm, especially by attracting programmers from other venues. For instance, Alf Bold, a film programmer at Berlin's Kino Arsenal, screened a selection from the 1984 NYFFD program at the Collective for Living Cinema when he was a guest curator there. Although the Collective was located in Tribeca/SoHo, which is still in Lower Manhattan, it was considered "kind of a different thing" than the East Village.[85] And, as the following excursus into the NYFFD's international travels will show, it was the containment of diverse artistic energies within both the festival format and Downtown label that ultimately enabled the films' mobility, moving them from their original context to German cinemas or *Kinos*.

German filmmaker Jürgen Brüning befriended Troyano and Hughes-Freeland when he showed his Super 8 films and those of Berlin filmmakers at the Pyramid Club in 1983. Troyano remarked that the Berlin films were "similar to what we do here."[86] Indeed, much like the Downtown scene, the Berlin Super 8 scene showed films in squatter cinemas, or as part of "multi-media performances in clubs and cafés, . . . [where] there [was] no particular fetishizing of 'image quality,'" as Keith Sanborn noted.[87] The Berlin films must have felt familiar to Troyano, not only because of their similarity in terms of cheap aesthetics, noncommitment to genre, and subject matter (ranging from urban nightlife documentation to commentary on state violence) but also because they likewise pointed to a collaborative and indisciplinary scene practice. Similar to the collaborations between Downtown musicians and filmmakers, the songs of

German post-punk and new wave bands such as Fehlfarben, DAF, and Malaria provided the rhythm for Yana Yo's films; the artist collective Die Tödliche Doris collaborated on films, publications, performances, and music; and Axel Brand and Anette Maschmann teamed up as Brand-Maschmann, a "two bodied system" not unlike Bradley Eros and Aline Mare of New York's Erotic Psyche.[88]

The cinematic encounter between Berlin and New York spawned a friendship between Brüning, Troyano, and Hughes-Freeland, and in the spring of 1986, three years after their first meeting, they toured Germany with a selection from the second edition of the NYFFD. Starting at Berlin's Eiszeit Kino, which Brüning had cofounded in 1985, the NYFFD traveled to the Kommunales Kino in Hanover, Kino the Lichtwerk in Bielefeld, Dusseldorf's Filminstitut, the Mal Seh'n in Frankfurt/Main, Cologne's Filmhaus, and the Werkstattkino in Munich. Sanborn describes the Super 8 scene in Germany as having "no center. It has, rather, a multiplicity of centers which can be connected only by imaginary lines."[89] In addition to the activities of individual filmmakers and loosely structured groups, the multiple centers of this rhizomatic structure were the off-cinemas and *Kinos* that screened the NYFFD's CoT-heavy selection.[90]

In a 1989 interview, Canadian filmmaker Penelope Buitenhuis suggested that, compared to the United States and Canada, the Berlin press and public were more appreciative of films made with Super 8: "Berlin was one of the places where I have gotten critical attention. A big article about a Super-8 filmmaker in a daily paper in North America is practically unheard of."[91] Although the NYFFD received mentions in underground zines like *Underground Film Bulletin* or in local periodicals such as the *East Village Eye*, the more prominent newspapers had covered neither the filmmakers screening their work at the NYFFD nor the festival itself. By comparison, the response in Germany was sweeping. From the *Bielefelder Spiegel* to the *Berliner Tagesspiegel*, from west to east, newspapers and magazines responded to the festival tour with a variety of reports and reviews. The primary reason that mainstream newspapers in Germany covered the NYFFD program was thanks to the simple but crucial fact that the films were not shown in Downtown clubs, where "everyone seemed to know each other either by sight or by name," but in arthouse cinemas, whose programming was regularly covered by the arts and culture sections of local newspapers anyway.[92]

Though some responses were more favorable than others, all of them emphasized what they felt were dark, funny, or crude but, in any case, authentic depictions of Lower Manhattan. A critic from Bielefeld thought he had experienced "ein Streifzug für Entdeckungsfreudige durch die amerikanische Undergroundlandschaft" (a journey for those who are eager to discover the American underground landscape), while a reviewer from Berlin was glad to see not "the beautifully polished, melancholy poetry of Jim Jarmusch or Eric Mitchell . . . but the other, more original, direct, dirty New York."[93] Indeed, little was polished in the NYFFD program, which included campy and playful films like Ela Troyano and Uzi Parnes's *Loisaida Lusts* (1985) along with others that depicted

New York's gloom and ruin. For example, Michael Wolfe's *Bloody Stump* (1983), shot on black-and-white Super 8 film and set to a noise-rock soundtrack for DirectArt, tells the story of a traumatized war veteran living on the Lower East Side while Ivan Galietti's *Pompeii: New York Pt. 1: Pier Caresses* (1982) compares the graffiti of Manhattan's gay piers to the erotic frescoes of pagan Pompeii. Films like these apparently made the NYFFD's program a representation of a "more original New York." As much of a glorification as this claim might be, it does suggest that the films' grainy images had a specific appeal and possessed an imaginative power that made the East Village and Downtown, in the mind of the German *Kino* audience, "such a place."[94]

After the first German tour proved to be a great success, at least in terms of press coverage, the Downtown festival returned to Berlin in February 1988 with a three-hour screening of eighteen films at the Quartier Latin concert hall. And although the local magazine *tip* found the NYFFD to be the antithesis of Berlin's international film festival, the Downtown event still coincided with and even ended up entering, with Richard Kern's *Fingered* (1986), the Berlinale.[95] Jürgen Brüning had arranged for *Fingered*, which had screened at the NYFFD the previous year, to be shown in the Berlinale's Infoschau section (now Panorama). Since the festival was not equipped to show Super 8 film, Troyano had to make a new copy by filming the projected film with a 16 mm camera (which points to a divide between Super 8 and 16 mm that is not just symbolic).[96] Rumor has it that when *Fingered* had the last of its three screenings at the Berlinale, the festival director interrupted the screening, climbed on stage, and admitted that if he had seen the film in advance, he would not have allowed it to be shown. The drama continued when the film subsequently screened every day for an entire week at Eiszeit Kino, where, one night, a group of ten masked persons interrupted the screening. They stormed the cinema, knocked over the projector, emptied the box office, and sprayed "Kampf dem Sexismus" (fight sexism) on the wall.[97]

This incident underscores how the films labeled Cinema of Transgression, as presented by the NYFFD, perpetuated a certain image not only of the supposedly taboo-breaking New York scene but also of the general state of U.S. underground film. After all, the press referred to *Fingered* as an "Underground-Streifen" (underground flicker) and an "amerikanischen Underground–Porno" (American underground porn). Because it offers explicit, often brutal glimpses into the professional and personal life of a phone sex worker, *Fingered* was often considered pornographic and provoked audience protest on more than one occasion. Kern, aware of his film's ambiguous genre status and the repercussions it might have, provided *Fingered* with a slightly tongue-in-cheek content warning: "This film is an EXERCISE in the CAPITALIZATION of an EXPLOITATION that some may find unnecessarily VIOLENT, SEXIST, and DISGUSTING." Whether this preface was added to the film out of genuine concern for potentially triggered viewers or to further emphasize its shock value is a question of interpretation. In any case, it is evident that *Fingered* was, at least at some point, not intended for general audiences but for a niche audience that either endured, or found valuable, or even enjoyed the explicit depictions.

After its attention-grabbing exhibitions in Berlin, *Fingered* continued to circulate. It found international distributors, including the German label Artware in Wiesbaden, and was shown many years later as part of the group show *You Killed Me First* at KW Institute of Contemporary Art in Berlin. Recently, MoMA's film department acquired the film, apparently deeming it worthy of collection, preservation, and exhibition. Here we see how multiple actors and institutions, both local and international, are involved in the circulation and reevaluation of an underground film like *Fingered*, influencing its framing and reinterpretation, assigning value and different meanings to it. Additionally, and more importantly, however, the NYFFD's shift from clubs to *Kinos*, and through these German cinemas to an international film festival, also means that the program became cleaner, losing its inherent messiness. This is not least due to the fact that the *Kinos* that hosted the NYFFD screenings were predominantly dedicated to the showing of films. From Hanover's, founded in 1974, to Bielefeld's, founded in 1985, these venues originated thanks to student collectives or *Filmfreunde*, self-described cinephiles. (The primary exception here being Berlin's Eiszeit Kino, which also presented stage performances and concerts.) Although these cinemas were independently organized and open to alternative and experimental content, they still showed films in a conventional manner, that is, projected on a large screen in the darkened hall of a dedicated cinema space. Once they arrived in Germany, the films were no longer part of an ongoing program in which they were shown unfinished or mixed with live performances, dance, or multimedia events. This is not to say that the latter mode is the only or in any sense the truest way to experience these films. But what I hope to demonstrate here is that while the NYFFD functioned as a crucial platform for Downtown filmmaking and performance practices, it also helped to uncouple the films from that very context, to contain their spillover, and to reduce them to auratically charged imaginaries of New York City. What becomes clear, then, is how this particular film festival, in labeling films "Downtown," had a containment effect not unlike that of the Cinema of Transgression Manifesto in the UFB or the East Village–themed exhibitions discussed earlier. Intentionally or not, they all worked at some point to erase the messy, indisciplinary, spillover energy of the scene in order to create more easily marketable and consumable, but ultimately also more mobile and widely received, (film) objects.

3

Film Happens

■■■■■■■■■■■■■■■■■■■■■

"Performance and film stick together," declares filmmaker and New York Film Festival Downtown organizer Tessa Hughes-Freeland in the film section of the February 1986 issue of *East Village Eye*, referring to "ongoings in the realm of projection" at local night clubs.[1] Indeed, film and live performance combined there in various constellations. Film sequences were integrated into live events or made specifically for them, such as Anthony Chase's Super 8 films, which were projected during live solo performances by John Kelly; screenplays were acted out on stage if money was lacking to shoot or finish a film, as was the case for Nick Zedd's *Me Minus You* and John Jesurun's *Chang in a Void Moon*; and artists who mainly worked in the realm of live performance, such as Karen Finley, Phoebe Legere, Lydia Lunch, Kembra Pfahler, or Joe Coleman, appeared in films or tried their hands at filmmaking, bringing their individual performing styles to the film set.[2]

If, as Hughes-Freeland's statement suggests, there was indeed a close alliance between performance and film in the Downtown club scene of the 1980s, this chapter will investigate how these practices were informed by and engaged with each other, what forms these encounters took, and what historical precedents they built upon. I will look closely at productions that emerged from the various intersecting scenes out of which the Cinema of Transgression (CoT) was conceived. In doing so, I will show that scene participants did not limit their activities to the realm of film; their engagement with film always and necessarily involved exchange with other practices, scenes, and sites. By thoroughly complicating binary distinctions such as live/recorded, mediated/immediate, and past/present, these engagements ultimately highlight the fact that film and performance often became entangled, rather than remaining ontologically distinct, let alone mutually exclusive, categories.

In this context, let me emphasize that the 1980s Downtown club scene gave rise to a style of performance that differed both structurally and textually from earlier styles. Although by the 1970s the notion of performance art still referred more broadly to any type of live performance "outside the usual categories of theater, dance, or music," performance eventually began to be recognized as an art form in itself thanks to emerging institutional and academic frameworks.[3] In New York City at the time, performance took place in public spaces, artists' lofts, alternative art spaces, experimental theaters, and, increasingly, art galleries. The latter, in particular, associated performance with the visual arts; however, the performances that I refer to throughout this chapter were mostly produced and presented in small nightclubs, which were often housed in storefronts, bars, basements, or private apartments. In order to imagine how these clubs became "stages where the performance events erupt[ed] in the flow of an evening's drinking, socializing, being on the scene," it is helpful to visualize their spatial structures.[4]

The Pyramid Club serves as a great example since it was central to much of the performance scene at that time. When reading reviews of Downtown productions in academic journals or magazines, it is striking how many of them give detailed descriptions of the venues themselves. For instance, in the summer of 1983, a visitor to John Jesurun's "living film serial" *Chang in a Void Moon* describes the Pyramid's spatial specificities and its atmosphere as follows:

> The Pyramid Club is a nightclub and bar with a small stage in the rear where musicians and artists regularly appear. The elevated stage is approximately six feet deep, fifteen feet wide, and three feet high. The performance area for *Chang* extends in front of the stage to where the audience is seated either on folding chairs, the floor, or at the tables that line the club's walls. The performance space and the area that is used for seating are otherwise used for dancing. A trademark of the Pyramid Club is a raised seating area with tables and chairs along one wall—a design that is said to give the atmosphere of a 1930s-style cabaret.[5]

The stage's compact dimensions left little maneuvering room for performers and even less distance from the audience. That the performance spilled over into the seating area seems to be, in this light, more an inevitable result of the club's limited space than a conceptual choice. Moreover, given that the Pyramid was first and foremost a bar, performances were not necessarily the main event but rather happened as a sideline. John Hagan, who played the lead character Chang, emphasizes this in his recollections of the space. He remembers performing "amid a buzz of drink orders and conversations, in a haze of cigarette smoke from offstage and on, and with spectators cramming the entrance that separated us from the front room where drag queens were dancing on the bar to pulsating music."[6] Both descriptions try to convey the vibrant and intimate atmosphere of the Pyramid Club: what it smelled like, what it looked like, what it sounded like—in short, what it felt like to be there. And it seems that this intangible element, the club's mood, is intrinsically bound up with the performances that took place there.

Not surprisingly, in a multipurpose club like the Pyramid, where the performance space evoked the feel of a cabaret venue and was "otherwise used for dancing," performers drew on the rich repertoire of cabaret entertainment, such as striptease, comedy, impromptu singing or lip-synching, dancing, drag, and dress-up. The duo Dancenoise (formed in 1983 by Anne Iobst and Lucy Sexton), for example, lived up to their name with their short, costumed, and indeed noisy acts, dancing and brawling on club and theater stages. The fact that performers like Dancenoise felt closer to the world of music, experimental theater, and nightlife does not mean that visual art and performance were separate camps per se but that this particular kind of performance was, at least initially, not tied to the institutional or commercial art world. These performances arose from places where (night) life and art production naturally blended.[7] Sally Banes finds an apt metaphor for this merging when she writes that "the party [had] come to the performance."[8]

Indeed, what one might call the "party mood" came to be a defining feature of 1980s club performance. Seeing or staging a performance was a social event. The roles of performer, audience member, bar personnel, and club owner often alternated or overlapped. When people visited a club to catch a performance, they also did so to hang out with friends or to see those friends on stage. A critic reporting on a Carmelita Tropicana and Holly Hughes performance at Club Chandelier in 1984 mentioned that the show itself "becomes a party for spectators inclined to stay" and that "most spectators do remain in the club, since the atmosphere throughout the evening has been more like a party than a performance."[9] As an outside observer, the critic went on to comment that "the spectators mingle freely; many seem to know each other and are comfortable in the space. Performers are difficult to distinguish from spectators."[10]

Another explanation for the party quality of club performances is that they emphasized ephemerality and diversion and prioritized a combination of spectacle and theatricality that was influenced by mass media and popular entertainment. "In a society consumed by 'spectacle' on a daily basis," writes Jacki Apple, "the so-called 'real life' and the language surrounding it have been theatricalized.... The world is a television or film soundstage on which daily life is played out and played back. The presentation of image subsumes ideology and identity; performance is paramount."[11] What Apple means is that, in the United States in the mid-1980s, in a culture of mass media and with a movie actor as elected president, the notion of performance exceeded the realm of art and spilled into the everyday. The productions discussed in this chapter were created during a period in which the boundaries between what was "real" and what was performed or mediated became increasingly blurred. Given this, it makes sense that Downtown performance often involved playing with identity, character, and gender both on and off stage and that the films and performances I will be exploring in this chapter played with those conventions as well.

While performances of the 1970s were primarily processual and time based, often stretching the audience's sense of time in durational works that lasted several hours, performances of the subsequent decade were more concerned with movement and functioned according to another temporal regime: they presented "time [as] telescoped."[12] Writing about 8BC founder and manager Cornelius Conboy's vision of opening a performance-oriented club, one critic observed that Conboy "had understood, like others producing in the East Village, that audiences' esthetic perceptions were shifting, and that television had much to do with this. . . . They were used to a medium that allowed them to view a show, have a smoke and a drink, and get up and leave at any moment to talk to friends."[13] The clubs' tightly packed schedules, with performances, concerts, and screenings often following each other in intervals of as little as twenty minutes, attest not only to a merging of art production and (night) life and a commonplace crossing of genres and formats but also to the audience's desire for distraction and volatility.

By the 1980s, of course, performance and film had already been closely connected for several decades. In the context of U.S. and Western European art making, productions in which different media and practices, especially live performance and film, enter into a dialogue can be traced back at least to the early and mid-twentieth century. In the 1960s, however, a new wave of performances began to defy established categorizations. Bringing together dance, painting, music, film projection, and installation, they built on formal experiments such as those of the European Dada movement of the 1920s and the U.S. avant-garde of the 1950s.[14] Concepts like "intermedia," "expanded cinema," and "mixed means" emerged in response, seeking to provide an alternative to the notion of pure form. They aimed to account for "works which fall conceptually between media that are already known," the interplay of components in new forms of theater, and the various ways in which the format of the screen becomes the subject of interrogation.[15] Nevertheless, while this formal mixing and structural expansion attempted to illustrate decisively that the notion of separate media had become obsolete, all three concepts maintained their independent existences.

Yet the term "expanded cinema" is still used to describe efforts to "expand cinema beyond its institutionalized form." In the words of Erika Balsom, works in the 1960s and 1970s that foregrounded cinema as a live event and rejected standardized screening formats "reinjected a charge of contingency into a highly rationalized area, very much in dialogue with contemporaneous developments in music, performance, and experimental theater."[16] Paradoxically, however, the very notion of expanding cinema beyond itself suggests the existence of an original, singular form. On this point, Gabriel Menotti makes an important observation when he states that "to characterize a work as an addition to cinema makes it simultaneously removed from and likely secondary to the medium. In that sense, the concept of expanded cinema actually prevents the concept of cinema to be expanded." Instead, he claims, it functions as yet "a further stage in cinema's individuation."[17]

Likewise, the notion of cinema's liveness needs critical reexamination. Considering early cinema screenings, as well as avant-garde practices of the 1960s and 1970s, Balsom states that "moving pictures were live from the beginning" and consequently suggests understanding cinema as an event: "In conceiving of the event of projection, one is no longer restricted to the consideration of an inert, autonomous text but rather can begin to ponder all that occurs during the time of exhibition, as well as all that may change from one instantiation to the next."[18] While Balsom's emphasis on viewing cinema and film through the paradigm of liveness works toward destabilizing the binary opposition of live and mediated, recorded and performed, she at the same time manifests this opposition precisely by stating that "as a performing art, cinema ceases to be a reproducible object and becomes instead a singular experience."[19]

The assumption undergirding this chapter, and indeed the entire book, is that films are not singular, self-contained objects, but are crucially circumstantial and already performative in character, regardless of whether they are enhanced by or embedded in live performance. By the same token, in this chapter I will not be treating performance in terms of its supposed originality, singularity, and immediacy. The idea that performance is ontologically tied to the present moment, resists documentation, and "becomes itself through disappearance" is still widespread in art history and performance studies.[20] Rebecca Schneider argues against the equation of performance with loss, stating that performance is "both the act of remaining and a means of re-appearance and 'reparticipation'" and, picking up on Peggy Phelan's phrasing, "becomes itself through messy and eruptive re-appearance." This is not to establish a dichotomy between a lost past and a fetishized present moment, between appearance and disappearance, presence and absence. Rather, Schneider argues that the performative trace, among which she especially includes gestural acts (re)enacted live, eludes any neat opposition between such classifications. Instead, it marks performance as "indiscreet, non-original, relentlessly citational."[21] What will prove useful for this chapter is Schneider's notion that bodily, material traces ground performance in a past moment and at the same time point to future realizations and possibly endless iterations.

Returning to the aforementioned terms that emerged in the 1960s and 1970s, Richard Kostelanetz claims that, in what he calls "mixed means performances," elements such as painting, sculpture, music, dance, theater, and film are mixed but ostensibly function independently of one another. This poses the question of how an audience perceives and finds significance in such pieces. In response, Kostelanetz suggests that the "'meaning' of an event can be nothing more than the forms it offers."[22] And since such a piece speaks in "several languages at once," its comprehension thus "more closely resembles looking at a street or overhearing a strange conversation than deducing the theme of drama: The longer and more deeply the spectator dissects and assimilates its sound-image complex and associates the diverse elements, the more familiar he becomes with the work."[23]

Kostelanetz pleads for a dissection, a singling out of different elements and their respective (media) specificity in order to obtain a thorough, rather than a correct, understanding of the work—hence "meaning" is put in quotation marks. He assumes that by making each element intelligible in its own right, the recipients will be able to familiarize themselves with the complexity of the whole work and will become receptive to its multiple stimuli. Ironically, this approach sounds very much like an act of tidying up, unmixing, or even containing, since it implies that each element, each "means," must be untangled from the others and regarded in its own, supposedly pure form.

The cases that I will explore throughout this chapter were often collaboratively conceived, produced, shot, and staged in the context of the Downtown club scene of the 1980s and indeed belong to the tradition of expanded and mixed performances whose history I briefly sketch above. However, I will approach these hybrid forms not by dissecting their respective elements but by paying attention to their productive entanglement, to what Kostelanetz might have called their "strange conversations." The examples themselves presuppose such a procedure: as they make us read performance as film and film as performance, we will see that nothing sticks together, that film and performance are quite casually and sometimes even just by chance spilling into each other.

From Sticking to Spilling: *The Dagmar Onassis Story*

As an example of film and performance "sticking together," Tessa Hughes-Freeland mentions the performance ensemble Torture Chorus headed by Stephen Holman, as well as John Kelly and Anthony Chase's *The Dagmar Onassis Story*, a Super 8 film and performance that was presented weekly at the Pyramid Club in 1984. However, Hughes-Freeland does not specify whether it is the film or the live performance one would get to see at the Pyramid Club. Taking this as a cue, it would be worthwhile not to think of *The Dagmar Onassis Story* in terms of either/or, but to consider it a film that spills into performance as much as a performance that spills into film so that, in certain ways, it is both.

After quitting his career as a professional dancer in the late 1970s, John Kelly started performing in nightclubs. In his five-to-ten-minute pieces, a musical soundtrack or prerecorded narrative offered the framework for an otherwise mostly improvised character-based performance. The fast-paced, chronically crowded Pyramid Club, where he became a regular after performing at its

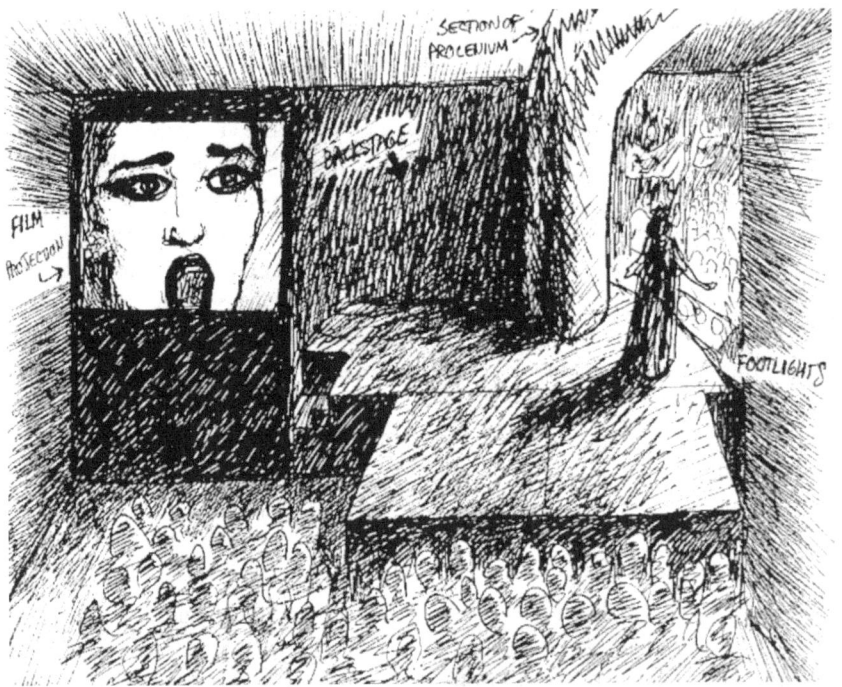

FIGURE 5 Set design for *The Dagmar Onassis Story*, 1984

opening night in 1981, informed his early work significantly: "The performances I created for the Pyramid's tiny stage allowed me to establish a vocabulary, a style. The weekly deadlines lit a great fire under my butt."[24] When *Dagmar Onassis* was staged at the Pyramid Club in 1984, the live action was performed in front of a hand-painted set by Huck Snyder and accompanied by projections of Super 8 film sequences by Anthony Chase. Snyder's sets, props, and backdrops, with their bright colors and distorted perspectives, made the stage look like a surrealist pop-up children's book, while Chase, a filmmaker working mostly with black-and-white Super 8 film, brought a strong German Expressionist film influence. They both frequently collaborated with Kelly, and *Dagmar Onassis* was their second joint project after *Mona Lisa* (1983), a film which developed from one of Kelly's performance pieces of the same name.[25]

Video documentation of *The Dagmar Onassis Story* from the Pyramid Club in 1984 begins with a hand-drawn sketch of the rather simple mise-en-scène. Sequences of the *Dagmar Onassis* film were projected center-left, while at center-right, a proscenium gave way to Snyder's backdrop, which, mirroring the club's own audience, depicted a painted audience dressed in formal evening attire, seated in a large opera or theater hall decorated with an ornamented gallery and a large chandelier (see Figure 5). The footage from the Pyramid Club shows that this painting is surrounded by a wrinkly red curtain that is folded to give the impression of spaciousness. One big spotlight illuminates both the painting and Kelly, who performs alternately facing the painted audience on the wall and the physical audience in the room. Later footage from a production at Studio Museum in Harlem in 1990 shows a somewhat tidier version of the mise-en-scène, featuring a more spacious stage with room for a row of bright footlights and a larger backdrop.

As Anthony Chase points out, clubs were "rowdy spaces" in the sense that, given their crowdedness and busyness, things did not always go as planned. Once Kelly started to perform his piece in East Village venues such as The Kitchen and La MaMa Theater that were more familiar with staging theatrical productions, the performances themselves became cleaner and more "controllable," if for no other reason than these venues could help set up the technical equipment.[26] In any case, the basic arrangement remained the same: the film projection on the left either alternated or was played simultaneously with the live action occurring on the stage to the right. For the following descriptions of *Dagmar Onassis*, I referred to both the Pyramid Club and Studio Museum recordings as well as to a digitized version of the twenty-four-minute color Super 8 film, which, at the time of this writing, was embedded as a YouTube video in an article published on MoMA's online magazine.[27] (MoMA had acquired the film for its collection in 2019).

The performance begins with the opening credits of the film. Dagmar Onassis is writing the title of the film/the performance with her dark red lipstick on a mirror, obscuring her own reflection. She turns to the camera with a sly but seductive smile, only to immediately turn back to the mirror and vigorously smear what she has just written. When the mirror is clean again, the cast list covers the surface name by name. Next, John Kelly appears on the floor of a room, surrounded by scattered records pulled out of their sleeves as well as a large gramophone and a small, black-and-white terrier (an image that immediately calls to mind Francis Barraud's nineteenth century painting of his dog sitting next to a gramophone, which became the iconic logo of the Gramophone Company and later entertainment retailer HMV). Kelly, wearing a plain white shirt and dark pants, is mesmerized by Maria Callas's high-pitched voice. He moves his head closer and closer to the funnel-shaped gramophone speaker until his whole head is inside it and the screen turns black. A photo of Callas herself appears next, then a slide show–like sequence of snapshots: Dagmar Onassis in various stage outfits, kissing, posing with friends, as well as baby and childhood photos—of Onassis? Of Callas? Of Kelly? While these photos are shown, Kelly's voice, talking over a crackling opera track, begins to tell Dagmar's story in the past tense, suggesting that the film is a gesture of commemoration:

> Dagmar Onassis brought back a style of singing which had long since been neglected. She literally changed the face of opera. It was a joke among us to divide the history of opera into . . . B.D. and A.D.—before, and after, Dagmar.

> She brought back the two main elements which make opera happen: tragedy and music. She was not born in Brooklyn, as many insist, but in the Margaret Hague hospital in Jersey City. She was christened Nora Sofia Anna Dagmar Kalogeropoulos and grew up an awkward and overweight child.[28]

At the moment in which Kelly-as-narrator tells us matter-of-factly that Dagmar had been an "awkward and overweight child," we hear laughter breaking out. It becomes clear that the film which we see is, in fact, a filmed screening, watched by another audience, in another place, at another time.

The story of Dagmar continues, and her companions and competitors are asked to betray secrets. "Diva" Tanya Ransom, a regular drag performer and host at the Pyramid Club, one of Onassis and Kelly's colleagues, sits on a metal frame bed (which is her actual bed in her apartment above the Pyramid Club). The camera pans her room and catches a glimpse of a painting that depicts Onassis in a lacy dress, with muscular biceps, voluminous blonde hair, and a spaced-out expression on her face. Ransom, adorned with a silky morning robe, pearls, and faux jewels, remembers Onassis: "That woman thrived on press. Bad or good. She got fat on it."

For the most part, the film features locations and people that connect to Kelly's life as a performer and scene participant. Social relations and artistic practice are always already intertwined in these scenes: Ransom lives right above the club where she is featured as a regular guest and performer. In this sense, the film also shows how the story of Dagmar's character, and thus Kelly's life as a performer, is interwoven with the Downtown drag performance and club scene. In the film, Kelly makes an appearance as yet another one of his characters, the Mona Lisa, who fondly reminisces about the time she spent with Dagmar in Paris. Again, the audience breaks out in laughter, obviously amused by Kelly's interpretation of da Vinci's masterpiece. The screen turns black, and the audience applauds.

Until this point, the documentation from the Studio Museum performance only showed the projection of the film. But as the film and live performance begin to overlap, the recording also shows the stage onto which Onassis makes an entrance. She faces the painted audience as she turns her back to the audience in the room. At the same moment that Dagmar appears on stage, a larger-than-life version of her face becomes visible on the screen. Here she enters the dark space of the frame, in which the wavy fabric of a theater curtain can only be faintly made out in the background. She moves her head slowly from left to right, bats her long eyelashes, shyly smiles, and lets her gloved hand rest on her chest before she begins her solo. The camera remains stationary as it takes in the satin red of her dress and lips, the sparkling of her earrings, the dramatic blue-green of her eye shadow, and the paleness of her face illuminated by a spotlight. Onassis on stage is performing the same solo as Onassis does on the screen, but they are doing so for different audiences. Onassis on stage is facing the painted *faux* audience, while Onassis on screen seems to be singing for the camera, for us, her audience, regardless of whether we are sitting in front of a computer screen in the 2020s, in the auditorium of the Studio Museum in Harlem in 1990, or on the floor of the Limbo Lounge in 1984, where the film that would later be screened as *The Dagmar Onassis Story* premiered under its alternative title *Dagmar Poisoned the Pizza* at the New York Film Festival Downtown.[29]

When the solo(s) end, a rousing chorus of applause and whistling comes from both the film's soundtrack and the audience in the room. At the same moment that Onassis on stage bows to the backdrop and turns to leave the stage, dragging her red stole behind her, the projected image of Onassis turns her head, and the screen goes black. I am now back in the world of the film again, in the room where Kelly, the fan, was listening to his collection of Callas records. Kelly's distraught expression changes. He pauses, seems to make a decision, then rushes out. The film cuts to the other side of the door, through which Dagmar is now entering, with a head of spiky blonde hair, pink cheekbones, dark and smudged eyeshadow, and screaming red lipstick—this is, in Kelly's words, "the coke-sniffing punk Dagmar," not "Dagmar as diva, mimicking her mother Maria."[30] Punk Dagmar begins to close the door to the room when a hand comes reaching out from behind it, which she forcibly pushes back in. Again, there is laughter from the audience. She dabs her lipstick dry with a piece of toilet paper and rushes off.

"We're at the Pyramid Cocktail Lounge, interviewing some of the thousands of fans who have come to see Dagmar Onassis." Approaching the queue of people lined up in the front of the Pyramid Club, a reporter holds his microphone up to a pale and red-eyed John Kelly. "What do you think is so great about her?" he asks, to which Kelly responds, "Well, she is the only star in opera today that has real glamour. She is a great star and a great actress." Kelly continues to praise her singing technique, her virtuosity, her overall magnificence. And then, there she is. On film, Dagmar is dancing immersed in red light, partying with friends in the backstage area of the Pyramid Club, alternately crying and laughing at an excessive dinner party in Ransom's apartment, sniffing cocaine until her long lashes are covered with white dust. On stage, she staggers back and forth, from screen to stage area, wearing a black cocktail dress and black pumps, her hair a fiery red. Onassis is slurring her aria rather than singing it. After the grand finale of her solo, she rolls around in the trail of white powder she left behind on the floor. The stage lights go out as church bells chime.

Onassis's portrait appears on the front page of the *Chicago Sun-Times*, attesting to her passing at the tender age of twenty-seven. The ending of *Dagmar Onassis* differs, depending on whether one watches the film by itself or (the recording of) the live performance. In the film, Kelly (as fan) comes onto the stage of the Pyramid Club, where he finds what remains of Onassis: a black stiletto, a pearl necklace, stockings, a red curly wig—markers of femininity as costume. Here, too, the stage's backdrop is Snyder's painted audience, but it is accompanied by text. Kelly silently scans the white capital letters that have been painted on black. They read, "Dagmar is a hybrid from lyp [sic] synch to the lips open out comes sound of the body making music of its own to achieve a resemblance of her tender moment ave Maria Callas." In this moment, Callas's voice, a ghostly presence, speaks: "I thank you for your love and I love you maybe more than you love me all. Thank you and good-bye." On the stage of the Harlem Studio, Kelly is not listening but lip-synching these exact same words. Recorded applause is followed by a last solo performance, this time not lip-synched but sung by Kelly himself. The film on the other hand closes with John Kelly, in his white shirt and pants, as he sings, here, too, with his own voice, Maria Callas's interpretation of "Ave Maria," extending his arm and resting one hand on his chest just like she did, addressing the painted audience.

In most of his works, Kelly deploys both lip-synching and live vocal production, which he calls "traditional drag craft."[31] He slips into the roles of Joni Mitchell, Mona Lisa, or Jacqueline Kennedy, invents characters like Dagmar Onassis (the fictive daughter of myth-enshrouded soprano superstar Maria Callas, born out of her brief love affair with the business magnate Aristotle Socrates Onassis), and performs as mythological or religious figures that transcend the notion of gender altogether, such as Narcissus and Saint Sebastian. Kelly's drag performance of these characters emphasizes the performativity of gender itself. Referring to the tradition of drag balls and contests, Judith Butler writes, "for a performance to work means that a reading is no longer possible or that a reading, an interpretation, appears to be a kind of transparent seeing, where what appears and what it means coincide."[32] What this implies is that if a reading is possible, meaning and appearance are not congruent, the artifice of the performance becomes tangible, and it does not work. However, Kelly's performance as Onassis, in *Dagmar Onassis* and elsewhere, is not intended to work, to succeed as passing or as any supposed realness. Instead, the inherent artificiality of the "as if" is actively and continuously highlighted, most notably when it becomes clear that Kelly is idol and fan at once. The cryptic wall text in the last scene of the film reads as an allegory for this: Kelly is and then isn't Onassis; his open lips are silently singing, forming words that another body sings, describing a moment of imitation. At the same time, his open lips, silently screaming and virtually prompting the sounds of his own body to escape the mouth, point toward the multiple fluid identities that are involved in this staged embodiment. It is in this moment that the artifice, and thus the inevitable ambivalence of drag performance, is emphasized and made productive.

C. Carr aptly describes Kelly's club pieces as "art about art, based on characters he could only know through film, recordings, or art history" and goes on to observe that "it was not deconstruction or parody. He showed how one could work with artifice to get to genuine emotional intensity."[33] In this sense, Kelly's performance as Onassis reads as a specific kind of fandom, a campy, and thus sincere, tribute to Callas's glamour and the excessiveness of the imagined

Onassis, not unlike the homage René Rivera aka Mario Montez paid to Dominican actress and gay icon María Montez when he based his stage name and fabulous style on her. Thus, Kelly's work must be seen not only in the context of performance, but explicitly in the context of the drag performance scene of the time, whose most notorious representatives were Brian Butterick (as Hattie Hathaway), Michael Norman (as Tanya Ransom), and James Roy Eichelberger (as Ethyl Eichelberger).

Like Kelly, these performers moved freely between different yet overlapping scenes, especially club culture and experimental queer theater.[34] Both Montez and Eichelberger, who also wrote plays himself, acted in plays ascribed to the Ridiculous Theatre, which was established in the 1960s and 1970s mostly through the work of actor and director John Vaccaro, playwright Ronald Tavel, and actor/director/playwright Charles Ludlam. Though they collaborated in various combinations and with different ensembles, each putting forward their own interpretation of the "ridiculous" in Ridiculous Theatre, there are shared elements among them. Not unlike the club performance style which I described in the beginning, the Ridiculous Theatre sensibility was less tied to theater traditions than it was to pop culture, 1960s performance art, experimental music, and, notably, filmmaking. In 1978, Gerald Rabkin writes that "beneath the surface camp and travesty there was seriousness. The Ridiculous refracted a genuine vision of reality, one shared by a community of artists and spectators."[35] Rabkin productively stresses that the Ridiculous Theatre was not so much a movement as a sensibility shared by audience, performers, and playwrights alike, indulging together "in what they like and [seeing] those things as being culturally valuable."[36] B-movies and early Hollywood cinema were popular references for cross-dressing performances, similar to the flamboyant films and performance rituals of Jack Smith, whose influence on and involvement with the Ridiculous Theatre productions is difficult to ignore.[37] Marc Siegel quotes Tavel, who wrote screenplays for Andy Warhol's films and developed plays with Vaccaro, in saying that "the Ridiculous is a proposal. It proposes, never supposes theatre." The Ridiculous thus also presents "a challenge to the ontological status of the play," as Siegel writes, since the script provides only a framework for a gathering, which may or may not "dissolve into the cinematic or theatrical event."[38] How scores and scripts were enacted or used as a framework for experimental filmmaking will be further explored in this chapter. For now, note that Kelly's performance practice and *Dagmar Onassis*, in particular, seem to share both the playful and decisively queer take on drag/cross-dressing performance and the oscillating between film, performance, and theater that characterized the work of the Ridiculous Theatre.

Whereas Eichelberger, Hathaway, and Ransom were known mainly by their chosen names, Kelly used his birth name and deliberately slipped in and out of character, on and off stage, allowing his characters a life of their own. Just as Mona Lisa had a guest appearance in *Dagmar Onassis*, Dagmar herself gave interviews and performed outside the framework of the piece.[39] Kelly and Onassis even performed (separately) at the same events, as an invite to a party at the Palladium indicates.[40] The March 1991 issue of *Outweek* features an interview with the title "Madame Dagmar Onassis Speaks (and Sings)!" In its introduction, the reader is prepared to find her speaking about "issues related to her career, her family and herself, never skirting the cul-de-sac conundrum surrounding her relationship to John Kelly."[41] This interview suggests not only that Onassis was by 1991 a known character, at least to the readers of a queer New York weekly news magazine, but also that Kelly and Onassis seem to relate to each other in quite a complicated way. There is a moment in the film that depicts what the *Outweek* interviewer jokingly calls a "cul-de-sac conundrum": Dagmar emerges from a room where John Kelly had just been listening to records. His arm and hand reach through the door but are harshly pushed back in by Onassis, as if saying *it is either you or me*. Performance, in the case of *Dagmar Onassis*, thus also means embodying multiple identities that are neither bound to the space of the stage nor to the frame of the film. In this unstable distinction between media spaces and characters, one agent has a particularly central effect, and that is the voice. Let me consider the role of the voice more closely before moving on to the next section.

The voice is performative by nature. Its evocativeness, that is, its disappearance at the moment of appearance, makes it dependent on the perception of others; its eventfulness requires the copresence of actor and recipient. Despite its ephemeral nature, the voice is always tied to a physical body, and at the same time transcends individuality, as it indicates belonging to a particular culture, social group, or gender.[42] Complicating the voice's corporeality and indexicality is crucial in drag lip-synching in general and in *The Dagmar Onassis Story* in particular. Here, the voice is not always easily traceable to the body from which it springs but upsets the play of sign and signified. In other words, the voice is not only performative but also excessive, bearing a potential for transgression. Sybille Krämer and Doris Kolesch summarize this in the following passage: "The voice is . . . not simply body or mind, sensuality or sense, affect or intellect, language or image, but it always embodies both. It is situated between two sides that enter into a relationship with each other within it. The voice eludes the disjunctivity of conceptual schemes, it undermines our binary categorizations to some extent and appears as a paradigmatic figure of transgression."[43] Note how transgression here is not understood as opposition or confrontation but in terms of ambiguity. By transcending the boundaries it itself establishes, whether those constituting the body, subjectivity, or signification, the voice is a kind of threshold phenomenon, characterized, in the words of Roland Barthes, by its atopic quality, that is, by its nonqualifiability.[44] As Kolesch says, "this non-qualifiability does not represent a lack, but a quality—the quality of the mixed, the composite, the mobile, fluid, manifold, transitory," and, one might add, the spilling.[45]

The performativity and transgressivity of the voice gain yet another dimension when considering the specific case of the operatic voice. For Sigrid Weigel, the voice in opera is a figure of reverberation in a double sense: as both the vocal trace of transcendence (in terms of an exaltation of speech and thus one's own discursive subjectivity) and as an echo of bygone cultic and religious moments in art, in which the voice often played a crucial role.[46] Conveniently, Weigel draws on Ingeborg Bachmann's unpublished text "Hommage à Maria Callas," in which the German writer asserts that Callas was extraordinarily present in her gestures, movements, and cries, and at the same time a "lever that turned a world around, . . . and one could suddenly *hear through centuries*."[47] In transcending time, as Bachmann describes so beautifully, the reverberation of the opera voice makes the past affectively present. Applied to *The Dagmar Onassis Story*, this is true in many ways: the voice of the dead opera diva, technically reproduced, is brought back to the stage and screen through John Kelly's reenactment, complicating the relationship between fan and star, man and woman, real and fake, audience and performer, as well as the already complex temporal and spatial matrix of this film as performance and this performance as film—which brings us back to the initial question of this chapter, namely how performance and film relate to each other.

In the context of his collaborations with Kelly and other performers such as Dancenoise and Jo Andres, Anthony Chase described his film sequences as being "woven into the performances" and thus "layering" them, meaning that they function as visual layers to bridge costume and set changes or as textual layers that help to carry the narrative forward.[48] However, it seems that neither the notion of a formal "sticking together" nor of a visual or textual "layering" aptly describe how film and performance relate to each other, not least since both wordings entail an understanding of each being singular entities, entities that might be glued together so tightly or might overlap in such a way that makes them almost inseparable. But entities whose inherent singularity, and the idea of their having fixed demarcations lines, still remains. *Dagmar Onassis*, however, cannot easily be contained within one category, medium, or form. Rather, it describes a moment in which film and performance spill over the stage, the frame, and also into each other, to a degree that makes it impossible, rather than merely difficult, to draw a distinct line between them. In the following pages, I will further explore processes of spilling between film and performance by looking, first, at the notion of live film in the work of Nick Zedd, and, second, at the film happenings of Ela Troyano.

Live Film: *Me Minus You*

1) Play tape #2. Play slides at 5 seconds each—Eric's monologue—2) Change to slide tray two. Go slower than 5 seconds each. Stop on Eric passed out by toilet.

> Turn projector off when screen goes down. Play tape +2 until music stops then put it on pause. Slides precede Chuck's entry onto the stage from the audience. He rips down the screen takes all of his clothes off, between swigs of cheap rot-gut. He then jumps into bed. Scene: Night. Bedroom. Two figures are in the bed fitfully attempting to make love. . . . [49]

The *Me Minus You* screenplay, written by Nick Zedd in 1985, begins with an instruction: Play tape #2. As can be gathered from what follows, the setup of *Me Minus You* invokes both the technology associated with the presentation of film as well and the markers of live performance; an audio tape with prerecorded music or dialogue, a tape player, slides, a slide tray, a screen, a stage, an audience, props, and actors all have a part to play in what could perhaps be described as a domestic drama on stage. Zedd, as his drag alter ego Nichole, starred in the lead female role; Eric Pryor, aka Rick Strange, took on the role of her abusive boyfriend Chuck; and Phoebe Legere, Jessica Jason, Tommy Turner, and Bunny Atlanta (now known as drag queen Lady Bunny) made guest appearances. After premiering at the Pyramid Club in April 1985, *Me Minus You* toured through various night clubs, film venues, and contemporary art spaces in New York City and Buffalo and was often shown as a double bill with one of Zedd's 16 mm or Super 8 films, such as *Geek Maggot Bingo* (1983). The flyer for an event at the Collective for Living Cinema announces that the audience would get to see a "Performance and Film" by Nick Zedd and gives *Me Minus You* the subtitle "expanded cinema performance." On other occasions, Zedd described it as an "ordeal," a play of his "Theater of Shame," a "performance thing," and a "live movie," suggesting that it ranges somewhere between theater, performance, and film.[50]

"Live movie" refers to the fact that *Me Minus You* was originally intended for the camera but was performed on stage due to budgetary limitations; calling the script a screenplay merely suggests that it is a play for the screen. So, *Me Minus You* is indeed an "unmade film," or rather, a film made by other means.[51] That this screenplay was taken to the stage to be performed "like a live movie," however, inevitably poses the questions of, first, what makes a film live and what makes a live situation film, and, second, how to talk about film as an event that does not leave much trace behind.[52] Since filmic or photographic documentation of *Me Minus You* is scarce, and the performance was not enacted again at a later point, my discussion of it is based not on documentation in the conventional sense of representation but instead on paratexts: a copy of the screenplay, a recounting issued in *Underground Film Bulletin*, statements in interviews, and promotional posters and ads, all produced by Zedd himself.[53]

Methodologically, I take my cue here from both Jonathan Gray's "off-screen studies" and Amelia Jones's proposition to study performance art "through their photographic, textual, oral, video, and/or film traces."[54] While Jones convincingly asserts that the experience of watching an artist perform live and the experience of viewing a photograph of said performance are arguably different, neither holds the "historical 'truth' of the performance," as both experiences are mediated in their own way, Gray makes a similar argument in the area of film studies.[55] Emphasizing the relevance of trailers, fan fiction, merchandise, and DVD bonus material, he considers such filmic paratexts "not simply add-ons, spinoffs, and also-rans: they create texts, they manage them, and they fill them with many of the meanings that we associate with them."[56] In so doing, he also makes the crucial ontological argument that the film or program itself does not constitute the entire text or form; instead, it is only a part of it, "always being a contingent entity, either in the process of forming and transforming or vulnerable to further formation or transformation."[57] The paratexts on which I will draw offer information on how *Me Minus You* was conceived, promoted, and perceived. As such, they are crucially involved in *Me Minus You*'s production, in rendering it experienceable, and giving it meaning. As indicated earlier, however, they go beyond merely framing the work, in the sense that they do not occupy a secondary position in relation to it. Rather, we should consider the texts and images of *Me Minus You* as part of the work's already unstable and contingent form, allowing it to spill out even more.

Let us start with the concept of "live film." To put the word "live" in front of "film" or "movie" was not a new idea in 1985. In fact, Jack Smith explicitly used the term, in capital letters, to describe his working method. LIVE FILM, according to Smith, implies that "some of the work goes on through the screening itself," meaning that corrections to the film and experimentations with sound take place during the film's screening and thus become part of the film.[58] This approach needs to be considered in the larger framework of Smith's processual, multidisciplinary, and gloriously messy artistic work, in which he lets performance, film, photography, and installation merge. When it came to his films, as Uzi Parnes writes, Smith "refused to believe in the sacrosanct quality of any individual movie. Instead, he felt that episodes, scenes, even individual shots could be moved around, deleted, or added each time the film was shown in order to create 'a new movie' for each show," or rather, a live film.[59] Note, however, that his refusal to produce films as single products was partly rooted in fear of their being duplicated and distributed against his will, or worse, confiscated and banned, as was the case with *Flaming Creatures* (1962–1963).

Whereas in Smith's work the film is assembled and literally happens in the moment of screening, namely through the interventions of the filmmaker himself, Zedd's live film is not based on a recording and is therefore not screened at all, but happens on stage, where it is performed in front of an audience.[60] The result is the same: By giving weight to its performativity, film becomes performance, at least momentarily. So, it wouldn't be entirely accurate to conclude that just because *Me Minus You* was billed as an expanded cinema performance, it was formally based on the events of the 1960s and 1970s; Zedd was less concerned with the formal extension of cinema than with its means of conveying a story. Thus, the fact that Zedd uses the term "expanded cinema performance" represents more of a recourse to established terminology and thus an incorporation into existing traditions.

Again, it is important to remember that this kind of questioning of the definition of "film" was often motivated more by economics than by concept. For instance, John Jesurun was introduced by a critic reviewing the stage version of *Chang in a Void Moon* as an "independent film maker who, lacking the money to continue producing films, decided instead to present his scripts on stage in what he describes as a 'living film serial.'"[61] Whether this remark fosters a romanticized vision of the chronically broke independent-filmmaker-cum-grassroots-theater-director is anyone's guess. It does, however, hint at the fact that economic conditions—and the need to work with or around them through improvising, detouring, and repurposing—factor into the determination of what is usually vaguely labeled as an "avant-garde" aesthetic. Zedd's and Jesurun's ventures into the realm of live performance can therefore be seen as attempts to make film by other means (which certainly also includes the economic sense of the word). So how did they realize these films on stage?

Chang in a Void Moon began as a twenty-minute Super 8 film in 1979 before it shifted to the stage in 1982. This "living film serial" has been perceived by viewers as being decisively cinematic: it achieves visual film-like effects, such as the impression of editing or shifting perspectives, as well as the sense of jumping in time and place, by "the simplest possible manipulations of the limited resources and effects available at the Pyramid Club."[62] For instance, a change of time and place was effected by a performer suddenly speaking another language or simply mentioning that, now, the action takes place in 1946 Saigon. The impression of a cut was produced by having one scene end abruptly and another start in a different area of the stage. In order to simulate a bird's-eye view, performers lay sideways on platforms to appear as though they were sitting around a desk with the camera hovering over them. Black cloth covered the platforms, which made them, thanks to well-adjusted stage lights, almost invisible against the black background. It did not matter whether a camera conveyed these scenes or not; as the audience replaced the eye of the camera, what mattered was that they read these scenes, based on previous visual experiences, as cinematic.

Me Minus You combines elements of film presentation with those of a live performance. In the beginning, slides that show Eric Pryor "passed out by toilet" depict, according to Zedd, his "characteristic life as a drunken wife beater and junkie" and thus function as an introduction to the piece. The story is mostly conveyed through dialogue and action on stage. The script includes idiosyncratically detailed indications for how actors should convey their lines ("deliriously happy") and which actions accompany ("empathically stomping down her dainty little foot") or follow their lines ("she has collapsed against the wall, and she cries louder and louder with a convulsive infantile hysteria"). Until the very last scene, there is no indication that *Me Minus You* actively involves its audience. However, after Nichole "shoots" herself and Phoebe Legere, Turner, who had been "sleeping" throughout the action on stage, makes an appearance: "Tommy wakes up. Stands. Examines the bloody mess. TOMMY: Oh man. What happened? (TO AUDIENCE:) What's going on? What are you just gonna sit here? Are you crazy? Oh Shit. (He walks out)." After this last scene, a slide shows the closing credits of this live film.

Zedd deploys a similar strategy in his Super 8 film *Bogus Man* (1980). Here, an anonymous, masked person continuously addresses the audience with a distorted voice, claiming to identify with the film's viewer. While watching allegedly secret CIA footage that unveils the unsettling cloning of the President of the United States, the audience is assured by the masked person that they know how it feels: "When I first saw this footage, I asked myself, Why? Why did my eyes have to see this? You're probably asking yourself that same question." At a later point, they begin again, explaining "The footage you are about to see..." but are interrupted by another voice that seems to give directions: "Wait, wait, wait... now... action!" In *Bogus Man* there is a constant interplay between fiction and reality. Uncertainty and ambiguity are not only discussed in textual terms but also become the formal strategy that emphasizes the constructedness of the film. Similarly, in *Me Minus You* Tommy Turner's address to the audience breaks with the presumed hermetic space of the stage while at the same time affirming the illusion of the story that is constructed in that very space, of which the audience becomes a witness and is called on to intervene.

In this context, the use of filmed footage on stage is worth pointing out as well. While the events in *Me Minus You* were to unfold in real time, Nichole's dream marks a temporal shift, or rather, a different field of consciousness. The screenplay gives instructions on how this dream would be conveyed: "1. Project slide 'Nichole's dream.' Cut off. 2. Project Super 8 film: play tape music with it the same music is on the film. 3. Cut projector off after the second of the vile shot ejaculating phallus goes off. [*sic*] 4. Put cassette on pause when music ends.— Nichole sits up."[63] A slide that read "Nichole's dream" was followed by an excerpt from Zedd's and Richard Kern's Super 8 film *Thrust in Me* (1985), a similar story of an unhappy relationship. Here, the apathetic female protagonist (played by Zedd in drag) commits suicide by slitting her wrists. Her boyfriend (also played by Zedd), who finds her dead in the bathtub, performs oral sex on the corpse. The climax of the film, in all its disturbing double entendre, features Zedd ejaculating onto his own dead face as the camera zooms in while the Dream Syndicate's song "John Coltrane Stereo Blues" plays, its lyrics foreshadowing the male aggression we see acted out on screen: "Don't tell me anymore 'bout the civilized world, baby / It's just you and me... / I said a man works hard all day / He can do what he wants to / At night... / She said hold me tight / I don't think that's what you want."[64] These verses mark the end of Nichole's dream, from which she wakes up startled: "What a horrible dream. Reminds me of a film I once saw."

The decision to use footage from this previously made Super 8 film made sense from a pragmatic perspective. Simply put, using existing material is cheaper than producing something new, and, as an entr'acte, the screening bridged possible costume or set changes. But using the film also allowed Zedd to augment the real time of the stage with the spatiotemporal structure of a dream, as he becomes haunted by his own work. In any case, the fact that *Thrust in Me* was reused in this way points again to, first, film being less a stable entity than something that, depending on usage and context, can materialize in varying forms and expressions, and second, that there is a casual but necessary switching back and forth between film, performance, and lived reality, that is, there is a spilling between these spheres and forms that blurs their markings. Similar to John Kelly's Dagmar Onassis, Nick Zedd's drag identity moved between different (media) settings. She appeared on screen, on stage, and occasionally at a friend's house.[65] In his performance *SHE*, just like in *Me Minus You* and *Thrust in Me*, Zedd wears the same black wig and the same dramatic makeup. A quick look at this performance will help to better understand his drag character.

SHE is based on a lyric Zedd cowrote with Lydia Lunch. Since the text is about his intense infatuation with Lunch, it stands to reason that his drag performance look is a copy of her signature style, with unruly black hair and makeup that emphasizes pouty lips and draws attention to the eyes. A press release for "Nick Zedd's Theatre of Shame" announces the piece as follows: "SHE articulates the lust and insane idolatry a man feels for a woman when he elevates her to the position of a goddess. Zedd will play the role originally portrayed by Lunch in its single performance on Dutch television in 1983. Bill Rice will appear as the narrator."[66] It is likely that this press release was written for a performance at the contemporary art center Hallwalls in Buffalo, New York, where *SHE* was followed by a screening of Zedd's films *The Wild World of Lydia Lunch* (1983) and *They Eat Scum* (1979) in September 1985. A taping of the performance shows Nick as Nichole (or as Lydia?) floating around a candle-lit and scarcely equipped stage, immersed in blue light. Zedd remains silent throughout the performance, dancing slowly while touching his body, which is wrapped in a morning robe and equipped with a pair of faux breasts. The movements seem improvised and, if scripted at all, only loosely to match the text, as it is read aloud by a male voice: "She is perfect . . . This woman who never ceases to be a child . . . raven and ravenous, eyes of blue fire, that burn holes in everything they look through . . ." In the last part, Nichole lounges on a couch and eats a banana, while looking at the audience, which, as the taping suggests, sits in proximity to the stage. This scene is of course reminiscent of Mario Montez in Warhol's short films *Mario Banana I* and *Mario Banana II* (both 1964), in which Montez looks invitingly into the camera while peeling and eating a banana with relish.

Zedd's drag character further compares to Rivera's and John Kelly's insofar as it is a performance identity that comes to the fore on stage or in front of a camera and which pays tribute to an admired and idealized woman. Dagmar

Onassis is Kelly's interpretation of Maria Callas; Mario Montez is Rivera's version of María Montez; and Nichole, although he never formulated this explicitly, surely can be regarded Zedd's embodiment of Lydia Lunch. This becomes clear in the text for *SHE*, which is an excessive, even obsessive panegyric to Lunch, but also in his drag character's looks. It seems as if Zedd's drag performance is, ultimately, motivated first and foremost by desire. The gentle admiration and the tragedy of unreturned love that is already palpable in Zedd's film *The Wild World of Lydia Lunch* (a travelogue about the summer Zedd and Lunch spent together in London and Ireland that ended their romantic relationship) reaches its peak in *SHE*, where admiration turns into quasi-religious worship. *Me Minus You* and *Thrust in Me* are not explicitly about Lunch, nevertheless, they implicitly continue the subject of the film and performance mentioned above by dealing with mental and physical power struggles in heterosexual relationships. So, while Kelly's and Rivera's drag are decisively queer performances that celebrate a heightened, idealized, and consequently artificial femininity, a kind of fandom that turns into camp stardom, Zedd's drag originates from a place of heterosexual desire. In a gesture of appropriation, Zedd becomes the woman who left him, dancing to the words of praise he wrote, touching his own body instead of hers.

There is now one final aspect of Zedd's script for *Me Minus You* to consider, which can also act as a segue into the next section of the chapter, and that is the question of improvisation and unpredictability. Even though the piece is in some respects characterized by a need to refunction and adapt, and thus has an inherent improvisational quality, the short and concise instructions in the script seem to leave little to no room for impromptu acting. This, however, does not mean that unplanned incidents did not happen; they were, in fact, embraced regardless. Indeed, when reading Zedd's account of the first performance of *Me Minus You* at the Pyramid Club, the accidents are precisely what constitute the event. Likewise, in an interview, Zedd spoke at great length and in detail about the outrageous behavior of his male lead, who, allegedly drunk, tore up his script onstage, was thrown off by Zedd, and began looking in the audience for a knife he had lost. "That wasn't scripted, but I was pleased that it occurred," concluded Zedd.[67] In the third issue of his zine *Underground Film Bulletin*, Zedd reported on this performance in a letter dated April 20, 1985, the day after the event. For the most part, the three-page-long hand-written letter is devoted to recounting the moments in which his performers forgot their lines, began to improvise, or fell out of character, including himself: "When I finally realized that he [Eric Pryor] was back onstage, I got really mad and ordered him off. He wouldn't leave so I picked him up and threw him off which hurt the illusion I was a woman as I did the whole performance in drag."[68] On the last page, a reply is printed: "Dear Son, The on stage performance of your play sounds strange." For the review of his "live film," Zedd deliberately chose the format of a letter, giving a subjective but informative report of what happened and how it appeared to someone we can assume was not a scene participant, namely his father. Whether we are reading an actual exchange between father and son is not relevant, for the letter is yet another enactment of *Me Minus You*, a performance of the performance, documenting and extending it, and, in Rebecca Schneider's words, rendering impossible "the pristine self-sameness of an 'original.'"[69]

Film Happenings: *Bubble People*

Troyano placed her camera in the middle of a loft where there were four sets—a volcano, a classroom, a beach party, and a stage draped in lamé. She wanted the actors to choose their own sets and props, and the camera would pan. She wanted someone from the crew to enter the frame occasionally, holding two extended sticks, and the camera would zoom in to this new frame. She wasn't interested in a film where the director made all the choices.[70]

What is described here is the making of Ela Troyano's first film *Bubble People*, shot in 1982 on 16 mm film in the loft of filmmaker and photographer Uzi Parnes. Parnes used his loft regularly as a venue for performances, screenings, and installations under the name Performances Staged. Most of the props, costumes, and sets for *Bubble People* came from Parnes's collection of gathered and self-made clothes and objects, which were often leftovers from past performances. The crew and cast of actors included Troyano and Parnes's friends and regular collaborators, such as Donna Death, Phoebe Legere, Ivan Galietti, Jack Smith, and Alina Troyano aka Carmelita Tropicana. As active participants in the Downtown improvisational music, performance, experimental/feminist theater, and filmmaking scenes, they were all used to performing, whether it be live, in front of a camera, or both.[71] In fact, Troyano specifically chose them because she "knew the people and had an idea of how they would behave."[72] As the account cited above indicates, the performers were encouraged to improvise with the given sets and props while the camera simply "pans." This suggests that the film was made by allowing and even encouraging some controlled randomness. Remember that a spill is neither intentional nor completely random but requires the right conditions for it to happen. In most cases, this means setting a framework and then accepting a loss of control. Similarly, Troyano's approach to filmmaking meant creating circumstances that allowed for experimentation and improvisation and thus for her films to happen either with or "without ever making it onto celluloid."[73] By looking closely at Troyano's two earliest films and their modes of production, exhibition, and enactment, I will outline their performance practices. Finally, I trace the productions of *Bubble People* to the present to identify under what conditions and for what reasons their messiness becomes contained.

For now, however, we will stay at the set of *Bubble People* in Parnes's loft. Rather than directing her actors, Troyano asked them to move through the four continuous sets and to interact freely with each other and the given props (inflatable beach balls, pastel-colored tulle, shimmering plastic foil, large paper fans), costumes (blue and purple wigs, bead chains, corsets, and floral dresses), and sets (made from rows of shiny draped fabrics).[74] The action was organized not according to a narrative logic or storyline but by having performers improvise in different formations, as a solo, duo, trio, or group, to a loose script and music. This approach derived from improvisational music, more precisely from Troyano's collaboration with musician and composer John Zorn.

In the early 1980s, before making *Bubble People*, Troyano worked as a projectionist in nightclubs, where she manipulated and mixed filmed footage, three-dimensional objects, and color transparencies by hand, often during a concert or party. When Troyano made projections for Zorn's pieces, he provided her, as well as the other projectionists and musicians, with a score to improvise from, either alone or in sets of twos, threes, fours, fives, and so on.[75] This was a continuation of the *Game Pieces* Zorn began developing in the late 1970s, which he described as "complex systems harnessing improvisers in flexible compositional formats."[76] His score for *Cobra* (1984), for example, proposes the concept of free improvisation. Here, Zorn invited musicians to play his composition as a game. *Cobra* consists of a set of cues and corresponding rules—which can signify body movements, a change in tempo, a pause, or a fade-out—that are noted on cards, which are in turn held up to the players by a prompter. As the number of players, the instrumentation, and the length of the piece are undefined and the players are always improvising, *Cobra* will not only sound different from performance to performance, but it will also look different. It is worth mentioning that Troyano was introduced to Zorn by playwright Richard Foreman, in whose *Rhoda in Potatoland* (1976) she appeared, and that Zorn in turn introduced her to Jack Smith when he did the sound and light for Smith's performance *The Secret of Rented Island*. Troyano attended the New York premiere in 1976 and was invited by Smith to participate in the performance on the following day. These connections not only document the networking logic of scenes as such but also help to clarify the encounters that prompted the spillover between the theater, music, performance, and filmmaking practices in question.

Bubble People's script, which functioned as a sort of score, was based loosely on the dialogues of George Cukor's *Let's Make Love* (1960). In this musical comedy, Marilyn Monroe stars as the lead in a Broadway show. In *Bubble People*, Parnes plays the part of Monroe, whose character Troyano imagined as a multiplied "Einstein-like genius, [who is] teaching everyone to become more like her and Bubble People that had always traveled passing through walls, everywhere."[77] Troyano described the atmosphere on set as "very backstage. . . . Like playing dress-up."[78] Indeed, there is a lot of seemingly mindless puttering around, silliness, and charming clumsiness, but also awkward and even boring moments in which not even the performers themselves seem to be entirely sure what is going on. While most scenes in *Bubble People* have such an air of messiness and confusion, there is one scene that especially expresses the film's constitutive glitches.

Before he comes into view, his distinctive voice can be heard. Jack Smith, who performed the main role of the Bubble Goddess together with Legere, is asking, "Action? Are you sure if there is enough light?" And someone answers him, "No." Smith goes on, "Uh . . . no? Now, hand me the script. 'Cause I haven't seen the script yet." Meanwhile, the camera zooms in on his body and moves up slowly from his feet to his chest, showing an arrangement of glittery fabrics, feathers, tape, and beads half-covering his body. A voice comes from offscreen: "Is there a script somewhere? Uzi? Is there a script? A movie without a script?! Well, where is it?" Then, adding in an overly ironic tone: "Oh, thank god, it's here." The camera is out of focus, and the screen shows a purple blur as we hear Smith again: "You have to tell me when the tape has begun . . . then . . ." We see his hands, adorned with heavy silver rings, holding pieces of paper. "I need a script to show what a great actor I am." The camera reaches his face. Wearing several necklaces, small-framed sunglasses, big golden earrings, and blue glitter in his beard, he is scanning the paper in his hand.

When presented as a double projection, the second screen on the left shows a scene in which Legere sits with the script between her legs, glancing at the text while she performs for the camera. Her voice is softly audible in the background, making Smith's already mumbling voice even harder to understand. Cut. Smith is standing on a pile of fabrics, surrounded by transparent foils, shimmering as if underwater. He declares: "All I know is I AM THE BUBBLE GODDESS." A hand reaches into the frame and hands him the script again. He takes it, pauses to read over it, then leans in toward the person on his left, points to the paper, and asks: "What is this?" The camera now only shows his hand, which is gesturing while Smith is addressing Troyano: "But what we talked about on the phone . . . the plan with the bubbles . . . that was much more interesting." Cut. The camera only shows his body up to the neck, and his hands are now holding the script and a big satin bra. He hesitates before he asks: "Now tell me the truth. Has the camera started?" Troyano, not visible in the frame, answers that the camera has indeed started. "Oh OK, because you know, we can get better results from each other if we're honest with each other and if we tell each other when the camera has started . . . I AM . . ." He pauses, and Troyano asks: "What are you?" Smith repeats: "I AM A BUBBLE GODDESS. Uh . . . As you can see, it was only after the tape has begun that I have even been handed the script." While previously Smith, Troyano, and the other people on the set only interacted with one another, it feels as if, with this last sentence, Smith addresses us, his audience, directly. It seems as if he were, though presumably half-joking, apologizing for not being able to give his best possible performance because, as we can see, it was only after the tape had begun that he was given the script.

Dominic Johnson sees this scene as an expression of what he calls a "sense of failure" that runs through Jack Smith's artistic practice. Smith tested both the upper and lower limits of performance, the potentialities of failure through excess and unmanageable maximalism, or, on the opposite end of the spectrum, through slowness, hesitation, and delay.[79] Smith's failure, then, is a queer failure, a virtuous refusal to comply with any kind of normative standards, and with "straight time" in particular.[80] For instance, in *The Secret of Rented Island*, the deliberate delays and the possibility of performance failure at any given moment were integral elements of the production. Smith asked arriving members of the audience to take on the roles of missing performers and made various, seemingly random adjustments to the set. When the performance began, he read his lines from a script in his hands, just like he did in *Bubble People*, and requested help to find the right passage when he was lost.[81] This was commonplace in his performances. In fact, Smith stated that, for him, an actor who can only memorize lines has no dramatic quality and is not a "good" actor.[82] It seems even more significant now that Troyano was introduced to Smith's work through *The Secret of Rented Island*, since failure through artifice and deferral, as well as Smith's very own notion of the dramatic, come, quite literally, into play in this performance, and are also distinctly tangible in Troyano's film.

For Troyano's second film, *Totem of the Depraved* (1983), there was no script at all, only a loose story framework. The film begins with codirector and protagonist Nick Zedd entering a room with brick walls. Dressed in a black suit and half-unbuttoned shirt, he sits down on a sofa bed decorated with tiger-patterned pillows. He looks around and then straight into the camera, asking, "Where is Ela?" to which a female voice responds, "Huh? What do you mean?" Zedd: "The director. There's supposed to be a director here. She's not here?" He nervously looks around the room until a voice from offscreen, which indeed belongs to Troyano herself, calls his name, making him look back into the camera. "Yeah, that's my name. Somebody told me something about a film. I am supposed to be playing... uh... a stud." The camera zooms into his face while he is speaking. He is interrupted by Troyano saying, "What the fuck do you mean, a stud? I mean, really..." while the camera zooms in closer and closer on his face (see Figure 6). "Why don't you look at the camera? Let me see. A stud you mean?" While Zedd wonders about the girls that would act in what he thinks will be a porn film, Troyano's camera zooms in and out of his face, studying its features and its expressions, just like she did with Smith, exploring the gestures of his hands through the lens of her camera while discussing the script, or lack thereof, and the roles of her actors, affirming that Jack Smith is the Bubble Goddess, affirming that Nick Zedd is Nick.

In *Totem of the Depraved*, Zedd and his costars were essentially playing themselves, improvising not based on a script but, as Troyano said, "improvising on life."[83] Zedd asking about the director and pretending to be at a casting session for a porn movie was improvised, a joke he may not have realized would be included in the film. Just before Zedd and Troyano got together to make the film, Zedd was thrown out of the apartment he shared with his ex-girlfriend and had to virtually seduce someone into letting him stay with them.[84] This endeavor became the basic plot of the film. By the time of filming, Zedd had already

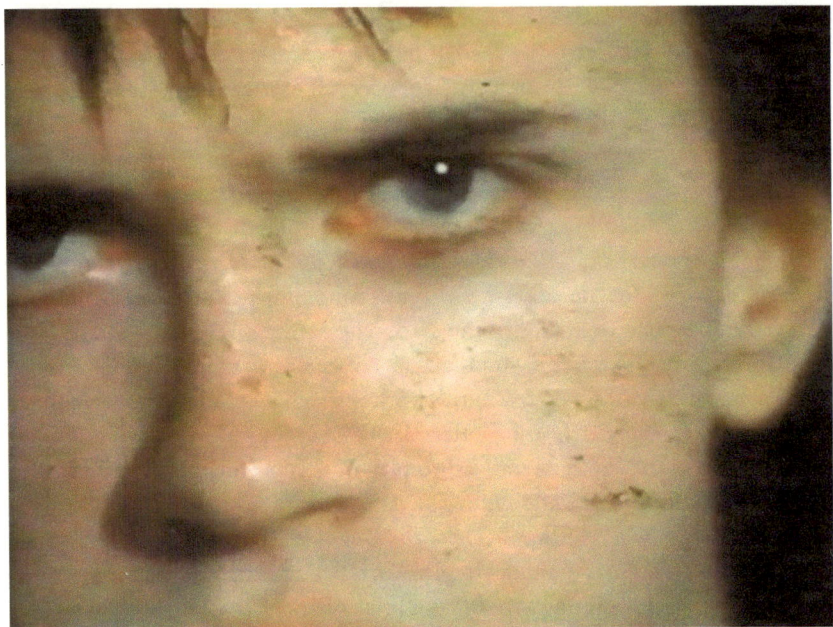

FIGURE 6 Nick Zedd in *Totem of the Depraved*, 1983

settled on an artist name, gained some notoriety as a filmmaker, programmer, and cartoonist, and was, with his signature unruly hair and black clothing, a familiar face in the scene. So having Zedd appear as Zedd meant that he was playing a role in the film that he played constantly in his daily life.

This blurring of life and film, as well as the renunciation of traditional notions of characterization, were common elements in the films that emerged from the Downtown scene in the late 1970s and 1980s. Performers did not necessarily "get into character," but more often appeared and acted as they would on a night out or when performing on stage. For instance, in Nick Zedd's *War Is Menstrual Envy* (1992), Kembra Pfahler appears in the outfit she regularly wore for shows with her band, the Voluptuous Horror of Karen Black: naked but painted blue (or orange, or red, or purple) from head to toe, with teased dark hair and thick black eyeliner. Similarly, whether Lydia Lunch was performing with a band, giving spoken-word performances, or acting in films by Downtown filmmakers like Beth and Scott B, Vivienne Dick, Richard Kern, or Nick Zedd, she was always unmistakably recognizable as the persona Lydia Lunch.[85]

The way the camera is incessantly fixed on Zedd's face in *Totem of the Depraved* also calls to mind the short portrait films of Andy Warhol. Produced between 1964 and 1966, the 472 films now known as the *Screen Tests* portray Factory visitors as they sit in front of Warhol's unmoving 16 mm camera. These three-minutes film reels depict what Callie Angell calls a feeling of being "trapped in the existential dilemma of performing as ... his or her own image" and what Jonathan Flatley describes as "dramas of self-presentation."[86] As musicians, actresses, poets, artists, and filmmakers invariably fail to maintain their pose, the screen tests capture and dramatize "each sitters' failure to hold onto an identity, the singular way that each person comes together and falls apart."[87] *Totem of the Depraved* is, at times, a drama of self-presentation in the Warholian sense. Zedd as Zedd seems to struggle to find his role, falling in and out of the identity he created for himself, holding on to the safety of an assumed character and the comfort of scripted lines.

Still sitting on the couch, Zedd leans back and says, "I don't understand, Ela didn't really give me a script. She gave me some scribblings here [picks up a piece of paper], but they mean nothing to me." Prior to making *Totem of the Depraved* with Troyano, Zedd had made the Super 8 films *They Eat Scum* (1979), *Bogus Man* (1980), and *Geek Maggot Bingo* (1983), all of which were based on detailed scripts and followed wacky yet somewhat fixed story lines, referencing B-movie, sci-fi, or horror cult film genres rather than adopting the score model of improvisational music and performance art. Even the "live film" *Me Minus You* followed a detailed screenplay. So he was naturally unaccustomed to making a film without a script, let alone doing so while being in front of the camera instead of behind it. For *Totem of the Depraved*, Troyano and Zedd asked Gia Gamba, Phoebe Legere, and James Richardson to interact and get physical with Zedd for ten minutes each while Troyano's camera was recording. The encounters are genuine to the point that they are both appealing and uncomfortable to watch, as the camera relentlessly documents the shyness, teasing, attraction, and awkwardness that unfolds between Zedd and his coperformers. For Zedd, the lack of a script seemed to be the defining element of the film, and of his experience of working with Troyano:

> Without the luxury of a script, I did the scene with Gia [Gamba] in which I examined her jewelry and then handcuffed her and proceeded to undress her until she whispered to me that she was a virgin. I asked her if I could move in with her and she said yes, so I told Ela to turn the camera off and left.... The next day, improvising a scene with Phoebe during the filming of the movie, I began to understand Ela's directorial approach. She'd turn on the camera and sit back and let us do all the work. She never gave any direction and we never knew what was going on; I had to figure it all out as the camera was rolling. In a daze, Ela dropped the camera and broke a lens. She must have forgotten she was filming. When she got the film back from the lab, instead of editing it, she just threw it on a projector and pronounced it finished.[88]

As contemptuous as Zedd's account may sound, it is revealing. It shows that for Troyano, directing did not mean taking the lead but creating a situation whose course or outcome remained open. Camerawork played a crucial role in this.

Troyano's camera was an Auricon 16 mm handheld, lightweight but still larger and more stable than a Super 8 camera, and it allowed her to feel more "anchored" while filming.[89] Indeed, in *Bubble People*, the camera is mostly placed in a fixed position. From there, it pans, zooms in for a close-up on an action, or spontaneously follows a performer's gestures or expressions. For instance, when one performer in a white men's suit passionately hugs another performer wearing a blonde wig and a tight red dress, his hips are circling and rubbing against the thighs of the man in the dress. The camera mimics this movement, zooming in and out rhythmically. In another scene, the camera keeps running while members of the technical crew walk into the frame, holding bulky headlights to illuminate the action.

In addition to her camerawork, there is a second vital aspect of Troyano's filmmaking practice to consider. Zedd stated that "when she [Troyano] got the film back from the lab, instead of editing it, she just threw it on a projector and pronounced it finished." Troyano had a habit of showing her films unedited, or rather, of editing them while they were being shot. Like Warhol, Troyano edited her films by literally turning the camera off and on again, even using the same camera model.[90] In Warhol's case, these jump cuts were described as "stroboscopic," visibly segmenting the filmstrip and deliberately counteracting any sense of continuity in films like *Bufferin* (1966) or *I, a Man* (1967): "The shutter blinks its eye and this wink leaves a trace on the filmstrip."[91] The use of strobe light in Warhol's *Exploding Plastic Inevitable* produces a similar effect, cutting the onstage action into single frames and creating a stop-motion effect. The filmic cut, associated with the operation of montage, usually serves to combine disparate parts into a coherent whole. Instead of stringing together scenes to create as coherent a narrative as possible, the editing in *Bubble People* resembles early television editing or the experience of zapping through television channels. When the cuts appear as a "reframing of a single, continuous image from a fixed point of view," we are reminded of the "immediacy, the sense of a continuous perceptual experience unfolding in real time that television shares with theater."[92] When they are abrupt and disruptive, taking us unexpectedly from one set to the next, it is as if someone got bored and changed the channel. The cuts are accompanied and thus accentuated by an audio signal. And while the sound of the cuts in Warhol's films has been likened to a "whip moving rapidly through the air or a turntable scratch," in *Bubble People* a whooshing *zap* gives the film its peculiar sonic rhythm, allowing its audience not only to see but also to hear the very act of recording.[93] Finally, Troyano's single-system sound-on-film camera enabled her to record image and sound simultaneously, facilitating fast development in the lab and rendering subsequent editing unnecessary. In this process, mistakes and glitches that highlight the film's materiality were not intended but deliberately maintained. For example, accidentally shooting on outdated film stock added flashes of light to a solo scene of Legere in *Totem of the*

Depraved and an incorrectly loaded lens resulted in blurry, appropriately bubble-like images in *Bubble People*.[94]

Instead of dismissing this as amateurism or even coquetry, I regard this approach as an expression of the productive dilettantism outlined by Erhard Schüttpelz. To produce as a dilettante means to not yet create the actual work or to not create an actual work at all, but to experiment, to play, to joke.[95] Remember that Troyano described the set of *Bubble People* as having a feeling of being backstage, of playing dress-up. It is precisely this air of rehearsal and screen testing that leads both *Bubble People* and *Totem of the Depraved* to implicitly reject the idea of film as a finished work. What is emphasized instead are their performative and processual qualities. "She must have forgotten she was filming": Zedd's assumption now makes sense. The presence of the camera on the set of *Bubble People* and *Totem of the Depraved* was certainly crucial, as it motivated the action it intended to record to happen. However, it seems as if the act of filming itself was secondary. Perhaps Troyano wanted to forget that she was filming as the actions unfolded, rejecting the conventional role of the director: "I gave my back to the camera.... [On the set of *Bubble People*] I was interested in having the camera stop a lot more, having a scene continue and then start again. Rather than starting, shooting and coming out again."[96] The film happened either way, whether she recorded it or not.

C. Carr describes the two films as "the closest things I've ever seen to film as performance." In her 1985 text "Loisaida Talking Pictures," she acknowledges the unpolished quality of Troyano's work, describing her multiple projections as "unrepeatable movies made on the spot" and *Bubble People* as a "wild vaudeville hippie mess. By choice."[97] And yet, by comparing the films to performances, and saying that they are performances (but not really), she suggests that she considers the two to be separate ontological categories that, being mutually exclusive, can only approximate each other. Such an assumption is based on a misguided understanding of film in terms of "recorded reproducibility" and therefore intrinsically antithetical to the immateriality, immediacy, and bodily presence of both performers and audience at an "original" event conventionally associated with live performance.[98] This certainly oversimplified binary opposition of the live and the mediated has been productively complicated in recent film and performance scholarship, showing how the very attempt to clearly delineate and separate film from performance and vice versa is as outdated as it is unproductive.[99] Troyano's films make this all the more clear. As performance and film spill into each other, each moves away from its respective singularity. In this sense, *Bubble People* is highly ephemeral. But whether it remains in this ambiguous state or is assigned to a specific medium and thus cast in a fixed form depends not least on the context in which it appears.

When *Bubble People* is performed in its "live film version," two reels of 16 mm are projected side by side, one starting a little earlier than the other, yet at no predefined moment. The soundtrack is mixed live from sonic improvisations of the performers in the film, from recorded dialogue from *Let's Make Love*, from other film and musical soundtracks, from records played live, and, sometimes, from a violin performance by the jazz and improvisational musician Polly Bradfield. This rather elaborate setup made performances rare and led to *Bubble People* often only being screened in excerpts. (For instance, the program of the 1984 New York Film Festival Downtown at Limbo Lounge listed "Excerpts from *Bubble People*," and at a Danceteria screening organized by Zedd, he only showed the solo appearances of Jack Smith.) As *Bubble People* looks and sounds different with each iteration, it emphasizes the notion that film can be enacted, that it can continuously be performed and thus remains open to alterations and modifications. A terminological note: André Lepecki's suggestion is relevant here, when he writes, with reference to Deleuze, that one *re*-enacts "not to fix a work in its singular (originating) possibilization, but to unlock, release, and actualize a work's many (virtual) com- and incompassibilities."[100] However, it might prove even more productive to drop the prefix. While terms such as reenactment or restaging connote a returning to a past event, an enactment accentuates the generative act of continuing a particular life cycle of a work rather than restoring, reconstructing, or repeating it.[101] The three recent performances of *Bubble People* in Berlin and New York that I will briefly address in the following are such enactments. There is no attempt to return it to any presumed original form. However, at the same time, there seems to be a desire to reenact the elusive elements and ephemeral practices that informed its production.

In 2009, at the *LIVE FILM! JACK SMITH! Five Flaming Days in a Rented World* festival in Berlin (at HAU and Arsenal, October 28–November 1, 2009), *Bubble People* was mixed with a slide show of photographs taken by Uzi Parnes of Downtown performers. It was shown in a program together with another slide show by Parnes (*Exotic Dreams*, 1982–1989) and a short home video entitled *Cocktails with Jack* (1983) that documented a night with Jack Smith at Troyano and Parnes's venue Club Chandelier. Some years later, in 2016 at the Drawing Center in New York, *Bubble People* was enacted in the context of the *Basement Performance* program curated by John Zorn, a series focusing on multimedia performances that included film and improvised music. Here, the double-screen projection was accompanied by a combination of recorded and live soundtrack featuring Bradfield and was followed by another Troyano-Parnes-Zorn-collaboration, *The Silence of Marcel Duchamp*. This "live cinema performance" shows photos from New York City's piers, a site of gay cruising in the 1970s and 1980s, which are superimposed with projections of found photographic footage or three-dimensional objects. The visuals are joined by Zorn's *BeuysBlock*, a sonic meditation on the conceptual work of Joseph Beuys, whose *Aktion Das Schweigen von Marcel Duchamp wird überbewertet* (The silence of Marcel Duchamp is overrated) (1964), lends the performance its title.

Both at the Berlin festival and the New York art institution, *Bubble People* was neither announced as a film nor screened in a conventional sense. Instead, it was performed, and the performance involved a double projection, live music, different slide shows, and, notably, the presence of the filmmaker. In addition, the respective framings of the performances explicitly articulated the social and artistic connections to Smith and Zorn and also highlighted the ongoing collaboration between Troyano and Parnes, aspects that are crucially embedded in *Bubble People* itself. To conclude this section, I want to focus on one last example that will require a more extensive contextualization and discussion.

In 2014, Parnes and Troyano, together with Carmelita Tropicana, staged a two-day live exhibition at New York University's 80WSE gallery titled *Recycling Atlantis* (November 12–14, 2014). The exhibition's name is a direct reference to Jack Smith's first theatrical performance, *Rehearsal for the Destruction of Atlantis*, which premiered in 1965 at the Astor Film-Maker's Cinematheque as part of the New Cinema Festival *Expanded Cinema*. Organized by Jonas Mekas, this festival featured, amongst others, John Vaccaro, Barbara Rubin, and Mario Montez. *Rehearsal* combined a costume-heavy live performance with projected imagery, and, as Mekas said, "was loose and relied on chance, on coincidences, on conglomerations." Although shown at a festival for cinema, Mekas thought that Smith's *Rehearsal* had "little to do with cinema," but was instead an "exercise in the Artaud Theatre," whereby cinema, meaning the projections, merely functioned as "an auxiliary of the theatre."[102] *Rehearsal for the Destruction of Atlantis*, not unlike *The Dagmar Onassis Story* and *Bubble People*, makes categorization difficult, as it dwells in the muddied space where theater, performance, and cinema spill into each other. Smith cleverly circumvented such labeling altogether by calling his piece "A Dream Weapon Ritual."[103]

"Jack Smith's version of Atlantis," as José Esteban Muñoz writes, "glimpsed in much of his film and performance work, disidentified with the constraining and phobic limit of the present." Muñoz sees Smith's work, and his vision of Atlantis in particular, as a queer "world-making project."[104] In his one-page manifesto "Capitalism of Lotusland" (1978), Smith dreams up another utopia, a place where artistic production is free from capitalist restraints and art is stunning and glamorous but also useful, "loaded with information," and available to all. He proposes a "free paradise of abandoned objects" and a "community movie set," an idea that he elaborates on in the performance *What's Underground About Marshmallows* (1981).[105] Smith's artistic utopia is also an explicitly socialist critique of *landlordism*. This neologistic umbrella term for ownership, private property, and Manhattan rent sharks is recurrent in his work and ultimately fueled his visions of alternate places and temporalities.

The manifesto "Capitalism of Lotusland" was the conceptual starting point for the exhibition *Recycling Atlantis* and informed its spatial organization. An excerpt of the manifesto was displayed on one of 80WSE's walls, forming the background for an array of donated items spread out on pedestals and the gallery floor. Dried autumn leaves, glasses, books, women's shoes, a water hose, a flatiron, and other abandoned objects were waiting to be picked up, to become props in the film, and to be taken home by visitors. Three of the gallery rooms were turned into a "community movie set." In one space, a camera recorded improvised performances featuring the visitors, Tropicana as one of Smith's recurring characters "Yolanda La Pinguina," abandoned objects as props, and Smith's texts as scripts. The shooting area blended into the temporary editing studio, where Troyano and Parnes mixed, layered, and merged footage from past collaborations with Smith and Tropicana, including *Bubble People*. A third area continuously screened live footage from both Parnes and Troyano's studio as well as from the movie set.

The exhibition text states that the gallery space was turned into "a site for live film, existing in a permanent state of development, in which the boundaries between design, production, and presentation are dissolved."[106] Here, two crucial connections can be made. First of all, the term "live film" was used by Smith and later by Troyano to emphasize the performative element in their film presentations. Smith is thus distinctly framed not only as a collaborator and friend but also as the primary precursor to Troyano's filmmaking practice. Second, in regard to the blending of production and presentation, the text refers explicitly to the making of *Bubble People* at Parnes's loft. The lack of distinction between backstage and movie set, and the fact that costumes and objects were freely available to be tried on and interacted with, were re-created at 80WSE Gallery. That this tradition of loft performance again brings us back to Jack Smith is only hinted at by the text when it mentions that his home and film sets were "often one and the same." But there is more to say about this.

In December 1969, Smith moved into a two-floor loft space in a red brick building on the corner of 36 Greene Street and 89 Grand Street in SoHo. He "turned it [the space] into a twenty-four hour film set, theater, living space, and trash heap," a "queer Hollywood-esque studio and lounge-space for frequent collaborators," which he dubbed The Plaster Foundation.[107] Smith created a performance area by removing the ceiling of the 15 × 500 ft. space to install rafters for lighting the central stage, rendering it "a fantastic accumulation of refuse and junk atop a mound of plaster," including empty bottles, Christmas trees, crutches, teddy bears, and a toilet—abandoned objects, indeed. The performances that took place amidst this continuously growing environment reportedly felt like the enactment of "no more or less than Smith's daily existence."[108] Scheduled every Saturday at midnight, they often lasted until the break of the next day. His collaborator John Matturri remembers that

> Smith's shows typically began hours late and then involved lengthy periods of arranging sets and lighting in front of the audience. What in conventional theater would be the performance proper often involved open reading from

scripts, as well as out of character interactions between Smith and his performers. In counterpoint to the dialogue, Smith would spontaneously rewrite, direct, ask for variant readings, and comment and argue with performers, technicians, and others. There would be continued rearrangement of sets and lighting and, not infrequently, onstage attention to nonfunctioning equipment. The performances would proceed spasmodically, be subject to frequent interruptions and collapse, and might finally end, often in the early hours of the morning, quite arbitrarily.[109]

Matturri's description of Smith's frequently interrupted and spontaneously altered performances evokes Smith's notion of live film, as well as his appearance in *Bubble People*. Stepping in and out of character as the Bubble Goddess in Parnes's loft, having discussions with the director and co-performers, asking for the script and then questioning its content, he treated the making of the film just like a midnight performance at his loft, prone to improvisation, experimentation, excess, and failure.

With *Recycling Atlantis*, the artist-as-curator's mission was to recover, reuse, and reclaim the utopia that sums up Smith's artistic, philosophical, and political visions and to do so from the position of collaborator, friend, and artistic successor. The exhibition became a form of reenactment, aiming to make the ephemerality of Jack Smith's unsubdued filmmaking and performance practice, which is echoed in *Bubble People*, visually present and physically experienceable. In the end, however, the effect of *Recycling Atlantis* is more akin to upcycling: by being shifted into the White Cube setting of this (educational) institution, not only Smith's but also Troyano's, Tropicana's, and Parnes's work seems to undergo a cleaning, and a reconditioning, presenting contemporary visitors with a more polished version of what was once a much messier affair. Here, once again, the dilemma of archiving and subsequently presenting indisciplinary Downtown works becomes apparent, as was already discussed with regard to the exhibition *You Killed Me First* and the Fales Library's Downtown Collection. On the one hand, the processing and presentation of these works is important and certainly desirable; on the other hand, they pose their own particular challenges. The ephemeral, messy, and exuberant quality of this scene is, by its very nature, impossible to reconstruct. The aspiration to create an "authentic" experience can therefore only fail (though perhaps this is a good thing).

Now to briefly summarize: In this chapter, I have examined cases whose modes of production, presentation, and reception bring film and performance together in ways that productively transcend the logic of combination and layering. I suggested understanding this exchange as a process that lets film and performance, whose clear distinction from each other, as we have seen, is, in any case, an illusion, spill over and into the other even more. In the productions explored, spilling was encouraged thanks to the way they were created in a collaborative, genre- and format-transgressing scene that happened in venues that both testified to and facilitated this mode of indisciplinarity. And while this scene developed its very own style of club performance, it also built on experimental filmmaking and performance traditions that date back at least to the practices of the 1960s, with Jack Smith being an essential precursor. Filmic experimentation, in this context, can be understood as a deliberate form of letting go, as in Troyano's case, or as a way of eluding the process of filming altogether, as in Zedd's. The spilling of film into performance and vice versa ultimately results in an understanding of film as something that can happen, something that can be performed and staged and sometimes recorded, something that can be fleeting and materially manifest, ephemeral, and reproducible at the same time. This, in turn, calls into question dualisms that reinforce the ontological distinction between film and performance, namely recorded/live, mediated/immediate, past/present. At this point, the conversation becomes productively strange.

4
Afterlife Formats
■■■■■■■■■■■■■■■■■■■■■

In 2000, the British Film Institute (BFI) released the Cinema of Transgression (CoT) on videotape. A compilation of ten films originally released between 1979 and 1993, the tape was part of the BFI's *A History of the Avant-Garde* series, which also included the compilations "Britain in the Twenties" and "Britain in the Thirties" along with collections of works of Hans Richter, Man Ray, and Kenneth Anger. The filmmakers' names are listed in pink letters against a black background on the tape's cover, with a small BFI logo in the upper corner. "A History of the Avant-Garde" appears in grey and "Cinema of Transgression" is printed in white. The sleeve's minimal design and simple font exude a generic, subdued punk chic, exchanging the messy playfulness of the era's collaged and Xeroxed posters and zines for a sense of order and establishment. On some editions, a yellow sticker gives warning of explicit content; on others, the number 18, the recommended minimum viewing age, sits discreetly in the bottom left corner (see Figure 7). The back of the sleeve provides a description of each film and a general synopsis of the compilation by referencing Zedd's manifesto. Similar to how the exhibition text for *You Killed Me First* announced that these films transcend "all moral or aesthetic boundaries," the synopsis on the tape's sleeve describes the CoT as a "movement looking to transform values by breaking all taboos of cinematic expression."[1] Thus, both the contemporary film and art worlds, exemplified by these two institutions, reproduce, perpetuate, and ultimately manifest, rather than critically frame, the narrative established by Zedd's informal historiography.

The BFI's compilation was a rather late release from its home video division. Although it did not launch *Connoisseur Video* until 1990, by 1982 the institution

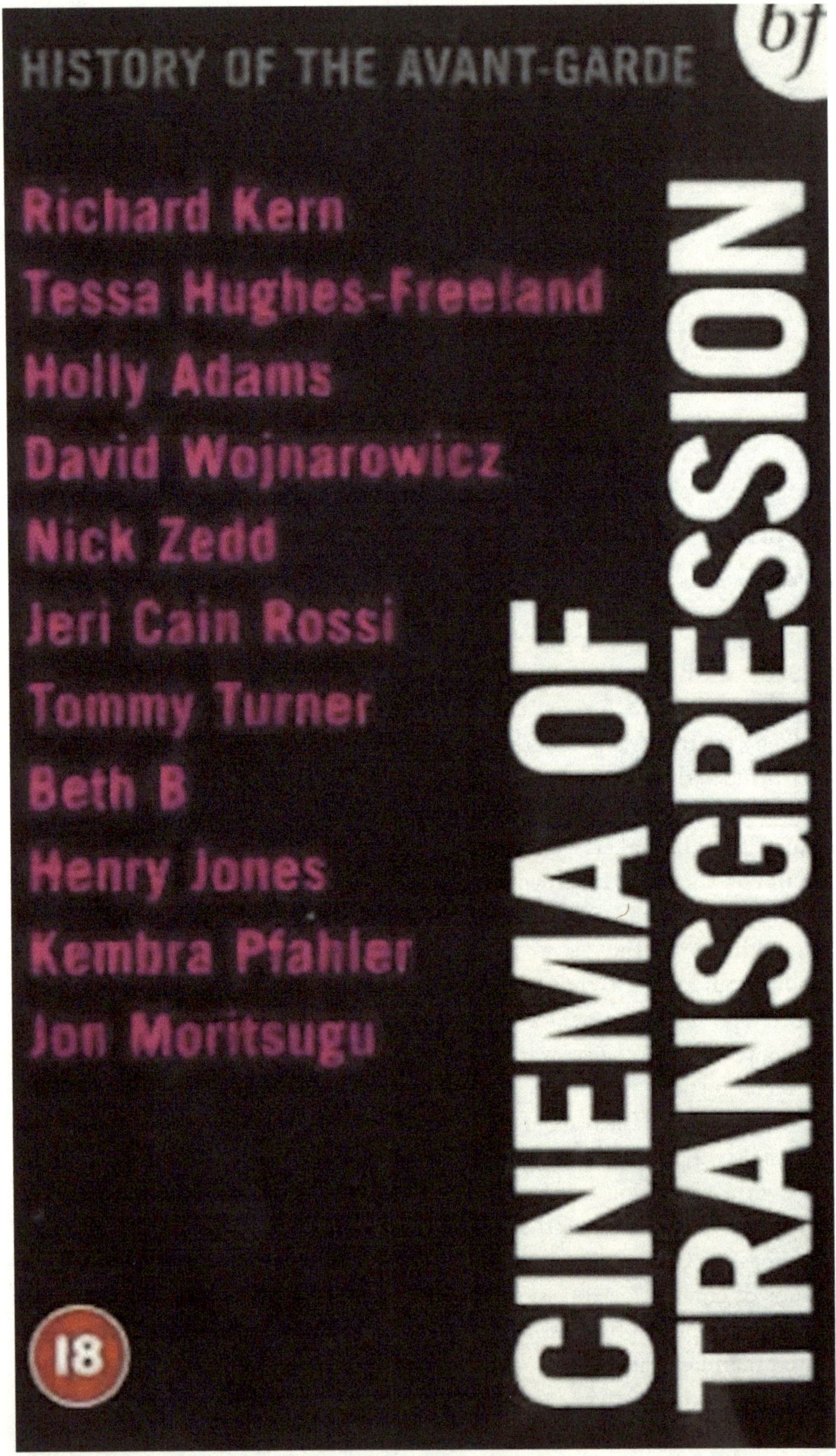

FIGURE 7 *The Cinema of Transgression Vol. 1*, BFI compilation

had already begun to recognize the potential of domestic video, imagining that a home videocassette label, "if mounted with flair, could bring the Institute into contact with a wider audience than it can currently engage either through non-theatrical distribution or its existing cinemas."[2] The assertion that a home video series by the British Film Institute, a long-standing national cultural institution, would need to be "mounted with flair" not only explains the subtle cover design of the CoT compilation, it also speaks volumes about the institution's attitude toward video, which is apparently caught between connotations of mainstream Hollywood cinema, B movies, or pornography on the one hand and its promise to reach a wider and potentially new audience on the other.

Unsurprisingly, however, the BFI wasn't the first to compile on tape films that emerged from the 1980s Downtown art, film, music, and performance scenes under the label Cinema of Transgression. Fifteen years before the collection's release, Nick Zedd selected eleven works by nine filmmakers that had been produced between 1979 and 1985, put them together on VHS and Betamax tapes, and offered them via his one-person production and distribution business, Weirdo Video.[3] The name of his company already frames the films as products of a cultural niche, quite the opposite of the BFI's attempt to market them in a way that would appeal to the acquired taste of a film connoisseur. Zedd's cover further suggests that he conceived the tape as the first part of an ongoing series, since the label "Cinema of Transgression" is followed by the addition "vol. 1." At least to my knowledge, though, no second volume was ever produced. For the cover, Zedd chose a pink monochrome photo of himself in drag, which he pasted on a yellow background. The back of the box lists the filmmakers and films. A synopsis quotes Orion Jeriko, Zedd's alter ego and editor of the *Underground Film Bulletin*, praising the alleged movement's grand gestures.

These two video compilations signal another paradoxical moment of spilling and containment in the CoT's history. By assembling films under the collective term "Cinema of Transgression," the compilers of these tapes attempt, albeit from different critical perspectives and at different points in time, to periodize and contain the films within the CoT descriptive, preparing them for inclusion in a film historical canon. At the same time, they circulate the films beyond their local context of reception, taking advantage of video technology's promise of access and wider distribution. After all, video as format or "technical infrastructure" enables flows that are informal and thus often elusive and obscure, more in line with the messy quality of a spilling.[4] However, marking a more general shift in the construction of the concept of CoT as it moves from Super 8 mm and 16 mm film to video, and later to televisual and digital formats, they also suggest that the work of constructing the CoT label not only neglects the plethora of activities, practices, media, and formats that spilled over at the time but also specifically obscures the significance of video and television. Video and television were in fact important means of artistic exploration and intervention—in the form of public access television programs, video screenings, and club events centered on television culture—and also crucial means of distribution. In this chapter, I thus consider what I will call the "afterlife formats" of the Cinema of Transgression: VHS tapes, public access television broadcasts, and the analog and digital media objects that are sold, shared, used, or archived online. While on the one hand, these situate the CoT in a past marked by certain media and technical formats, on the other hand, they also determine the conditions of further engagement and the films' ongoing circulation—in other words, the CoT's afterlife beyond museums or institutional archives. In the following, and in looking at these afterlife formats, I am curious to explore the potential messiness of circulation and displacement as well as the possibilities for containment that certain formatting practices afford. And by formats, I mean "specific formal and aesthetic configurations of media" that not only maintain the (in)operability of media but also "point to specific communities of practice."[5] I am inspired by Benoît Turquety here, who evaluates the operability of "media" against that of "formats." He convincingly argues that the former term "is too wide and too abstract to describe specific 'configurations of film,'" meaning both their material embodiment and their embeddedness within "local material cultures, local modes of representations, and the local physical environment."[6] Formats, in other words, account for the ways in which film moves and is displaced, which is one of the central concerns of this book.

All on One Tape

Before returning to the two VHS compilations, I want to briefly consider the reconfiguration of the use and meaning of video between 1970 and 1980 as fundamental to the crucial changes in screening and viewing practices that resulted from the conversion of film to video in the Downtown scene. Initially seen as akin to television (and its promise of liveness and immediacy), video was then reimagined as a recording medium. As portable video cameras and recorders became available to individual consumer-producers, it presented an alternative to, and was thus distinct from, television. However, while video technology in the early 1970s still held an emancipatory potential for creating and sharing media content, both for artists and amateur users, in the 1980s there was a definite turn toward video as a medium for (home) entertainment.[7] Hence, what happened in the late 1970s, and thus preceded both Zedd's self-distribution activities and the BFI's home video label, was, according to Christina Bartz, a "conversion of video as a medium of interactive communication and decentralized participation to a distribution device," particularly for movies.[8] Again, while video technology fluctuated between associations with television and cinema, respectively, "it was only at the beginning of the 1980s that video ... was clearly transferred to the processing chain of the medium of film," as Tobias Haupts notes.⁹ Joshua M. Greenberg traces this development in the United States in his book *From Betamax to Blockbuster: Video Stores and the Invention of Movies on Video*. He shows how video technology becoming more affordable and thus widespread throughout the late 1970s and early 1980s led to the emergence of a hobbyist video culture as well as a growing consumer market for prerecorded videotapes. Similarly, while videocassettes and videocassette recorders were initially displayed in electronics stores alongside other appliances such as television sets or microwaves, the retail spaces for video began to change between 1977 and 1980. Not only were tapes given more display space in electronics stores but specialized video rentals and stores also started to open. In the East Village, M/W/F (Monday/Wednesday/Friday) Video Club, an initiative by the artist group Colab Inc., presented the first sale and rental place for artist video and film in New York City. Its catalog, which is now accessible online, includes analog films transferred to video, including Zedd's compilation and films by Tessa Hughes-Freeland and Kembra Pfahler, as well as artist TV programs produced for public access cable television, which I will turn to in the next section of this chapter.[10] Greenberg makes the crucial point that while the video shop "framed movies on videocassette as artifacts, tangible objects to be displaced and sold to consumers for their own use," the rental "reconceived the relationship between product and customer" by offering videocassettes not as "things to be bought, but as experiences to be rented."[11]

By the beginning of the new decade, video had thus become an increasingly common consumer phenomenon, with the effect that "[v]ideotapes themselves became understood less in terms of their technical nature as interchangeable parts of the VCR and increasingly in terms of the texts that they carried" and the experience they enabled, namely watching a movie at home.[12] Equally, the VCR, which had already begun entering U.S. households in the mid-1970s, transformed from a machine that records television into a machine that plays prerecorded cassettes, mainly movies.

Video and VCRs bring film into the viewer's home, both in the sense that film turns into a haptic, collectible consumer object and that it enables a viewing experience that is private and domestic rather than collective and public. This situation invites both distraction and heightened attention. At home, a film might be watched while eating, socializing, or as a secondary activity. While this mode does not equate to passivity, it does contrast with the focused (and idealized) viewing situation usually associated with the darkened auditorium of a movie theater.[13] At the same time, video, which can be paused, rewound, and watched again, allows for a more concise film viewing that turns the spectator from hurried to "pensive," as Raymond Bellour would say, and prompts a mode of repeat viewing that marks a crucial shift in the overall practices of film reception toward a "personalization of the relationship between film and spectator."[14] Uma Dinsmore-Tuli even speaks of a "domestication of the cinematic text through repeat viewing," which "may facilitate a level of engagement with, love for, and knowledge about movies that exceeds or extends that which it is possible to achieve during cinematic screenings."[15]

With respect to the CoT compilations, rewinding the tape and skipping violent or sexual scenes that were carefully classified as "explicit content" on the BFI tape amounts to sanitizing the films of their offensive content. But does stopping the tape not have a similar effect? The fast-forward button may make the film's images rush by in a hectic haze, too fast for affects such as disgust, horror, or shame to register. The pause function, on the other hand, renders them graspable and controllable, ready to be examined thoroughly until they lose their power to shock. The private and potentially repeated viewing—especially in comparison to screening practices at clubs, festivals, and other small or alternative cultural spaces—therefore points to domestication (or, rather, taming) and, more importantly, containment: compiled on tape under the name Cinema of Transgression, the films are stripped of their messy entanglements for the sake of being contained within a reproducible, haptic object attributed to home video entertainment, however niche that kind of entertainment might be considered.

In this regard, it is not insignificant that the videotape is an object that can not only be read like a book in a figurative sense but can be collected, stored, and displayed like one as well.[16] Thinking about the formal similarities between the VHS and the book brings us back to the compilation, a format typically found in the literary domain, and to the practice of compiling itself. Like the album and the anthology, the compilation is a specific mode of collecting, dedicated to the selection and arrangement of content. However, since the album is, in the words of Roland Barthes, an "artificial ensemble of elements, whose order, whose presence or absence is random," it needs a cover or a sort of binding to organize the disparate material into a coherent ensemble.[17] This is certainly true of compilation. But compilation is not only about accumulation, it is also about production. Its etymological roots lie in the Latin word *(com-)pilare*, which translates to stealing or looting. Generally speaking, *compilare* may mean excerpting or copying other texts in order to create something new, "plowing through a multitude of different stocks of text and material, tearing out passages, accumulating them and rearranging them under a new theme or with poetic motivation."[18] Crucially, this process involves not only the selection and arrangement of material but also its assessment. In this regard, it seems most productive to think of compiling in terms of what Petra McGillen identifies as a double procedure of concentration and liquefaction.[19] According to this understanding, compiling enhances the mobility of individual objects by removing them from their original contexts to secure or emphasize what is exemplary or otherwise worthy of preservation from a larger pool of material. In the context of this chapter, we can read this as a structuring act that contains unruly phenomena within a more compact form or format.

Against this (cultural) technical background, it is now easier to see where the impetus behind the two CoT compilations lies, namely in the relocation of films in order to contain and retain them. While Zedd's tape was the first to take films from different sources and present them together under the Cinema of Transgression label, the BFI followed suit fifteen years later, when said label had already been tested and established. Both tapes suggest that their selection of films not only exemplifies the transgressive nature of this supposed movement, but also, especially in the case of the BFI, that they are worthy of being seen and valued as a piece of film history. While Zedd's compilation singles out films in order to place them in a specific grouping, the BFI goes a step further by manifesting this specific view of the CoT and also claiming its place in the history of avant-garde film, where it ranks alongside the likes of Dadaist filmmakers Hans Richter and Man Ray.

Interestingly, the BFI frames the CoT as avant-garde rather than underground, which is the more common attribution made by authors like Jack Sargeant and Nick Zedd himself. As I discussed in chapters 1 and 2, Zedd sought to situate his notion of the CoT in a (slightly edited) genealogy of underground filmmakers like Jack Smith, Kenneth Anger, and others, while dismissing the 1960s avant-garde as elitist and close minded. The distinction between avant-garde and underground film in the U.S. context is also crucial for scholars like Duncan Reekie, for whom avant-garde cinema sparked an "experimental cinema project that is not (avant-garde) art but a fusion of the radical elements of anti-art and popular cinema."[20] Underground cinema thus developed within the larger framework of an "emergent counter-culture; a heretical and mercurial combination of experimental film, amateur cine culture, pop, beat, camp, radical agit-prop and anti-art."[21] "Underground" certainly still evokes resistance rather than sophistication. Placing the CoT in the history of avant-garde cinema thus not only singles out film amongst the many practices and media involved, but also, metaphorically speaking, removes the spills of a much messier underground. Here we see how distributors such as the BFI can function as "cultural intermediaries and tastemakers," not only facilitating our access to films but also playing a key role in maintaining or building what is considered important and canonical.[22] By releasing and marketing the CoT compilation under its prestigious label, the BFI is ultimately making a claim to its value and canonical potential. I imagine that Zedd would have appreciated this gesture, especially since the BFI tape remains consistent with his own conception of the CoT. However, during the preparation of the release, there were disputes, especially over authorship and fees. In Fales Library I found a letter from Zedd to the BFI with the following complaint: "The contract you sent me is entirely unsuitable.... As one of several prospective filmmakers included in the compilation I would then be getting 25% of what? The entirety of what is left after dividing it up between the other filmmakers and you?... In short, I do not intend to be hoodwinked by any institution or solicitor interested in exploiting the product of my labor."[23]

It figures that by "product of my labor" Zedd refers to his efforts to invent and promote the Cinema of Transgression, in part by compiling the 1984 videotape on which the BFI's compilation is clearly modeled.

In any event, both tapes operate a form of historicization that also entails periodization. The BFI, with its selection of films made between 1979 and 1993, contains the CoT within a definite time frame. The compilation itself, produced almost a decade later in 2000, comes across as a somewhat authoritative gesture of retrospection, of ordering and stabilizing a history that is in fact much less straightforward. Zedd's tape, on the other hand, had a slightly different message. Rather than retroactively manifesting the existence of the Cinema of Transgression, his compilation helped to create it in the first place. He first promoted the tape in the fourth issue of the *Underground Film Bulletin* (UFB) in 1985, which also featured his "Cinema of Transgression Manifesto." The "new generation of filmmakers" named in the manifesto—Richard Kern, Tommy Turner, Richard Kleman, Manuel DeLanda, Bradley Eros and Aline Mare (aka Erotic Psyche), and Zedd himself—are also among those whose work is included on the tape, which is meant to support the manifesto's claim of an existing movement. In asking the respective filmmakers for permission to put their works on the tape, Zedd openly framed the compilation as promotion for the CoT.[24] Indeed, the selection of films shaped the general impression of who was part of the "movement" and who was not, which means that its construction coincided with—and is thus inextricably linked to—Zedd's self-organized publishing and distribution activities. This is also to say that, from the beginning, it spilled over any strictly defined category of film, existing across different media and formats.[25]

With all this in mind, I will investigate how strategies of self-organized, video-based distribution developed into, and sometimes existed in parallel to, formal distribution on an international scale, and how these can be placed within the broader history of independent film, video art, and home video distribution. I begin by taking a closer look at the UFB as a place for advertising not only films, but specifically films on tape.

One ad for *The Cinema of Transgression Vol. 1* in the sixth issue of the UFB (1987) came in the form of an unfolded and duplicated tape sleeve, with the note that the films in question had been "condemned by [film critic] J. 'Ostrich' Hoberman" and "banned from the EZTV." Such rhetoric of exclusion was a common trope in the zine. Interviews and articles were often accompanied by comments that other magazines had refused to print them, just as it was pointed out when certain venues refused to show films that carried the CoT label. In this case, the tape was allegedly condemned by Hoberman, a staff film critic who specialized in writing about experimental and underground film for local alternative newsweekly the *Village Voice*, and was banned from EZTV, a center for community-based production and exhibition of video art, microcinema, and multimedia performances in Los Angeles.[26] The fact that Zedd chose to mention Hoberman rather than a writer for a major newspaper, and EZTV rather than a more established institution, indicates that he may not have been looking for commercial or highbrow attention. The lack of recognition by the alternative scenes caused, if not necessarily disappointment, at least a degree of defiance. Another instance of rejection can be found in the UFB in the form of a letter from someone named Darrell who tried to convince the independent distributor MPI Home Video to include Richard Kern and Lydia Lunch's *Fingered* (1986) in their catalog. After breaking the news that MPI had rejected *Fingered* on the grounds of pornographic content—which is almost ironic, given that pornography was already one of the largest genres of film distributed on home video at the time—Darrell advises Kern and Lunch to establish an "actual counter-culture (stop thinking of hippies!)" that occupies its own submarket and distribution system. He mentions that MPI might fund such an alternative distribution network, but "for now, at least, the answer . . . is no thanks. Sorry. It'll end in tears."[27]

In light of the obvious difficulties in inserting films ascribed to the CoT orbit into artistic or commercial distribution systems, it is logical that in-scene zines like the UFB functioned as primary sales platforms for films on tape, indeed following Darrell's advice to establish a countercultural submarket and distribution system. Along with Zedd's compilation, the UFB promoted various independent films that had been transferred from 16 mm or Super 8 to videotape. Nick Zedd himself regularly ran advertisements for Weirdo Video, and later Penetration Films, offering films on VHS or Betamax for between fifteen and thirty dollars. Although these ads usually included text and images for each available title, there must have been frequent misunderstandings as to what type of film was being offered. In the "Penetration Films" folders in his papers at Fales Library, there are several requests for gay porn films, as well as a template for a note that Zedd presumably sent in response: "Hello and greetings from Penetration Films. We regret to inform you that at this time, we do not offer any kind of male or gay videos. Nick Zedd's films are indeed raunchy but pretty hetero all the same."[28] While the note alludes to the prevalence of porn in video distribution circles, it also reflects the self-image of Zedd and Penetration Films. While in reality a one-man operation, the note gives the impression that there is an entire team behind the label. Also, although the note is written in a humorous, friendly, and not-at-all homophobic tone, Zedd, like Kern and Lunch, had to make a point of distinguishing his work from the so-called adult film sector.

Ads for VHS mail-order by other filmmakers and independent distributors, such as Kembra Pfahler, Directart, Richard Kern's Deathtrip Films, We Got Power Films, or Atomique Film International, appeared in the UFB as well. These often looked like pages from a video catalog, with a box to check next to each film title requested and a blank space to fill in the shipping address and desired format (either VHS or Betamax, which were still competing formats in the mid-1980s). By transferring their films to videotape and setting up their own mail-order distribution systems, in which underground zines played an important role, Downtown filmmakers participated in the very commodity culture and "culture of the private" that video technology was then resonating with.[29] Indeed, when Richard Kern and Lydia Lunch collaborated on *Right Side of My Brain*, the Super 8 film "was made specifically to be released on video for the home market." As Kern explained to me: "This was in 1983 and home video was just starting. Lydia [Lunch] pointed out that only Hollywood movies or old B movies were being released, and there were really no underground or alternative movies for people to buy or rent."[30] He adds that while *Right Side of My Brain* was released on both Betamax and VHS, once VHS prevailed on the market, he released his other films, which had all been shot and edited on Super 8, only in that format. He did this under the handle Deathtrip Films, a one-man operation that he ran out of his apartment.

It becomes increasingly evident that the domestic sphere had by this time become the site not only for the consumption of film-on-video but also for its production and distribution. When Kern's tapes were advertised in the UFB or in his own zines *Dumbfucker*, *Heroin Addict*, and *Valium Addict*, each ad included a note to contact "deathtrip films, P.O. box 1322, NY NY 10009 for info." This information then consisted of "xerox printouts describing each film with an order form on the bottom with a statement 'I am over 18 years old' that they had to sign." Although the zine network generated considerable tape sales, Kern recalls that "most sales were through word of mouth."[31] This is yet another indication of how individually organized, small-scale distribution often works: decidedly informal, unofficial, and within existing networks.

However, by making use of the home video market for the distribution of their films, Kern and Zedd also took advantage of distribution strategies common to earlier avant-garde filmmakers, such as those initiating the first film co-ops. The New American Cinema Group, for example, in its 1961 "First Statement," expressed the need to implement alternative infrastructures for independent film in general and to form a cooperative distribution center in particular.[32] A year later, the New York Film-Makers' Cooperative opened, which was soon followed by the London Film Makers' Co-operative (LFMC), founded in 1966, and the Canyon Cinema in San Francisco in 1967. As Erika Balsom notes, the principles guiding these distribution systems were access and autonomy, favoring dissemination over rarity and reaffirming cinema's potential for collectivity.[33] Filmmakers deposited their works with the cooperatives, which rented them out for screenings and exhibitions, charging a per-screening fee that was then split between the artist and the organization.[34] Among the avant-garde filmmakers of the 1960s, 16 mm was generally the format of choice. And yet, many began to turn to 8 mm for reasons similar to later Super 8 filmmakers' perspectives on video: in addition to the promise of accessibility and reproducibility, the benefits of private and repeated viewing included a more intimate engagement with the viewer, as well as circumventing censorship and the costs and implications of licensing processes. The New York Film-Makers' Cooperative, for example, tested the idea of selling reduction prints of 16 mm films along with their rental model in the 1960s, as 8 mm became more widely available in color and with sound. Stan Brakhage strongly advocated for the idea of producing 8 mm films and offering them as collectibles for a more intimate and individualized home viewing experience, while Jonas Mekas proposed the idea of a "private home cinema" in a 1964 article on censorship he wrote for the *Village Voice* in response to the seizure of Jack Smith's *Flaming Creatures*. However, since interest remained sparse and printing costs high, the project never really took off.[35]

Video, then, promised to solve the problem of expensive print production and provide a solution to the issue of worn-out single prints. Although it was still a widely held notion that the electronic image produced by video technology was inferior to that of projected film, throughout the 1970s, distributors increasingly turned to video for its ease of reproduction, portability, and handling, once again favoring access over quality.[36] This turn to video for distribution purposes coincided with video becoming an artistic medium itself. For women artists in particular, video had an emancipatory potential. Not only was it free of a history of production dominated by men, but it also allowed artists like Joan Jonas, Letícia Parente, Martha Rosler, and Ulrike Rosenbach to produce and modify representations of female bodies and expressions autonomously, thanks to closed-circuit and editing possibilities.[37] As more and more work was not just transferred to tape but specifically made on tape, the cooperative model soon established itself in the realm of video art. Nonprofit organizations like Electronic Arts Intermix (EAI, founded in New York City in 1971) and London Video Arts (LVA, formed in 1976), set out to advocate for video works produced from the mid-1960s onward by supporting and facilitating their production, exhibition, and distribution. In 1973, EAI's Artist's Videotape Distribution Service was established to ensure circulation beyond the limited-edition model of the commercial galleries. The LVA launched its distribution catalog in 1978 with a similar goal, renting out videotapes to exhibition galleries and colleges. Initiatives like these reflected the belief that video was a democratic medium that could be reproduced for and accessed by all.[38]

This brief excursus shows that by the time the generation of filmmakers who had worked primarily with 8 mm in the 1980s Downtown scene turned to video distribution, various distribution systems had already been tested and reshaped, not just in the realm of video art and experimental/independent film but also in the growing home market for mainstream cinema as well as niche genres such as horror and porn. Filmmakers like Zedd and Kern, by distributing their independently produced films (which themselves often borrowed from adult genres like exploitation, pornography, or horror) on VHS via mail order, thus merged the idea of video as home entertainment with that of self-organized video distribution as an alternative to being formally represented by a cooperative or an organization. Although Kern initially distributed his films himself, primarily within his local network, he was soon represented by smaller companies around the world. Kern recalls that

> [my] films were licensed to Haxan Films in France, Radium Films in Sweden, several companies in Italy, a company in Japan and Artware in Germany. I would do the deals for 2–5 years and when they ran out, sell them to someone else. These were generally low budget deals where they would pay 1500 up to 7000 [US dollars] for rights to sell certain films. In the USA, after I released them, Film threat [sic] started releasing films and did well with them... and they have been at Music Video Distribution (MVD) out of Philly [Philadelphia] since DVDs started.[39]

Missing from Kern's listing, however, is Essa Distribution, based in the small seaside town of Husum in the German state of Schleswig-Holstein. Essa released two Kern compilations in 1993: *Deathtrip Vol. 1* and *Deathtrip Vol. 2*, containing six and ten films respectively, ranging from earlier black-and-white Super 8 works such as *The Manhattan Love Suicides* series (1985) to films from the early 1990s such as *Nazi* (1991). The tape sleeves indicate that while these films are "from the Deathtrip" (a play on words that directly references Kern's production and distribution business, Deathtrip Films), the filmmaker should not be contacted at his New York residence, but rather through Film Threat Video in Los Angeles.[40]

Slightly more populous than Husum, though not exactly known as a hotspot for underground film culture either, Wiesbaden in Germany is not only one of Europe's oldest spa towns but also the birthplace of the underground culture label Artware. Founded by Uwe Hamm-Fürhölter and Donna Klemm in the mid-1980s, Artware was a production and distribution company for industrial, experimental, and noise music.[41] However, as a self-proclaimed "Spezialist für abseitige Unterhaltung" (specialist for marginal entertainment), Artware's extensive mail-order catalogs also included clothing, zines, and videotapes.[42] The label distributed films by Kern, Lung Leg, and Zedd and enthusiastically promoted the Cinema of Transgression concept in Germany. Hamm-Fürhölter, a musician who performed under the pseudonym Kim Il Jung, was introduced to the idea of the CoT when Jürgen Brüning organized a 1986 tour of the New York Film Festival Downtown program through German arthouses and off-cinemas, which I discuss in chapter 2. In addition to including filmmakers in the Artware catalog whose work often carried the CoT label, Hamm-Fürhölter wrote articles for film magazines and organized Zedd's screening tour through Germany.[43]

In March 1990, a flyer announced "Nick Zedd penetrates Germany," specifically the arthouses and independent cinemas of Nuremberg, Frankfurt, Stuttgart, Berlin, Bremen, and Hamburg, with his "16mm and Super 8 films... plus more of the 'Cinema of Transgression.'"[44] It was during this tour that Johannes Schönherr, a programmer at Nuremberg's Kino im KOMM and a sort of film activist who had already taken an interest in New York's underground film scene, became more involved with the CoT concept. He booked a screening of Zedd's films at Kino im KOMM and deliberately promoted it as a provocative and scandalous event. Unsurprisingly, a group of feminist protesters interrupted the screening of Zedd's "spliced Super-8 originals" by throwing eggs and cat litter at the screen. The next day, the protest made headlines in Nuremberg's tabloid press, which was quick to pick up on the material quality of the protest: EIER GEGEN CHAUVIS (eggs against chauvinists), PROTESTE GEGEN SEXFILME: FRAUEN KIPPEN MÜLL INS KINO (Protests against sex films: women dump garbage in cinema), JENSEITS DES GUTEN GESCHMACKS (beyond all good taste). Rather than condemning the intervention, Schönherr saw the protest as an affirmation of the transgressive potential of Zedd's cinema, drily commenting that by turning the cinema into a garbage dump, the protestors had "given the place a design appropriate for the dirty movies [they were] about to watch."[45]

Clearly there is some spilling going on here, a very literal sort of mess involving all sorts of sticky materials. But is there also containment? And what is the role of video distribution in general in this dialectical relationship between spilling and containment? Looking back at the issues of production, exhibition, and distribution discussed in previous chapters, recall how the New York Film Festival Downtown (NYFFD) initially foregrounded spilling and messiness within an indisciplinary scene. However, once the festival enabled its films, many of which were associated with the CoT, to move from the local scene to an international scene and distribution system, the messy quality was contained not only in the CoT but also in the Downtown label that the NYFFD, willingly or not, marketed. Around the same time, Nick Zedd founded the *Underground Film Bulletin*. Much as the NYFFD subsumed dance, performance, and slide shows into film, the UFB was a film zine that implicitly presented film as intertwined with a wide range of artistic practices and scene activities. However, given that it was initially conceived as a marketing tool, used to publish "The Cinema of Transgression Manifesto" and to promote the first Cinema of Transgression VHS compilation, it was also essential in both constituting and reinforcing Zedd's conception of the CoT.

Similarly, VHS distribution channels, whether self-organized or not, may have enabled new connections, expanding the local scene into a transatlantic network with new hubs and nodes. Through their distribution, the films also experienced new contexts and audiences, becoming objects of protest in the eyes of German feminist activists and framed as marginal entertainment in European distribution catalogs. However, the spilling that VHS distribution and the resulting elusive circulation initially suggest often goes hand in hand with compilation, marketing, commodification, and thus a kind of containment. Moreover, distribution almost always implied that the concept of the CoT would be reduced to individual films and filmmakers, necessarily excluding that which spills over the rigid boundaries set by notions of authorship or the singular constitution of a filmic work. Ironically, Artware's video distribution even initiated Kern's and Zedd's reentry into German arthouses and off-cinemas, where their films were once again screened on actual projectors, since they were prime representatives of the CoT, and, by extension, of a seemingly outrageous American underground film genre. But while all of this was happening, the Downtown scene was not just turning to video as a medium for the home video market. It had also long since begun to make inroads into television, both bringing televisual programs and practices into the Downtown club scene and, as we will see, bringing the scene onto the television screen.

Changing Channels

Let us keep in mind that the interest in video as an artistic medium was not new in the 1980s. As I mentioned earlier, the late 1960s and early 1970s saw the emergence of video art and performance, particularly by a large number of women artists, and the formation of video art distribution services. While many of these early works dealt with television structurally (and critically), artists began experimenting with producing actual television content, too. Here I am, however, more explicitly concerned with the increasing examination and appropriation of TV formats and culture in the Downtown scene, lasting from the 1970s until the early 2000s. With cable networks and broadcasts on New York's public access channels developing into important means for showcasing experimental content, including films, gallery tours, interview shows, news videos, public service announcements, "and, by extension, [for] constructing the Downtown scene itself," these early televisual experimentations are an intriguing facet of indisciplinary, scene-generating practices.[46] These efforts are particularly important as forerunners for Nick Zedd's public access series *The Adventures of Electra Elf*, which aired on the Manhattan Neighborhood Network from 2005 to 2008. In looking at a television series from the early 2000s as part of my discussion of the various conceptions of Cinema of Transgression, I want to pay attention to what is not easily contained within the label. In other words, with *Electra Elf*, the seemingly solid boundaries of the CoT unravel even more. But how did the Downtown scene come to television in the first place? And how did television come to the Downtown scene? What were the circumstances of this alliance?

As early as 1971, Manhattan was the first major metropolitan area to grant franchises to the two cable companies, Sterling Manhattan and Teleprompter, on the condition that each would set aside two channels for public access programming, meaning that they would offer free and virtually uncensored airtime on a first-come, first-served basis.[47] Although cable television itself had already been introduced in the early 1940s, it took until the mid-1980s for cable systems and their subscribers to grow to significant numbers.[48] In Manhattan, the areas south of 14th Street (East Village, SoHo, and Tribeca) were not wired for cable until 1976.[49] William Hohauser, producer of the public access *Vole Show*

(1977–1997), remembers that "in the '70s, cable television was a small thing, less corporate. Cable companies hadn't gotten this ridiculous idea that they would be content providers. They were just operating as big antennas."⁵⁰ Religious, civic, and fraternal organizations, as well as activists and artists, took advantage of the still relatively open terrain of cable television and began producing content, often in the spirit of what TVTV's founder Michael Shamberg dubbed "guerrilla television."⁵¹ This content was coordinated by time slot and channel, with Channel C reserved for series and D for specials and one-offs. No commercials were allowed, and shows had to be either submitted on twenty-eight- or fifty-eight-minute tapes or broadcast live.

Within this newly emerging amateur television environment, a number of programs were also produced in and around the Downtown scene. For instance, *All Color News* (1977–1978) by Collaborative Projects, Inc. (Colab) was a community news service interspersed with artist-created content that ran for twelve weeks on Manhattan Cable Channel D.⁵² Paul Tschinkel's *Inner Tube* (1974–1984) featured taped music shows from the (post-)punk and No Wave scenes and reports on the art and filmmaking scene, showing concerts by Klaus Nomi, DNA, or the Cramps, as well as Nick Zedd's *They Eat Scum* (1979). Many of the live shows, such as Coco Crystal's *If I Can't Dance You Can Keep Your Revolution* (1977–1995), billed as "an hour of talk, telephone, and technical failure," or artist Jaime Davidovich's *The Live! Show* (1979–1984), a program hosted by his alter ego Dr. Videovich featuring performances, live phone-ins, and home-shopping segments, were produced at ETC/Metro Access. Opened by Jim Chladek in 1973 and located near Union Square in Downtown Manhattan, this studio offered basic, low-budget equipment for live broadcasting and tape recording at an affordable price.⁵³

Among the often short-lived and mostly informal and improvised ETC/Metro Access productions, *TV Party* (1978–1982) is particularly noteworthy for this context. Cablecast live on Channel D at 12:30 A.M. on Tuesday nights, it was hosted by Glenn O'Brien, a columnist for *Artforum* and *Interview*. Blondie guitarist Christ Stein cohosted and filmmaker Amos Poe directed the show, which was taped by a rotating crew that included artists Jean-Michel Basquiat and Fab 5 Freddy, filmmaker James Nares, and *BOMB* magazine editor Betsy Sussler. Just as *Interview* and *BOMB* were centered around conversations with and between artists, musicians, and actors, *TV Party* was loosely structured around the talk show format, with hosts and guests from the Downtown scenes "sipping cocktails, chatting, playing music, and taking telephone calls." This was set on a studio stage that was "barely raised above audience level," with the result that audience, guests, and crew members were often indistinguishable from one another—not least since, as Benjamin Olin noted, "*TV Party* guests were generally picked from the same Downtown milieu of artists and musicians that filled the studio and the control booth." Olin goes on to write that "the festive and frequently chaotic atmosphere depicted on *TV Party* spilled into the control booth, directly inflecting the show's formal composition. The live production of *TV Party* was approached . . . as an improvised jam in which the mixing desk was commandeered as a musical instrument."⁵⁴ *TV Party*'s set seems to mirror the indisciplinary, performance-oriented Downtown clubs. At the Pyramid or Club Chandelier, the party atmosphere structured the events happening there, as they often spilled over from the tiny stage into the party and bar areas. And just as the club performances often blurred the lines between film and live performance, *TV Party* was a talk show that spilled over the boundaries of its own format. With its sense of unpredictability and improvisation, the show took the idea of party as performance (and vice versa) from the club to the studio, or rather, to various television sets in Manhattan. It is also worth considering how the show's format manifested the scene structures from which it emerged, as Olin notes: "*TV Party* can . . . be understood as the collective expression of a 'group consciousness,' an audio-visual rendering of the affective connective tissue that structured Downtown life."⁵⁵ In this light, it only made sense to take the party out of the studio and back into the club. So the *TV Party* crew recorded several shows at the Danceteria, the Peppermint Lounge, and the Mudd Club, while many Downtown clubs incorporated television and video into their own genre- and discipline-bending programs, with Club 57 making the exploration of American television culture its signature feature.

In the catalog accompanying MoMA's 2017 *Club 57* exhibition, Ann Magnuson, the club's manager and programmer, reflects on her vision for the now infamous venue: "Besides being a fresh take on the Surrealist cabaret, I also saw the club as a giant TV set, where every night was a different channel. For our generation, the first weaned on television, it was also a place to collectively exorcise the TV demons we had grown up with—the most harrowing having been broadcast on the nightly news."⁵⁶ When considering Magnuson's statement and the constant back-and-forth between club and television, it seems not farfetched to think of the club "as a giant TV set" and thus as a medium in and of itself. At Club 57, the TV set emanated "TV demons" needing to be exorcised, but it was also a source of nostalgia to be collectively and semi-ironically indulged in. So on four dates in 1980, its "Channel 57" programming unit presented *Television-Nostomania!*, a selection of 1960s sci-fi series like *Lost in Space* (1965–1968, CBS) and *My Favorite Martian* (1963–1966, CBS), served up with "vintage commercials, popcorn and Swanson dinners!"⁵⁷ The dictionary defines *nostomania* as the "irresistible compulsion to return home."⁵⁸ In this case, returning home apparently meant returning to the TV dinners served in compartmentalized tinfoil trays popularized in the 1950s, and thus to the simplicity of the early days of television. Michael Z. Newman writes that "when television was new enough to be considered magical, like something out of the world of science fiction, TV representations of space and of the futuristic gear of space travel . . . implicitly conveyed the medium's power to overcome old limitations of time, space, and vision."⁵⁹ Notably, the first iteration of Club 57's *Television-Nostomania* brought back precisely those shows that explored visions of the future and outer space at a time when television itself was being experienced as a technological and cultural novelty.

This heyday of television is also evoked on the flyer promoting *Bad Music Videos*, a show hosted by performance artist Karen Finley and the *East Village Eye*'s art editor Carlo McCormick at Limelight in 1986 (see Figure 8). On the front, the text of the invitation appears on the screen of a Philco Predicta tabletop television. This 1959 model featured the company's signature freestanding swivel-screen, shaped and mounted like a mirror, on a cabinet equipped with an automatic timer. Advertisements for the model emphasized the set's elegant design, presenting it as a domestic object that would blend seamlessly into an equally chic interior decor. Like the TV dinners served at Club 57, the appearance of this machine on the flyer for a club/TV event turns a crucial moment in the history and discourse of television and the home into a moment of generational (dis-)identification. Many of the 1980s scene's participants, like Finley and Magnuson, were born in the postwar years, when the television set became a fixture in more than half of all U.S. households. At the time, magazine ads went beyond producing images that idealized a White, gendered, middle-class suburban lifestyle (after all, it is a White, generically feminine woman who is adjusting the TV screen in many of these promotional materials). These ads also marked the television set as both "household object and entertainment form," evoking what Lynn Spigel calls the "theatricalization and specularization of domestic space."[60] Spigel goes on to note that in the context of the 1950s' "extreme preoccupation with the merging of indoor and outdoor space," one of the promises that television held was to function as a 'window into the world,' an idea that figured television as "the ultimate expression of progress in utopian statements concerning man's ability to conquer and to domesticate space."[61]

So the "space-merging" quality of television, that is, the idea of the deflation of interior and exterior within the television space popularized in the 1950s by models like the Philco set, finds a new interpretation in the show *Bad Music Videos*.[62] Produced by Danceteria's video jockey Michael Overn, *Bad Music Videos* comprised six thirty-minute episodes that aired on Wednesdays at 9 P.M. on Manhattan's Public Access Channel C. Most of the shows were filmed in clubs and in front of a live audience, while others were recorded in Overn's private loft with invited guests. Hosts McCormick and Finley presented "the worst videos ever seen" (such as "David Bowie and Cher longing for each other through clouds of colored smoke") and commented on them much to the delight of the audience.[63] Each episode also had a special theme and guests, such as Lydia Lunch, Wiseblood (JG Thirlwell), Karen Finley, Andy Somma, or John Kelly, who was invited to perform a "bad music opera" for the show.[64] In her *Village Voice* review of the show's Love Club edition in April 1986, C. Carr wrote: "Bad music video is a natural in the clubs, where so many performances have worked the post-television vein, mining the 'ironic richness of banality.' In contrast to the

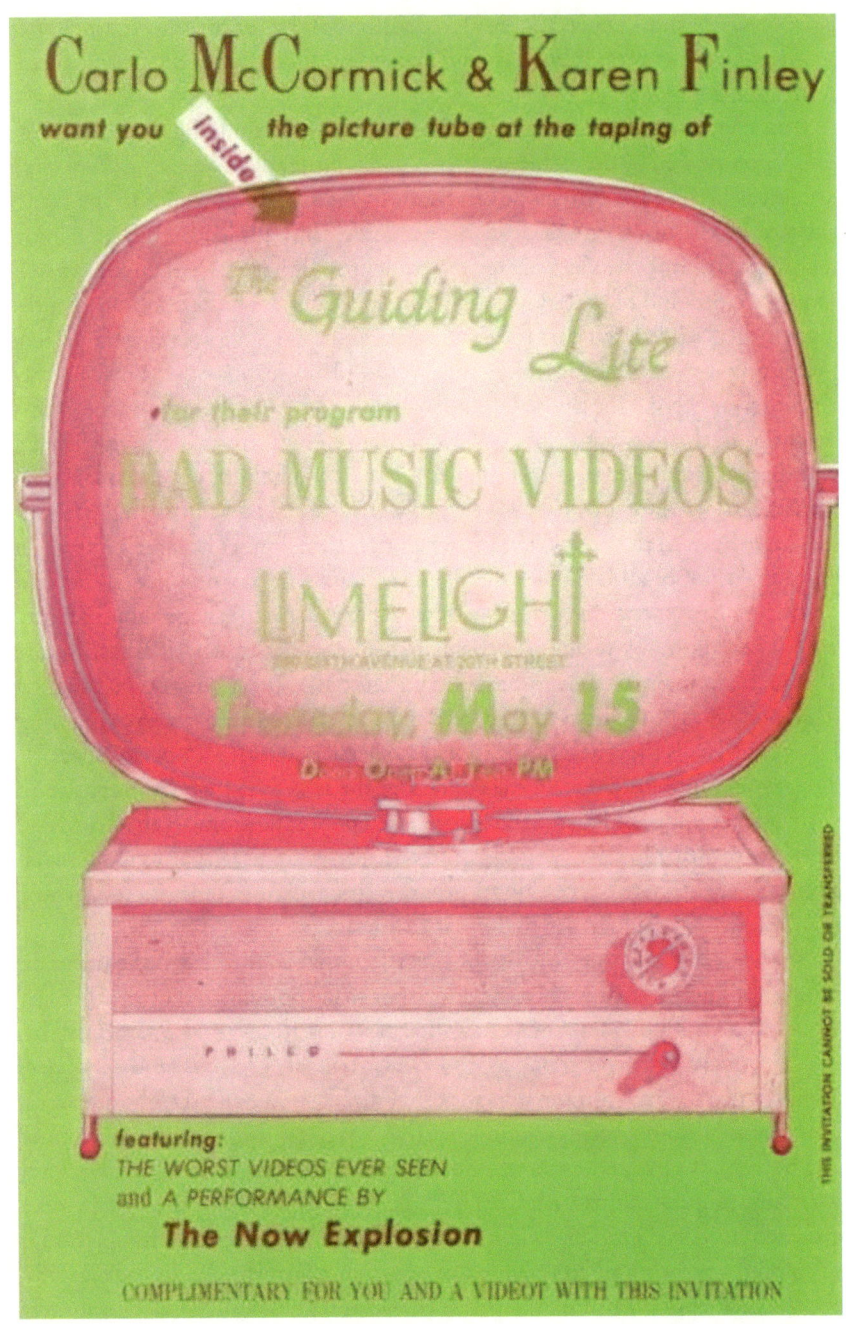

FIGURE 8 Flyer for *Bad Music Videos* at Limelight, 1986

electronic product (which at least aspires to slickness) and the careful on-air packaging that usually surrounds it, veejays Finley and McCormick are appropriately rude and unrehearsed."[65]

Carr places *Bad Music Videos* in what sounds like an already established tradition of "post-television" culture in the Downtown club scene. However, by contrasting the unrehearsed live taping against the "careful on-air packaging" and slickness of electronic products—by which, I assume, she means high-budget pop music videos—she confirms the very binaries of liveness versus recorded, immediate versus mediated that *Bad Music Videos* undermines, or at least complicates. For the show ironically celebrates 1980s pop kitsch precisely by transforming television viewing into a live spectacle, a collective rather than private experience. In this sense, *Bad Music Videos*, like Club 57's *Nostomania*, can be seen as a moment in which the Downtown community bonds over both shared TV memories and contemporary TV phenomena. Only, in the case of *Bad Music Videos*, this experience is also extended to and shared with an audience that is not present in the club but is sitting in front of their television screens at home.

It is also telling that a venue like Club 57 not only presented ironic and often critical explorations of television content, what Carr called "working the post-television vein," but was also compared to a TV set in terms of its structure. As Magnuson stated, the club's busy schedule, where "channels" changed every night, switching from performances to costume parties, film screenings, and video nights, was modeled on the experience of watching television. Given that television played such a crucial role in the club culture's spirit of indisciplinarity, it makes even more sense that Downtown scene participants not only turned to video as an artistic medium or means of distribution but also sought to conquer the sphere of television itself, actualizing the democratic and participatory potential that television and video, respectively, had initially promised as a "medium of immediacy and directness."[66] These TV activities reveal another plane of the Downtown scene's artistic energy: an absolute openness to create in defiance of disciplinary, medial, and format boundaries. And it is precisely this energy that is constrained by labels such as Cinema of Transgression.

Having moved back and forth between the 1970s and 1980s, from party television to TV parties, I will now enter Manhattan's early 2000s public television culture with *The Adventures of Electra Elf*. Through an exploration of Zedd's TV series, I want to draw a line between the shift from film to video in the 1980s and the resulting channels of distribution and circulation into the more recent past, though I also wish to articulate more explicitly the CoT's spillover into the realm of video and public access television.

Coproduced and directed by Nick Zedd, *Electra Elf* aired on Sundays at 11:30 P.M. on Manhattan Neighborhood Network's (MNN) Channel 2.[67] The show marked Zedd's first foray into television, as well as his first time working in a serialized format, after making short and feature-length films and videos since the late 1970s. Founded in 1992, MNN is a nonprofit organization that operates five public access television cable channels in Manhattan (of which MNN2 is the "Lifestyle Channel," dedicated to exploring the everyday interests of New Yorkers). MNN also provides production and training facilities, and, as of 2016, hosts a digital channel. MNN makes a point of emphasizing its liberal and independent policy; its mission statement lists access, collaboration, community, empowerment, freedom of expression, diversity, inclusion, and sustainability as fundamental values and goals.[68] In this regard, the station echoes the idea of community-based programming that provided the base for Manhattan's first public-access cable stations. Zedd himself described *Electra Elf* in an interview as "an attempt to reach people in their living rooms by way of ghetto television channels."[69] Read in a friendly way, Zedd's description of MNN as "ghetto" is an acknowledgment of its local and indeed niche nature. This framing also suggests that in the early 2000s, an era in which "video as digital moving image media has grown to encompass television and film to function as the medium of the moving image," and in which content sharing had become facilitated by the Internet, public access television channels still held a potential for disseminating cultural products that fell through the cracks of other exhibition and distribution systems.[70] Zedd chose this particular channel to launch what one Reddit user, in a post on the site's age-restricted ObscureMedia community, aptly called a "more-than-low budget cable access TV show."[71]

Across two seasons of ten half-hour episodes, *The Adventures of Electra Elf* is set in a fictionalized version of the East Village and centers on Jennifer Swallows (played by Reverend Jen Miller, cocreator of the series), a reporter for *Art Star Scene Magazine A.S.S.* by day, superhero Electra Elf by night. Together with her pet Chihuahua, she fights "corrupt senators, sleazy frat-boys, satanic cults, landlords, zombie-tourists, and other miserable malcontents."[72] Unlike earlier Downtown TV productions, which were often talk-, event-, or news-based, the series follows a fictional narrative. What connects *Electra Elf* to the Downtown TV programs of the 1970s and 1980s, however, is its intimate involvement with the local scene. Similar to *TV Party*, the show is built around the lives of members of the Lower East Side's creative communities. Reverend Jen Miller, for example, is a columnist, writer, founder of the real *A.S.S. Magazine*, and a participant in the Lower East Side's and Williamsburg's performance scenes of the early 2000s. She has appeared in most of Zedd's later video works, including *Thus Spake Zarathustra* (2001), *Elf Panties: The Movie* (2001), *Lord of the Cockrings* (2002), and *Electra Elf: The Beginning* (Parts 1 and 2, 2005). When interviewed by *New York Magazine* in 2010, she responded to the question, "Are you sort of a neighborhood fixture?" by saying, "Yes. No one down here even asks me about my elf ears anymore."[73]

The plots of the episodes often revolve around the increasing gentrification of the East Village. An example is *Maggot on a Hot Tin Roof* (season 1, episode 2, 2005), in which the director of the troll museum, a quirky longtime resident of the East Village (known in the show as Hummerville), is visited by Swallows for an interview for *A.S.S.* Both women feel terrorized by the masses of European zombie tourists flooding Hummerville's streets and worry that the museum director will be forced out of the neighborhood. This episode turned out to be a glimpse into the future. Reverend Jen Miller herself ran what she called the Lower East Side Troll Museum out of her apartment for sixteen years, until she was evicted in 2016. As in the show, the museum, which housed shelves stuffed with hundreds of troll dolls, was only accessible to those who knew which doorbell to ring.[74]

A feature on Zedd by the online magazine *Vice* called *Electra Elf* his "most popular work" and "greatest success": "It was far from the cinema of transgression, but Zedd liked the lighthearted direction his art was taking."[75] By framing *Electra Elf* as distinctly post–Cinema of Transgression, the *Vice* article suggests that the series was able to garner a considerable fan base precisely because it felt removed from Zedd's CoT-related doggedness, and thus more accessible than his previous "filmic freak-outs." Despite its campier tone, however, *Electra Elf* shares various traits with Zedd's earlier films that more readily fit the Cinema of Transgression rubric. For instance, the series carries the same sense of anger at urban politics, merges fiction and reality, and references cartoon and fantasy aesthetics. Likewise, the B-movie acting style and low-budget cardboard sets recall films like *They Eat Scum* or *Geek Maggot Bingo*. But the series not only links to previous Downtown public-access shows and the sensibility of Zedd's own earlier work, which is more commonly associated with the CoT, but also conflates several generations of Downtown scenes. In addition to Reverend Miller, who only came to New York in 1990, *Electra Elf* features guest appearances by underground actress Brenda Bergman, porn star and performance artist Annie Sprinkle, artist Marguerite Van Cook, and experimental filmmaker and actor Taylor Mead, all of whom were active in New York's Downtown art scenes of the 1970s and 1980s (and in Mead's case, since the 1960s, when he appeared in several Warhol films).

At this point, I would like to reiterate that the conception of CoT that needs to be reframed is strictly oriented to the limiting narrative of a 1980s film movement united by the desire to cross aesthetic and moral boundaries in and through filmmaking. As an early 2000s public access television production reminiscent of the Downtown film and video productions of previous decades, *The Adventures of Electra Elf* does not fit neatly into the narrative of a 1980s countercultural film movement, yet it cannot be considered in isolation from it. It is precisely this ambiguity that makes the series such an appropriate case for this text, which seeks to rearticulate the CoT as a shape-shifting phenomenon rather than a closed chapter in the history of underground film. In other words, *Electra Elf* is evidence that the medial and temporal boundaries of the CoT continue to loosen with each spill. In order to follow the CoT's spills into the present moment, in the next and final section of this chapter, I will turn to the context of digital formats.

#cinemaoftransgression

Since *Electra Elf* went off the air, fans have uploaded individual episodes to video-sharing sites such as Vimeo, Dailymotion, and YouTube. Similarly, many of the films produced in the CoT orbit in the 1980s and early 1990s, initially transferred from Super 8 to VHS for distribution purposes, have since undergone another format change when they became DVDs or were digitized and uploaded to video-sharing platforms. However, original videotapes and DVDs also appear on online sales sites such as Amazon or eBay, where sellers present them as rare, obscure, and even obsolete media items and price them accordingly. For example, in February 2023, Pennsylvania seller frenzy.finds listed a copy of *The Cinema of Transgression Vol. 1* on VHS for $225 in "used but good condition," adding that the "tape works well for being an amateur recording." Not long before that, Nick Zedd had also developed an online sales practice for tapes and ephemera that could be considered as "amateur" as the videotapes themselves, distributing them through his social media channels.

While working on earlier drafts of this chapter in 2020 and 2021, such sales posts appeared on both my Facebook and Instagram feeds. On Facebook, Zedd was offering DVD copies of early films such as *They Eat Scum* (1979) as well as more recent productions like *Lord of the Cockrings* (2002). The photo accompanying the post shows the DVDs lined up on a table, in a cluttered space whose function or location remains undetermined. Zedd provided no further information other than that the DVDs could be ordered via e-mail, would be shipped from Mexico, and cost twenty dollars each—effectively a bargain compared to eBay or Amazon prices, as another Facebook post from the same year shows. Below a screenshot of an Amazon listing of the DVD compilation *Abnormal: The Sinema of Nick Zedd* for $105.61, Zedd wrote "Why pay $105.61 to someone on Amazon when you can buy it from me for $30?" When I started following Zedd on Instagram, I often clicked through similar images where he offered illustrations, signed photos, and DVDs for sale, having tagged them #cinemaoftransgression.

On the one hand, this kind of informal distribution ties back to the logic of early mail-order VHS, where no agency or label acted as an intermediary, and Zedd, like many other underground filmmakers, packaged his films in handmade sleeves and shipped them from home. On the other hand, it raises new questions regarding the attribution of value, contextualization, and (digital) circulation of the objects that are being offered. For some, the online sales may simply be proof that Nick Zedd had indeed "stayed underground" (as *Vice* put it in a headline for a 2014 feature on him), meaning that he still held a radical anti-commercialist stance. However, the tale of the bankrupt but "authentic" underground artist distracts from a very real urgency.[76] A few years before his death in February 2022, when his sales posts became more frequent, Zedd was actually battling various illnesses.[77] So what looked like a somewhat defiant attempt to sell memorabilia online could also have been an effort to raise funds for medical treatment and, more incidentally, to place his legacy in the hands of friends, fans, and followers (rather than only in institutional archives). Strikingly, what Zedd sold online was exactly the kind of paratextual material that he sold to NYU's Fales Library in 2011, where his papers became part of the Downtown Collection catalog and thus the archival historiography of New York's Downtown scene. This situation demonstrates once again how objects and documents of a marginal art practice like Zedd's can occupy different positions, straddling distinctions that lose their stability in the process: depending on the context or "institutional cue," a drawing or a VHS tape can be both a valuable, hard-to-access archival object and ephemeral, even "cheap" fan memorabilia.[78] The social media activities described above, then, provide one thing above all—a clue to the CoT's curious and volatile afterlife. I will explore some of these digital facets in more detail below.

After the rather accidental and fleeting encounter with the aforementioned social media posts, my exploration of what remains of the CoT online continued with a more targeted search. Typing "Cinema of Transgression" into an online search engine quickly led to UbuWeb, a self-described "pirate shadow library" for avant-garde media.[79] Abigail De Kosnik would place UbuWeb in the category of "rogue archives," as it is a nonprofit online repository available for and accessible to all Internet users, free of charge and liberated from copyright restrictions.[80] Run by author and conceptual artist Kenneth Goldsmith with the help of other "rogue memory workers" like fans and pirates, the library has been collecting video, sound, and text works by various artists and making them available online since 1996. While some of these artists are "better known for other things" than what is associated with them on UbuWeb (for example, there are films by both German left-wing militant Ulrike Meinhof and French sculptor Niki de Saint Phalle), the library's agenda is not only based on accessibility but also proposes a "revisionist art history based on the peripheries of artistic production" and what Goldsmith calls a "muddying" of the avant-garde.[81] As he elaborates, "UbuWeb's large, boundary-blurring archive of the avant-garde necessarily alters what is meant by avant-garde, a term saddled with the legacies of patriarchy, hegemony, imperialism, colonization and militarization. . . . When you assemble a collection of the avant-garde, you run the risk of replicating everything wrong that is associated with it. I deployed impurity as a way of muddying, *détour*ning, and playfully reimagining the avant-garde, twisting and warping the rigorous, hard-baked grids of modernism into something more fluid, organic, incorrect, and unpredictable."[82] Goldsmith does this by employing a "casual mode of accumulation" that privileges coincidence, subjectivity, and fragmentation over any presumed accuracy, expertise, and completeness.[83] Within its collection, UbuWeb maintains a list of twelve films under their entry for "Cinema of Transgression (1979–1993)." The selection is predictable yet at the same time arbitrary. It includes filmmakers regularly associated with the CoT, like Richard Kern and Tessa Hughes-Freeland, though their own individual entries also feature additional films. It also includes works by those who were more retrospectively ascribed to the group, such as Jeri Cain Rossi, Jon Moritsugu, and Beth B. And while M. Henry Jones is represented by three films, Nick Zedd is missing from the list entirely. At the bottom of the list there appears a single quote from Zedd ("If it's not transgressive, it's not underground. It has to be threatening the status quo by doing something surprising, not just imitating what's been done before") followed by his manifesto. Though Zedd's own entry in the UbuWeb film library is quite extensive, with ten films and a two-part compilation ranging from 1979 to 2005, in the context of the CoT listing, however, he appears less as a director than as a film philosopher whose writings have given a name and a shape to a transgressive underground zeitgeist that the included films are meant to illustrate. So while the entry itself, and especially the presence of the manifesto, enshrines the existence of the CoT as a movement, the arbitrary selection of the twelve films simultaneously seems to destabilize this conception. This is not least due to the fact that the UbuWeb's historiography of the avant-garde differs radically from that of, for example, the British Film Institute, which I discussed at the beginning of this chapter in terms of the video compilation *Cinema of Transgression* that was released as part of its *History of the Avant-Garde* series. While the BFI certainly sought to inscribe the CoT within an otherwise established canon of avant-garde film, UbuWeb's ever-growing repository increasingly demystifies any historical avant-garde canon. Its listing of the CoT may perpetuate Zedd's manifesto narrative. But while it provides a unique opportunity for easy access to the films, it also allows them to be considered in a cross-decade, cross-disciplinary, multimedia context that is more in keeping with their own spilling character. And by that I also mean their reformatting and subsequent dissemination.

Take, for example, Nick Zedd's *Bogus Man* (1980). When streamed on UbuWeb, the film bears visible traces of its original materiality along with evidence of its multiple reformattings, with its necessarily lossy compression. Flashes of light suggest the use of outdated stock in the production of the 16 mm film, while the black bars at the edges and the flickering lines across the image indicate a conversion to video or an adaptation to digital formats. These traces not only add to the already messy quality of digitally circulating images that metaphors like "flow" or "stream" tend to obscure, whether that's low resolution, buffering, or unclassifiable content or obscurity due to the sheer volume of ephemeral networked imagery.[84] Yet *Bogus Man*'s glitches also prove that this is not a digitization for the sake of institutional preservation or exhibition but a reformatting primarily aimed at making the film accessible to a broader public, here specifically in a digital context. Kenneth Goldsmith wryly admits that "in terms of quality UbuWeb's films are truly a disaster."[85] This is largely due to the library's "piracy as preservation" policy. Many of the films hosted on UbuWeb come either from underground video stores "such as Kim's [Video and Music] in New York [which was] full of sloppy VHS rips of underground film" or from university film and video programs, which in the 1980s, as Goldsmith notes, "with their budgets being slashed, found it cheaper to rent 16mm film one time from places such as Canyon [Cinema] and then make copies of it for their libraries.... These rips—first on VHS, then on DVD, and finally as Audio Video Interleaved files (AVIs) and MP4s—were, in turn, copied by students and faculty members who first circulated them among themselves and then released them on file-sharing networks."[86]

In describing the process of reformatting, Goldsmith also makes the point that pirate infrastructures have a decidedly generative quality. In Brian Larkin's terms, this means that they have the potential to circulate media goods, to give rise to new economic and social networks, and also to generate a certain aesthetic, specifically "a set of formal qualities that generate a particular sensorial experience of media marked by poor transmission, interference, and noise."[87] In this sense, the traces of reformatting and duplication in *Bogus Man* on UbuWeb read as inscriptions of a pirate infrastructure and as markers of what Lucas Hilderbrand, in reference to video technology, calls an "aesthetics of access."[88] Hilderbrand argues that the specificity of videotape, its rewritability and ability to circulate, is only revealed through its inherent properties of degeneration. *Bogus Man* on UbuWeb thus illustrates how the audience's affective engagement with the film and their active participation in its distribution become inscribed in the very material of the film.[89]

A structurally different but similarly significant affective-material engagement can be observed when viewing David Wojnarowicz's Super 8 mm film projects *Beautiful People* (ca. 1988) and *Heroin* (ca. 1981) in their online versions, available on the YouTube channel of artist and musician Jesse Hultberg.[90] Hultberg and Wojnarowicz were both members of the post-punk band 3 Teens Kill 4 and also collaborated on filmmaking. In *Beautiful People*, Wojnarowicz's camera follows Hultberg as he dresses in glamorous drag and, equipped with a toolbox filled with small toy figures, makes his way from his New York apartment to a remote forest lake. Back when the film was shown at East Village venues like La Mama Theatre, Hultberg and Wojnarowicz performed the film's soundtrack live.[91] With its air of incompleteness, *Beautiful People* evokes the notion of a film happening, and thus the kind of spillover between film and (live) performance that I discussed in chapter 3. In their state of liminal uncertainty, such films resist finality and instead invite the performance of further, perhaps different, iterations. One such iteration was realized in 2011 when Hultberg trimmed the material from about thirty minutes to seven, adding sound, the song "Special Reserve" by 3 Teens Kill 4, and opening credits. He first showed the result at a 3 Teens Kill 4 concert at the HOWL! Festival in New York and later uploaded it to YouTube.

Hultberg then turned his attention to another film project that was left unfinished. In 1979, David Wojnarowicz began filming three friends, including

Hultberg and Brian Butterick (of 3 Teens Kill 4 and also known as drag performer Hattie Hathaway), as they roamed the abandoned warehouses and West Side piers along the Hudson River—sites of cruising, guerrilla exhibitions, but also drug use—and staged scenes of them shooting heroin and pointing guns at each other. One version of the film, now titled *Heroin* and listed on the membership-based streaming site Mubi, is a three-minute black-and-white Super 8 short from 1981.[92] Hultberg revisited the material yet again and in 2018 released *Heroin* in a slightly longer color version and with one of the earliest recordings of 3 Teens Kill 4, a song called "3 Teens Kill 4 No Motive." Fittingly, the cover of the band's first album features the same still life that appears briefly in the film, its elements symbolizing the fatal shot, whether from a gun or a syringe: on a mosaic floor are images of handguns, a dartboard, two photographs of a person holding a doll's head that is wrapped in a dark cloth as if awaiting a killing bullet, and a cigar box containing dried poppy seeds. Beautiful in a sentimental yet seemingly innocent way, the seeds appear here as sources of morphine, one of the main active ingredients in heroin.

In releasing new versions of these hitherto little-noticed films, Hultberg goes beyond underscoring his own role in their production/performance during Wojnarowicz's lifetime. Above all, he emphasizes his friend's indisciplinary and collaborative practices, of which filmmaking and music making were only two of many (and arguably the least recognized, since he is known today primarily for his painting and his role in the AIDS movement). Hultberg also clearly believes that these films should reach a wider audience, as is evident in the brief blurb that appears below the YouTube stream of *Heroin*. In it, Hultberg thanks Marion Scemama, another Wojnarowicz collaborator, for "salvaging" the film from Fales Library, where the original material is kept, making it sound as if the film had to be dug out from the depths of the archive before it could finally be given the exposure it deserves online.

Indeed, Hultberg's commentary on Fales seems to confirm the often assumed dualism of local analog archives and global online platforms (an antagonism that YouTube itself promotes by marketing the site as the antithesis of mainstream broadcasters and brick-and-mortar archives), where the latter is a facilitator of cultural production and preservation rather than a gatekeeper.[93] Of course, this framing obscures the fact that the Google-owned platform in fact does control and standardize platform-based interaction by imposing a "governance framework" in the form of (copyright) regulation, curation, and moderation.[94] And yet, YouTube's multiple affordances, that is, its invitation not only to watch but also to share and add content, are significant here. Hultberg's editions of Wojnarowicz's films may be acts of remembrance, but they are open ended rather than self-contained; Hultberg is not simply restoring the films that he and Wojnarowicz began, but rather continuing them. And it is precisely because these films, edited and reformatted, now appear on YouTube, with its billions of users, that they are likely to enter into further stages of reproduction and dissemination.

For, as De Kosnik puts it, "each media commodity becomes, at the instant of its release, an archive to be plundered, an original to be memorized, copied, and manipulated... rather than an end unto itself."[95] And this applies not only, but perhaps especially, to those media objects that circulate in the digital sphere.

I have already pointed out that digital images are often messy in more ways than one, not least because their seemingly uncontrolled circulation renders an overview or classification virtually impossible. In the realm of social media, one attempt to get a handle on this messiness and organize digital content and its circulation is the collective practice of hashtagging. Since its introduction on Twitter in 2007, and on Instagram in 2010, the # symbol has effectively turned words into labels and slogans, or rather "networked keywords," that facilitate gathering of these slogans and their associated images into clusters of similarity.[96] This operation of the hashtag leads back to the aforementioned social media activity of Nick Zedd. In his Instagram story, one of the photos showed a pile of different media in a variety of formats spanning his film, drawing, and music work. There were DVD copies of his films *Geek Maggot Bingo*, *They Eat Scum*, *War Is Menstrual Envy*, and the compilation *The Cinema of Transgression Vol. 1*, a framed ink drawing promoting a music event in San José, and a 7-inch vinyl record of the single *Consume and Die/Generation Z*, which was a collaboration between Zedd and the noise punk band Zyklon Beatles from the year 2000. Zedd made use of Instagram's ability to overlay an image with text and add a hashtag: "if interested send me an email at mrnickzedd@yahoo.com #nickzedd #cinemaoftransgression."

Clicking on the hashtag brings up more than a thousand images, a number that does not exactly make it a trending hashtag (for comparison: #dogoftheday has over 81 million posts) but still indicates a certain level of activity. The images it gathers fall roughly into three categories. First, there are a large number of photos from the personal accounts of Zedd and his wife, either documenting (and commemorating) their family life in Mexico or sharing images related to Zedd's artistic work (#kingofunderground #lowbudgetfilms #deathrockstyle). Here, as in many other instances, the Cinema of Transgression label remains closely tied to the life and work of Nick Zedd, though at the same time it joins a series of other labels among which there is no hierarchy. Second, there is content related to the broader Downtown scene of the 1980s, often posted by fans of underground culture or initiatives like New York's Boo-Hooray, which processes personal archives related to subcultural phenomena (#counterculturerarities #ratedx). These images tend to capture archival content like party flyers, zines, or film posters, often packaged in plastic sleeves to emphasize their unique status as rarities. And then there is a miscellaneous third category, with images including a still from Sergei Parajanov's *The Color of Pomegranates* (#experimentalcinema), a Polaroid of a young John Waters on the occasion of his birthday (#nowavecinema #punkmusic), or glossy soft-core photography (#nudeart). The way users employ the hashtag in combination with or as a synonym for other cultural genres and moments, or as a general descriptor for daring visual content (and possibly without ever having heard of Zedd's manifesto), is proof that hashtags have completely upended the concept of authorship. Put more simply, anyone can tag their post #cinemaoftransgression, adding it to the growing collection of content that the hashtag itself accumulates, linking it to other more or less related hashtags. Notably, this indexing happens independently of the actual semantic or hermeneutic connection between the hashtag and the image and without any authority to regulate or validate its use. The # symbol thus reemphasizes the already tag-like quality of the Cinema of Transgression concept, as it is now "an index and a slogan at the same time."[97] In this sense, and not unlike the video compilation with which I began this chapter, the hashtag is an operator of both containment and spilling. For the purposes of mobility, classifiability, and visibility, it contains diverse elements within the neat boundaries of the keyword. Interestingly, however, the decision about what the keyword subsumes is now in a collective hand. Once again, any user can employ and circulate the hashtag, thus confirming, contradicting, or at least obscuring its originally intended meaning. As such, the hashtag is symptomatic of the curious afterlife of the CoT that I have discussed in this chapter. For it ultimately shows that the Cinema of Transgression—as a concept but also as a collection of all the material it covers—is still spilling over today and will most likely continue to do so, never in a linear fashion but messily, back and forth and in all directions, taking on new forms, collecting new meanings, and forming all kinds of constellations.

Coda

■■■■■■■■■■■■■■■■■■■■■

Keep on Spilling

In this book, I have attempted to reactivate the spillover of the Cinema of Transgression while identifying the various processes of containment and their effects that have contributed to its consolidation and canonization over the past forty years. The idea of an underground film movement from the gritty East Village of the 1980s, united in its commitment to the project of transgressing boundaries, has never fully entered the commercial mainstream, nor has it received much attention in academic discourses. Yet it remains an effective and, above all, seductive narrative, now readily embraced and reproduced, and not only by the art world where I first encountered the CoT.

One question that constantly accompanied the writing and thinking process of this project, therefore, was the following: how does one, metaphorically speaking, get rid of the object of research? Leaving behind preconceived notions of underground film in general and the CoT in particular, precisely by attempting to get closer to it, is an endeavor that has proven to be challenging in more ways than one.[1] What has become clear over time, however, is that the CoT concept is alluring not only because it transports one to the "good bad old days" of the capital of collective imagination but also because it offers compressed versions of what actually defies strict categorization. In other words—and this is also where the CoT differs crucially from other moments of artistic production within the rich history of Downtown movements, venues, and institutions—though its concept is designed to be uncomfortable, even offensive, in its supposed agenda, it ultimately creates a paradoxical sense of comfort in its simplification and stabilization of complex, even messy, matters. First, there is the matter of transgression, the crossing of boundaries, which is too often equated with the display of violence, drugs, rebellion, sex, and blood. This is boundary crossing for the sake of "easy frisson" rather than provoking "zones of implosion" where boundaries themselves are no longer of interest.[2] This applies to body fluids, sure, but what about all the other things that flow and spill over? For then there is also the question of film. The label "Cinema of Transgression" presents film as singular, work and author bound, as ontologically fixed—nothing spills over. As I have shown in chapter 2, the CoT was constructed from an indisciplinary scene, in which different scene activities like zine making, DIY programming, nightlife, and club culture, as well as practices involving film, performance, spoken word, dance, music, video, and television production, which became the focus for chapters 3 and 4, respectively, not only stuck together but inevitably spilled over into one another. The label contains precisely these spillings along with the contexts that configure and negotiate film in ever new and, above all, situated ways. In this sense, the CoT label ultimately not only stabilizes a concept of film that never actually existed, it also suggests that the CoT exists solely in the past tense, as a chapter of underground film history whose radical spirit is waiting to be evoked in exhibitions like the one which I used as the entry point for my investigation. However, as my observations on the more recent channels and contexts of the films' circulation make clear, while the CoT's spilling is continuous by its very nature, so too are the efforts to contain and stabilize it within more graspable and also marketable forms.

These spills have also led me to consider the ways in which my own perspective and writing are necessarily limited, and that the format of a scholarly book might contain the unruliness of its subject, and thus at least some of its spills. *Films That Spill* is therefore not intended to be conclusive. Instead, it offers novel perspectives that I hope will stimulate new discourse on the CoT and beyond. I imagine how the methodology and vocabulary developed here for studying the CoT will themselves spill over into other projects, informing those seeking to ask how artistic movements and scenes are described, historicized, and perhaps become contained within a particular narrative framework. Finally, I want *Films That Spill* to encourage reflection on the role of media such as film as integral elements of complex, elusive, and ever-changing constellations that are literally all over the place. In other words: this book will, I hope, inspire a more messy approach to film and media studies.

Appendix

List of Interviews

Interview with Jürgen Brüning, November 7, 2018, Berlin.
Interview with Anthony Chase and John Kelly, June 2019, via phone and email.
Interview with Manuel DeLanda, September 16, 2018, New York City.
Interview with Bradley Eros, October 13, 2018, New York City.
Interview with Karen Finley, May 22, 2019, via Skype.
Interview with Tessa Hughes-Freeland, September 13, 2018, New York City.
Interview with Richard Kern, October 4, 2018, New York City.
Interview with JG Thirlwell, September 26, 2019, New York City.
Interview with Ela Troyano, September 7, 2018, and October 2, 2019, New York City.

Many of the initial interviews listed above were followed by email correspondence.

List of Archive Collections Included

Downtown Collection, audiovisual holdings, Fales Library and Special Collections, New York University
The Poetry Collection of the University Libraries, University at Buffalo, The State University of New York.
Pyramid Club Flyers Collection, Fales Library and Special Collections, New York University

David Wojnarowicz Papers, Fales Library and Special Collections, New York University

Nick Zedd Papers, Fales Library and Special Collections, New York University

Acknowledgments

From its very beginning, many individuals and a variety of institutions provided invaluable assistance in the development of this project.

I want to begin by thanking my colleagues in Oldenburg, Mainz, and Frankfurt, particularly the first cohort of the DFG (Deutsche Forschungsgesellschaft) graduate research program Configurations of Film at Goethe University Frankfurt: thank you for your stimulating intelligence, humor, and collegiality; our years together truly became a time of intellectual and personal growth for me. To my thesis advisor Marc Siegel especially: thank you for being immensely generous with your time and thoughts and for giving me critical advice and gentle support along the way.

I also want to thank the kind and helpful staff at the Fales Library and Special Collections at New York University for doing such great work. My research trips to New York City would not have been possible without the financial support of the DFG and the Deutscher Akademischer Austauschdienst (DAAD).

To my wonderful family, partner, and friends (you know who you are!): thank you for your love, support, and motivation and for never doubting that what I am doing is relevant. I appreciate it so much.

Last but by no means least, I would like to express my gratitude to all the fantastic individuals who were kind enough to share their memories and time with me. Jürgen Brüning, Anthony Chase, Manuel DeLanda, Bradley Eros, Karen Finley, John Kelly, Richard Kern, Tessa Hughes-Freeland, JG Thirlwell, and Ela Troyano: your anecdotes and insights proved incredibly valuable. Thank you.

Notes

Introduction

1. Orion Jeriko [Nick Zedd], "The Cinema of Transgression Manifesto," *Underground Film Bulletin*, no. 4 (1985): 3–4.
2. Duncan Reekie, "The Underground Cinema Resurgence: From the New York Cinema of Transgression to the New London Underground 1991–2006," in *Subversion: The Definitive History of Underground Cinema* (London: Wallflower Press, 2007), 187–199.
3. Matthew Yokosbosky, "No Wave Cinema, 1978–87—Not a Part of Any Wave: No Wave," in *Captured: A Film/Video History of the Lower East Side*, ed. Clayton Patterson (New York: Seven Stories Press, 2005), 179–184. For other mentions of the CoT in relation to No Wave and underground film, see also Mark Benedetti's PhD dissertation "Beneath New York: The Formations and Effects of Canons in American Underground Film Movements" (Bloomington: Indiana University, 2013) and Barry Spunt, *Heroin, Acting, and Comedy in New York City* (New York: Palgrave Macmillan, 2017), 5.
4. Nick Zedd, "Nick Zedd," in *Captured: A Film/Video History of the Lower East Side*, ed. Clayton Patterson (New York: Seven Stories Press, 2005), 273–274.
5. Casandra Stark Mele, "Why I Left the 'Cinema of Transgression' Behind, Or Why It Left Me," in *Captured: A Film/Video History of the Lower East Side*, ed. Clayton Patterson (New York: Seven Stories Press, 2005), 277–279.
6. Cricket Delembard, "The Cinema of Transgression: Where Are They Now? A Recollection," in *Captured: A Film/Video History of the Lower East Side*, ed. Clayton Patterson (New York: Seven Stories Press, 2005), 272.
7. Patricia Mellencamp, "Receivable Texts: U.S. Avant-Garde Cinema, 1960–1980," *Wide Angle* 7, no. 1–2 (1985): 78.
8. Natalie S. Loveless, "Reading with Knots: On Jane Gallop's Anecdotal Theory," *S: Journal of the Jan van Eyck Circle for Lacanian Ideology Critique* 4 (2011): 24.
9. Sarah Schulman, *Gentrification of the Mind: Witness to a Lost Imagination* (Berkeley: University of California Press, 2012).
10. Thurston Moore in *"Llik your idols,"* KW Institute for Contemporary Art, March 10, 2012, https://www.kw-berlin.de/en/llik-your-idols/.

11 John Law, *After Method: Mess in Social Science Research* (London: Routledge, 2004).
12 Law, *After Method*, 5.
13 Friedrich Weltzien, "Von Cozens bis Kerner. Der Fleck als Transformator ästhetischer Erfahrung," in *Ästhetische Erfahrung: Gegenstände, Konzepte, Geschichtlichkeit*, ed. Sonderforschungsbereich 626: Ästhetische Erfahrung im Zeichen der Entgrenzung der Künste (Berlin: Free University of Berlin, 2006), https://www.geschkult.fu-berlin.de/e/sfb626/veroeffentlichungen/online/aesth_erfahrung/aufsaetze/weltzien.pdf, my translation.
14 Esther Leslie, *Liquid Crystals: The Science and Art of a Fluid Form* (London: Reaktion Books, 2016), 154.
15 Alexis Pauline Gumbs, *Spills: Scenes of Black Feminist Fugitivity* (Durham, NC: Duke University Press, 2016), xxi–xxii.
16 Zaina Alsous, "'Spill' Maps a Future in Which Black Women Inherit the Universe," *Bitch Media*, October 13, 2017, https://www.bitchmedia.org/article/spill-scenes-black-feminist-fugitivity/alexis-pauline-gumbs.
17 Georges Bataille, "Formless," in *Visions of Excess: Selected Writings, 1927–1939*, ed. Allan Stoekl (Minneapolis: University of Minnesota Press, 1985), 31.
18 Yve-Alain Bois, "The Use Value of 'Formless,'" in *Formless: A User's Guide*, ed. Yve-Alain Bois and Rosalind E. Krauss (New York: Zone Books, 1997), 18.
19 Johanna Schaffer, "Formlos wie Spucke," in *Radikal ambivalent: Engagement und Verantwortung in den Künsten heute*, ed. Rachel Mader (Zurich: Diaphanes, 2014), 212, my translation.
20 Mary Douglas, *Purity and Danger: An Analysis of Concepts of Pollution and Taboo*, vol. 2 of *Collected Works* (Routledge and Kegan Paul, 1966; London: Routledge, 2003), 36. Citation refers to the 2003 edition.
21 Brooke Erin Duffy and Jeremy Packer, "Wifesaver: Tupperware and the Unfortunate Spoils of Containment," in *Re-Understanding Media: Feminist Extensions of Marshall McLuhan*, ed. Sarah Sharma and Rianka Sing (Durham, NC: Duke University Press, 2022), 115.
22 Duffy and Packer, "Wifesaver," 115.
23 Bataille's understanding of transgression and expenditure can be found in several of his theoretical and literary works. I refer mainly to the writings originally published as *The Notion of Expenditure* (1933), *L'expérience intérieure* (1943), and *L'Erotisme* (1957).
24 The Instagram profile of the Greer Lankton Archive, maintained by Lankton's husband, Paul Monroe, published a photo in 2015 of Lankton as Dee Dee Lux at a Chicago nightclub in 1978, wearing sunglasses, a wig, a fur stole, and leopard-print panties. Monroe writes that Lankton created the character when she was sixteen and wore the costume not just when going out but also to "yard sales and to her local Woolworth's in Park Forrest [sic] Illinois." See https://www.instagram.com/p/5qNwh3vj4X/?taken-by=greer_lankton_archives_museum.
25 Linda Williams, "Film Bodies: Gender, Genre, and Excess," *Film Quarterly* 44, no. 4 (1991): 2–13.
26 Edward Buscombe, "Generic Overspill: A Dirty Western," in *More Dirty Looks: Gender, Pornography and Power*, 2nd ed., ed. Pamela Church Gibson (London: BFI Publishing, 2004), 26.
27 Nicholas Baer, Maggie Hennefeld, Laura Horak, and Gunnar Iversen, "Introduction: Envisioning the Unwatchable," in *Unwatchable*, ed. Nicholas Baer, Maggie Hennefeld, Laura Horak, and Gunnar Iversen (New Brunswick, NJ: Rutgers University Press, 2019), 5.

28 Lauren Rabinovitz, *Points of Resistance: Women, Power and Politics in the New York Avant-garde Cinema, 1943–71*, 2nd ed. (Urbana: University of Illinois Press, 2003), 14, 15.
29 Here I refer to the already mentioned writings of Bataille and to Friedrich Nietzsche's *Die fröhliche Wissenschaft* (1882, 1887) and *Also sprach Zarathustra* (1882–1892) and Michel Foucault's "A Preface to Transgression" in *Language, Counter-Memory, Practice: Selected Essays and Interviews*, ed. and trans. Donald F. Bouchard (Ithaca, NY: Cornell University Press, 1977), 34. Originally published in *Critique: Hommage à Georges Bataille* 195–196 (1963): 751–770.
30 Michel Foucault, "A Preface to Transgression."
31 Lawrence K. Altman, "Rare Cancer Seen in 41 Homosexuals," *New York Times*, July 3, 1981, 20, https://www.nytimes.com/1981/07/03/us/rare-cancer-seen-in-41-homosexuals.html.
32 Ann Magnuson, "Club 57," *Artforum* 38, no. 2 (1999), https://www.artforum.com/print/199908/club-57-840.
33 "Keith Haring Paints Mural on Berlin Wall," *New York Times*, October 24, 1986, 9, https://www.nytimes.com/1986/10/24/arts/keith-haring-paints-mural-on-berlin-wall.html.
34 Douglas C. McGill, "Art Boom Slows in the East Village," *New York Times*, July 25, 1987, 13, https://www.nytimes.com/1987/07/25/arts/art-boom-slows-in-the-east-village.html.
35 Juan A. Suárez, *Bike Boys, Drag Queens and Superstars: Avant-Garde, Mass Culture, and Gay Identities in the 1960s Underground Cinema* (Bloomington: Indiana University Press, 1996), 218.
36 Douglas Crimp and Adam Rolston, eds., *AIDS Demo Graphics* (Seattle: Bay Press, 1990), 34.
37 "AIDS in New York: A Biography," *New York Magazine*, May 26, 2006, http://nymag.com/news/features/17158/.
38 Paula A. Treichler, "AIDS, Homophobia, and Biomedical Discourse. An Epidemic of Signification," *October* 43 (1987): 32.
39 Simon Watney, *Policing Desire: Pornography, AIDS, and the Media*, 3rd ed. (Minneapolis: University of Minnesota Press, 1997), 12–37.
40 "Script for Fear of Disclosure Video, 1989," David Wojnarowicz Papers, Series 3, Subseries F, Box 6.261/ 6.262, Fales Library and Special Collections, New York University.
41 David Wojnarowicz, "Losing the Form in Darkness," in *David Wojnarowicz: Tongues of Flame*, ed. Barry Blinderman (Normal: Illinois State University, 1990), 65, 67.
42 Hal Foster, *Bad New Days: Art, Criticism, Emergency* (London: Verso, 2015), 3.
43 Marvin J. Taylor, "I'll Be Your Mirror, Reflect What You Are: Postmodern Documentation and the Downtown New York Scene from 1975 to the Present," *RBM: A Journal of Rare Books, Manuscripts, and Cultural Heritage* 3, no. 1 (2002): 35.
44 Tim Lawrence, *Life and Death on the New York Dance Floor, 1980–1983* (Durham, NC: Duke University Press, 2016), x.
45 Lawrence, *Life and Death on the New York Dance Floor*, x.
46 Michel Foucault, *Discipline and Punish: The Birth of the Prison* (Portland: Peregrine Press, 1979), 25–26.
47 Maria Lind, "The Collaborative Turn," in *Taking the Matter into Common Hands: On Contemporary Art and Collaborative Practices*, ed. Johanna Billing, Maria Lind, and Lars Nilsson (London: Black Dog Publishing, 2007), 16, 17.

48 Lind, "The Collaborative Turn," 18.
49 Erhard Schüttpelz, "Akademie der Dilettanten (Back to D.)," in *Akademie*, ed. Stephan Dillemuth (Cologne, Germany: Permanent Press, 1995), 40, my translation.
50 Schüttpelz, 55, my translation.
51 Schüttpelz, 55, my translation.
52 Schüttpelz, 55, my translation.
53 Will Straw, "Scenes and Sensibilities," *Public* 22, no. 23 (2001): 252.
54 Kate Eichhorn, "Copy Machines and Downtown Scenes: Deterritorializing Urban Culture in a Pre-Digital Era," *Cultural Studies* 29, no. 3 (2014): 4. The map, in turn, can be understood with Deleuze and Guattari as an analogy of the rhizome, meaning a nonhierarchical structure with no predetermined beginning or end, without a center—or rather, with multiple centers, multiple points of entry, and ongoing potentials of multidirectional connectivity (Gilles Deleuze and Félix Guattari, *Rhizom* [Berlin: Merve, 1977], 21).
55 Benjamin Woo, Jamie Rennie, and Stuart R. Poyntz, "Scene Thinking," *Cultural Studies* 29, no. 3 (2014): 288–289.
56 André Gaudreault and Philippe Marion, *The End of Cinema? A Medium in Crisis in the Digital Age*, trans. Timothy Barnard (New York: Columbia University Press, 2015), 10.
57 Gaudreault and Marion, *The End of Cinema?*, 2–3.
58 Charles Acland, *Screen Traffic: Movies, Multiplexes, and Global Culture* (Durham, NC: Duke University Press, 2003), 46.
59 Miriam De Rosa and Vinzenz Hediger, "Post-what? Post-when? A Conversation on the 'Posts' of Post-media and Post-cinema," *Cinéma and Cie* 16, no. 26/27 (2016): 10.
60 De Rosa and Hediger, "Post-what? Post-when?" 10.
61 Rembert Hüser, "Agent im Kreis," in *Handbuch Filmanalyse*, ed. Malte Hagener and Volker Pantenburg (Wiesbaden, Germany: Springer VS, 2020), 1–16, https://link.springer.com/referenceworkentry/10.1007/978-3-658-13352-8_18-1, my translation.
62 Heather Love, "Queer Messes," *WSQ: Women's Studies Quarterly* 44, no. 3–4 (2016): 345.
63 Asbjørn Grønstad, "The Two Unwatchables," in *Unwatchable*, ed. Nicholas Baer et al. (New Brunswick, NJ: Rutgers University Press, 2019), 152, 153.
64 Erika Balsom, *After Uniqueness: Film and Video Art in Circulation* (New York: Columbia University Press, 2017), 18.
65 The term "nontheatrical" has been productively examined by Barbara Klinger in "Cinema's Shadow: Reconsidering Non-theatrical Exhibition," in *Going to the Movies: Hollywood and the Social Experience of Cinema*, ed. Richard Maltby, Melvyn Stokes, and Robert C. Allen (Exeter, UK: University of Exeter Press, 2005), 35–36, and by Haidee Wasson in *Museum Movies: The Museum of Modern Art and the Birth of Art Cinema* (Berkeley: University of California Press, 2005).
66 Gray takes this term from Gerard Genette's *Paratexts: The Thresholds of Interpretation*, trans. Jane E. Lewin (Cambridge, UK: Cambridge University Press, 1997).
67 See for instance Vinzenz Hediger, *Verführung zum Film. Der amerikanische Kinotrailer seit 1912* (Marburg, Germany: Schüren, 2001); Jonathan Gray, Cornel Sandvoss, and C. Lee Harrington, eds., *Fandom: Identities and Communities in a Mediated World*, 2nd ed. (New York: New York University Press, 2017); Henry Jenkins, *Convergence Culture: Where Old and New Media Collide* (New York: New York University Press, 2006); John T. Caldwell, "Prefiguring Bonus Tracks:

Making-Ofs and Behind-the-Scenes as Historic Television Programming Strategies and Prototypes," in *Film and Television after the DVD*, ed. James Bennett and Tom Brown (London: Routledge, 2009), 149–171.
68 Jonathan Gray, *Show Sold Separately: Promos, Spoilers, and Other Media Paratexts* (New York: New York University Press, 2010), 6, 7.
69 Raiford Guins, *Game After: A Cultural Study of Video Game Afterlife* (Cambridge, MA: MIT Press, 2014), 12.
70 Charles Acland and Haidee Wasson, "Introduction: Utility and Cinema," in *Useful Cinema*, ed. Charles Acland and Haidee Wasson (Durham, NC: Duke University Press, 2011), 1.

Chapter 1 Forgetting the Cinema of Transgression

1 "You Killed Me First," KW Institute for Contemporary Art, Exhibitions, accessed August 6, 2024, https://www.kw-berlin.de/en/you-killed-me-first/.
2 Daniel Horn, "After Anger," *Frieze*, April 6, 2012, https://www.frieze.com/article/after-anger.
3 Arthur C. Danto, *The Philosophical Disenfranchisement of Art* (New York: Columbia University Press, 1986, 2004), 121.
4 Tim Lawrence, *Life and Death on the New York Dancefloor, 1980–1983* (Durham, NC: Duke University Press, 2016), xiii.
5 Jack Sargeant, *Deathtripping: The Cinema of Transgression* (London: Creation Books, 1995), v.
6 Beginning in the mid-1980s, Richard Kern produced and distributed his films on video with his own distribution company, Deathtrip Films. Nick Zedd did so in a similar manner with Weirdo Video and Penetration Films. In the recent past, MoMA's film and video library purchased films by David Wojnarowicz, Ela Troyano, Richard Kern, and Kembra Pfahler. Anthology Film Archives digitized some of Manuel DeLanda's films with support from the Andy Warhol Foundation for the Visual Arts. Electronic Arts Intermix distributes copies of films by David Wojnarowicz and Tommy Turner. PPOW Gallery in New York City represents the Estate of David Wojnarowicz, including most of his filmic work. UbuWeb lists twelve films under the entry for Cinema of Transgression; see http://ubu.com/film/transgression.html.
7 Janine Marchessault, "Film Scenes: Paris, New York, Toronto," *Public* 22, no. 23 (2001): 71.
8 Jack Halberstam, *The Queer Art of Failure* (Durham, NC: Duke University Press, 2011), 2, 15.
9 "Downtown New York," Exhibitions and Events, Collection 1980s–Present, Fall 2019–Spring 2021, https://www.moma.org/calendar/galleries/5129.
10 Dan Fox, "A Better View," *Frieze*, December 19, 2017, https://www.frieze.com/article/better-view.
11 For more information about *East Village USA*, see https://archive.newmuseum.org/exhibitions/421. After its time at Grey Art Gallery, the show traveled to the Andy Warhol Museum in Pittsburgh and to the Austin Museum of Art. It was accompanied by *The Downtown Book: The New York Art Scene 1974–1984* (Princeton, NJ: Princeton University Press, 2006), which was edited by Marvin J. Taylor and features critical essays on the Downtown music, performance, art, film, and writing scenes. For more information about *The Downtown Show*, see https://greyartgallery.nyu.edu/2016/05/press-release-Downtown-show/.

12 Lucas Hilderbrand, Alexandra Juhasz, Debra Levine, and Ricardo Montez, "Downtown's Queer Asides," in *Downtown Film and TV Culture 1975–2001*, ed. Joan Hawkins (Bristol, UK: Intellect, 2015), 250.
13 Richard Kern, in discussion with the author, October 4, 2018.
14 Horn, "After Anger."
15 Anja Dreschke, Ilham Huynh, Raphaela Knipp, and David Sittler, "Einleitung," in *Reenactments. Medienpraktiken zwischen Wiederholung und kreativer Aneignung*, ed. Anja Dreschke, Ilham Huynh, Raphaela Knipp, and David Sittler (Bielefeld, Germany: Transcript Publishing, 2016), 11, my translation.
16 Dreschke, Huynh, Knipp, and Sittler, 11.
17 Elena Filipovic, "The Global White Cube," in *The Manifesta Decade: Debates on Contemporary Art Exhibitions and Biennials in Post-Wall Europe*, ed. Barbara Vanderlinden and Elena Filipovic (Cambridge, MA: MIT Press, 2006), 79.
18 "Institution," About, KW Institute for Contemporary Art, https://www.kw-berlin.de/en/about/.
19 A critic writing for a local Berlin newspaper has repeatedly criticized Biesenbach for being the mainspring in the *SoHofication* ("SoHo-Effekt") of Berlin's downtown neighborhood; see Nicola Kuhn, "Berlins SoHo—nur so lala," *Der Tagesspiegel*, Kultur, March 12, 2000, https://www.tagesspiegel.de/kultur/berlins-soho-nur-so-lala-663307.html.
20 Caroline A. Jones, "Biennial Culture: A Longer History," in *The Biennial Reader. An Anthology on Large-Scale Perennial Exhibitions of Contemporary Art*, ed. Elena Filipovic, Marieke Van Hal, and Solveig Øvstebø (Ostfildern, Germany: Hatje Cantz, 2010), 68.
21 "Berlin/Berlin," Berlin Biennale, 1st Berlin Biennale for Contemporary Art, September 9–December 30, 1998, https://www.berlinbiennale.de/en/biennalen/5/berlin-berlin.
22 Charlotte Bydler, "The Global Art World, INC.: On the Globalization of Contemporary Art," in *The Biennial Reader: An Anthology on Large-Scale Perennial Exhibitions of Contemporary Art*, ed. Elena Filipovic, Marieke Van Hal, and Solveig Øvstebø (Ostfildern, Germany: Hatje Cantz, 2010), 388.
23 Jones, "Biennial Culture," 69.
24 Reza Abdoh's retrospective at KW in 2019 was held at the same time as a presentation of films and photographs by David Wojnarowicz and a survey of the work of curator Frank Wagner. Wagner had curated the first German exhibition on AIDS, titled *Vollbild Aids—Eine Kunstausstellung über Leben und Sterben* (at the Neue Gesellschaft für bildende Kunst in West Berlin, December 6, 1988 through February 13, 1989), which featured Wojnarowicz and Peter Hujar, among others. Wagner also organized *Close to the Knives—A Memoir of Disintegration. Ein Gedenkraum für David Wojnarowicz* at KW in 1992–1993 as a tribute to Wojnarowicz, who died of AIDS in 1992. Kenneth Anger's first institutional solo show in Germany (at Künstlerhaus Bremen in 2006) was curated by Susanne Pfeffer, who also curated Anger's 2009 solo show at PS1 together with Biesenbach.
25 Kern, in discussion with the author.
26 "Joe Coleman Internal Digging," KW Institute for Contemporary Art, Exhibitions, May 26–October 21, 2007, https://www.kw-berlin.de/en/joe-coleman-internal-digging/, emphasis added; "Kenneth Anger," MoMA PS1, February 22–September 21, 2009, https://www.moma.org/calendar/exhibitions/3808, emphasis added; "Reza Abdoh," MoMA, June 3–September 3, 2018, https://www.moma.org/calendar/exhibitions/3929, emphasis added.

27 Haidee Wasson, *Museum Movies: The Museum of Modern Art and the Birth of Art Cinema* (Berkeley: University of California Press, 2005), 22. In February 2005 in connection with the exhibition *East Village USA* at the New Museum, filmmaker Tessa Hughes-Freeland organized the *East Village USA Film Festival: Films from New York City's East Village in the 1980s*, which showed "rare hard-to-find shorts with cult classics by such underground artist-filmmakers as Manuel De Landa, Bradley Eros, Richard Kern, Kembra Pfahler, and Nick Zedd" ("East Village USA Film Festival: Films from New York City's East Village in the 1980s," Public Programs, Film and Video Series, February 16–21, 2005, https://archive.newmuseum.org/public-programs/759). In 2018, films by Richard Kern, Nick Zedd, Tessa Hughes-Freeland, and Manuel DeLanda were shown at MoMA. They were announced as "landmark examples of . . . [the] Cinema of Transgression" and presented in a survey titled *New York Film and Video: No Wave–Transgressive*, which was part of the museum's *Club 57* exhibition ("Club 57: Film, Performance, and Art in the East Village, 1978–1983," MoMA, Exhibitions and Events, October 31, 2017–April 8, 2018, https://www.moma.org/calendar/exhibitions/3824).

28 Kate Eichhorn, "Copy Machines and Downtown Scenes: Deterritorializing Urban Culture in a Pre-Digital era," *Cultural Studies* 29, no. 3 (2014): 10.

29 Orion Jeriko [Nick Zedd], "The Cinema of Transgression Manifesto," *Underground Film Bulletin*, no. 4 (1985): 4.

30 Amy Taubin, "The Other Cinema," *SoHo Weekly News*, June 7, 1979, 94.

31 Orion Jeriko [Nick Zedd], "Long Live the Cinema of Transgression," *Underground Film Bulletin*, no. 3 (1985): 3.

32 Jeriko [Zedd], "Long Live the Cinema of Transgression," 3.

33 Nick Zedd, *Totem of the Depraved* (Los Angeles: Two Thirteen Sixty-One Publications, 1996), 52.

34 Janet Lyon, *Manifestoes: Provocations of the Modern* (Ithaca, NY: Cornell University Press, 1999), 5.

35 Lyon, *Manifestoes*, 5.

36 Jeriko [Zedd], "The Cinema of Transgression Manifesto."

37 J. L. Austin, *How to Do Things with Words: The William James Lectures Delivered at Harvard University in 1955* (Oxford: Oxford University Press, 1962), 75; Gabriele Brandstetter, "YES! Das Manifest als künstlerische Praxis," in *"Clean the Air": Künstlermanifeste seit den 1960er Jahren*, ed. Burcu Dogramaci and Katja Schneider (Bielefeld, Germany: Transcript Publishing, 2017), 18.

38 Jasmine Sailing, "Nick Zedd Interview," *Cyber-Psycho's A.O.D.*, no. 3 (1993): 32.

39 Tessa Hughes-Freeland, in discussion with the author, September 13, 2018.

40 Ela Troyano, in discussion with the author, September 7, 2018.

41 Lyon, *Manifestoes*, 10.

42 The New American Cinema Group, "The First Statement of the New American Cinema Group (USA, 1961)," in *Film Manifestos and Global Cinema Cultures: A Critical Anthology*, ed. Scott MacKenzie (Berkeley: University of California Press, 2014), 60.

43 Jeriko [Zedd], "The Cinema of Transgression Manifesto."

44 Zedd, *Totem of the Depraved*, 84.

45 Lauren Rabinovitz, *Points of Resistance: Women, Power and Politics in the New York Avant-garde Cinema, 1943–71*, 2nd ed. (Urbana: University of Illinois Press, 2003), 14.

46 Scott MacKenzie, "Introduction: An Invention without a Future," in *Film Manifestos and Global Cinema Cultures. A Critical Anthology*, ed. Scott MacKenzie (Berkeley: University of California Press, 2014), 1; Rabinovitz, *Points of Resistance*, 15. It should

be noted, however, that the temporal dynamics of the manifesto form could likewise be considered in a much more complex way. Deeply anchored in present conditions, the manifesto conceives an often-impossible future, attempting to break with a past from which, however, it cannot completely separate itself. It is precisely this complexity—and the hopeful, imaginative, sometimes utopian moment inherent in it—that has made the manifesto an important tool in the context of queer and feminist art and politics, as well as an intriguing object for their theorization and historical analysis, as becomes clear in the work of Laura E. Guy, Felicity Colman, and Katy Deepwell. See Laura E. Guy, "Manifestos: Aesthetics and Politics in Queer Times" (PhD diss., Manchester Metropolitan University, 2017, https://e-space.mmu.ac.uk/618980/1/LEGuy_PhDThesis_FinalSubmission.pdf; Laura Guy, "I Want a Dyke for President: Sounding out Zoe Leonard's Manifesto for Art History's Feminist Futures," in *Feminism and Art History Now: Radical Critiques of Theory and Practice*, ed. Victoria Horne and Lara Perry (London: I.B. Tauris, 2017), 41–62; Felicity Colman, "Notes on the Feminist Manifesto: The Strategic Use of Hope," *Journal for Cultural Research* 14, no. 4 (2010): 375–392; and Katy Deepwell, ed., *Feminist Art Manifestos: An Anthology* (London: KT Press, 2014).

47 Ernie Blerk, n. t., *ZAT Magazine*, no. 5 (1985): 20–22; Bryan Bruce, "Pissing on the Cinema of Transgression," *CineAction!*, no. 3 (1986): 21–27.

48 I am referencing various international articles and screening announcements ranging from 1987 to 1990 that can be found in the Nick Zedd Papers at the Fales Library (series II, subseries D, box 8, folders 27, 28, and 29).

49 For instance, when C. Carr published an article in the *Village Voice* describing the films of Ela Troyano (such as *Totem of the Depraved*, which she made with Nick Zedd) as instances of the Cinema of Transgression, Zedd proceeded to make a case for officially excluding Troyano from it and proceeded to refer to her as the "late" Ela Troyano. See, for example, *Underground Film Bulletin*, no. 3 (1985): 47.

50 Rabinovitz, *Points of Resistance*, 6, and Patricia Mellencamp, *Indiscretions: Avant-Garde Film, Video and Feminism* (Bloomington: Indiana University Press, 1990), 10ff.

51 Rabinovitz, *Points of Resistance*, 16.

52 Constance Penley and Janet Bergstrom, "The Avant-Garde: Histories and Theories," *Screen* 19, no. 3 (1978): 118.

53 This synopsis was sent to me upon request by a BFI press officer (cultural program).

54 The VHS is not available via the BFI anymore, nor was the compilation ever converted to a digital format. When requesting information about the VHS, a BFI press officer directed me to their listings on Amazon, where only two tapes are offered for sale.

55 "The Cinema of Transgression (1979–1993)," UbuWeb, Film and Video, http://ubu.com/film/transgression.html.

56 Marlene Manoff, "Theories of the Archive from Across the Disciplines," *Libraries and the Academy* 4, no. 1 (2004): 10.

57 While I will distinguish between these two groups for the sake of clarity, the distinction is still more complex. This is not least because, as Jacques Derrida says, every archive is fundamentally external, situated, and thus virtually public. See Jacques Derrida, "Archive Fever: A Seminar by Jacques Derrida, University of the Witwatersrand, August 1998. Transcribed by Verne Harris," in *Refiguring the Archive*, ed. Carolyn Hamilton et al. (Dordrecht/Boston/London: Kluwer Academic Publishers, 2002), 42.

58 Richard Kern noted this in our conversation on October 4, 2018, about copies of *Dumbf—er*, a series of zines he published in the early 1980s.

59 Achille Mbembe, "The Power of the Archive and Its Limits," in *Refiguring the Archive*, ed. Carolyn Hamilton, Verne Harris, Jane Taylor, Michele Pickover, Graeme Reid, and Razia Saleh (Dordrecht/Boston/London: Kluwer Academic Publishers, 2002), 19.
60 Michel Foucault, "Of Other Spaces: Utopias and Heterotopias," trans. Jay Miskowiec, *Diacritics* 16, no. 1 (1986): 26. Originally published in *Architecture/Mouvement/Continuité*, no. 5 (1984): 46–49.
61 Tobi Haslett, "Modern Love: Gary Indiana Has Told the Story of His Life with Many of the Legendary Parts Cut Out," *n+1*, 26 (2016), https://www.nplusonemag.com/issue-26/reviews/modern-love/.
62 "Guide to the Nick Zedd Papers, 1963–2916," NYU Special Collections Search Portal, Fales Library and Special Collections, MSS.311, https://findingaids.library.nyu.edu/fales/mss_311/.
63 Mbembe, "The Power of the Archive and Its Limits," 20.
64 "Downtown Collection at the NYU Special Collections," NYU Libraries, Research Guides, Archives and Special Collections, https://guides.nyu.edu/downtown-collection.
65 Jacques Derrida, "Archive Fever: A Freudian Impression," *Diacritics* 25, no. 2 (1995): 9–63 (17).
66 Derrida, "Archive Fever," 40.
67 Marvin J. Taylor, "I'll Be Your Mirror, Reflect What You Are: Postmodern Documentation and the Downtown New York Scene from 1975 to the Present," *RBM: A Journal of Rare Books, Manuscripts, and Cultural Heritage* 3, no. 1 (2002): 38.
68 Taylor, "I'll Be Your Mirror," 45; José Esteban Muñoz, "Ephemera as Evidence: Introductory Notes to Queer Acts," *Women and Performance: A Journal of Feminist Theory* 8, no. 2 (1996): 7.
69 Taylor, "I'll Be Your Mirror," 49.
70 "Guide to the David Wojnarowicz Papers," NYU Special Collections Search Portal, Fales Library and Special Collections, MSS.092, http://dlib.nyu.edu/findingaids/html/fales/mss_092/.
71 Muñoz, "Ephemera as Evidence," 10–11.
72 Melissa Adler, *Cruising the Library: Perversities in the Organization of Knowledge* (New York: Fordham University Press, 2017), 14.
73 "Guide to the Nick Zedd Papers, 1963–2916."
74 "Nick Zedd Appreciation Society Materials, c. 1988," Guide to the Nick Zedd Papers, 1963–2016, MSS.311, Series II: Projects, Subseries B: Distribution, box 6, folder 69, mixed materials, Fales Library and Special Collections, New York University, https://findingaids.library.nyu.edu/fales/mss_311/contents/aspace_ref2/#aspace_ref17.
75 Abigail De Kosnik, *Rogue Archives: Digital Cultural Memory and Media Fandom* (Cambridge, MA: MIT Press, 2016), 66.
76 Derrida, "Archive Fever," 42.
77 Verne Harris, "Genres of the Trace: Memory, Archives and Trouble," *Archives and Manuscripts* 40, no. 3 (2012): 151–152.
78 Harris, "Genres of the Trace," 152.

Chapter 2 Downtown Images

1 C. Carr, "R.I.P. 8BC," in *On Edge: Performance at the End of the Twentieth Century* (Middletown, CT: Wesleyan University Press, 2008), 70.
2 John Irwin, *Scenes* (Beverly Hills: Sage, 1977), 27.

3. "Performativity" has become an umbrella term in linguistics and cultural and gender studies. First brought up by J. L. Austin in *How to Do Things with Words* (Oxford: Oxford Press, 1962), the term was further discussed and used by, among others, Judith Butler in *Bodies That Matter: On the Discursive Limits of "Sex"* (London: Routledge, 1993) and *Excitable Speech: A Politics of the Performative* (London: Routledge, 1997) and Jacques Derrida in *Limited Inc* (Evanston, IL: Northwestern University Press, 1988). Here, I am referring to a more general understanding of performativity as "self-reference of actions and their reality-constituting power," as defined by Erika Fischer-Lichte on page 29 of *Performativität: Eine Einführung* (Bielefeld, Germany: Transcript Publishing, 2012).
4. Janine Marchessault, "Film Scenes: Paris, New York, Toronto," *Public* 22, no. 23 (2001): 68.
5. Though I will not go deeper into the development of other areas of Lower Manhattan such as Greenwich Village, Tribeca, or SoHo, it should be noted that they also underwent processes of gentrification in which the art scene, real estate interest, and city government revaluation plans intertwined. For instance, SoHo and other areas that were more shaped by industry saw the creation of "loft living," where the lofts in which artists lived, performed, and worked in the 1950s and 1960s were made increasingly appealing to the imagination of middle-class tenants thanks to the growing fascination with artists' studios in the 1970s and 1980s. See Sharon Zukin's "The Creation of a 'Loft Lifestyle,'" in *The Gentrification Debates*, ed. Japonica Brown-Saracino (London: Routledge, 2010), 175–184.
6. Kathy Acker, "Getting the Alphabet Right," undated annotated typescript. Viewed in the exhibition *Kathy Acker: Get Rid of Meaning* at Badischer Kunstverein, Karlsruhe, Germany, October 5–December 2, 2018.
7. Manuel DeLanda, in discussion with the author, October 16, 2018.
8. Richard Kern, "Watching Thanateros," interview by Jack Sargeant, *Deathtripping: The Cinema of Transgression* (London: Creation Books, 1995), 97.
9. Jack Stevenson, "Grindhouse and Beyond," in *From the Arthouse to the Grindhouse: Highbrow and Lowbrow Transgression in Cinema's First Century*, ed. John Clide and Robert G. Weiner (Lanham, MD: Scarecrow Press, 2010), 141; Eric Schaefer, *"Bold! Daring! Shocking! True!": A History of Exploitation Films, 1919–1959* (Durham, NC: Duke University Press, 1999), 5.
10. David Church, *Grindhouse Nostalgia: Memory, Home Video and Exploitation Film Fandom* (Edinburgh: Edinburgh University Press, 2015).
11. For a more detailed examination of this growing infrastructure and the role Jonas Mekas played in it, see David E. James, *To Free the Cinema: Jonas Mekas and the New York Underground* (Princeton, NJ: Princeton University Press, 1992).
12. Harris Smith, "No New Cinema: Punk and No Wave Underground Film 1976–1984," in *Captured: A Film/Video History of the Lower East Side*, ed. Clayton Patterson (New York: Seven Stories Press, 2005), 173. The Downtown night clubs that opened in the 1960s and 1970s existed in close geographic proximity to numerous artist and performance spaces, theaters, and galleries including La Mama Experimental Theatre Club (est. 1961), The Performing Garage (est. 1968), and The Kitchen (est. 1971).
13. Matthew Yokobosky, "No Wave Cinema, 1978–87: Not a Part of Any Wave: No Wave," in *Captured: A Film/Video History of the Lower East Side*, ed. Clayton Patterson (New York: Seven Stories Press, 2005), 180.
14. Mark Benedetti, "Canonization and No Wave Cinema History," in *Downtown Film and TV Culture 1975–2001*, ed. Joan Hawkins (Bristol, UK: Intellect, 2015), 269–270.

15 Tim Lawrence, *Life and Death on the New York Dancefloor, 1980–1983* (Durham, NC: Duke University Press, 2016), 48.
16 Ela Troyano, in discussion with the author, September 7, 2018.
17 Tessa Hughes-Freeland, in discussion with the author, September 13, 2018; Lawrence, *Life and Death on the New York Dancefloor*, 22–23.
18 Joan Hawkins, "Downtown Cinema Revisited," in *Downtown Film and TV Culture 1975–2001*, ed. Joan Hawkins (Bristol, UK: Intellect, 2015), xix.
19 Troyano interview.
20 David Wojnarowicz, "Sidewalk Begging," *East Village Eye*, October 1985, 14.
21 Hawkins, "Downtown Cinema Revisited," xii.
22 Christopher Mele, "Forging the Link Between Culture and Real Estate: Urban Policy and Real Estate Development," in *The Gentrification Debates*, ed. Japonica Brown-Saracino (New York: Routledge, 2010), 129.
23 Lawrence, *Life and Death on the New York Dancefloor*, 263. Fun Gallery opened in 1981; 51X Gallery, Gracie Manson, Civilian Warfare, Nature Morte, and East 7th Gallery opened in 1982; and New Math Gallery, Piezo Electric, C.A.S.H. Gallery, International with Monument, and Pat Hearn Gallery opened in 1983.
24 Carlo McCormick, "Climbing: The East Village," press release, January 7–February 4, 1984, Hal Bromm Gallery, https://www.halbromm.com/climbing-the-east-village-1984.
25 There was the *East Village Artists* show at the Virginia Museum of Fine Art, *The East Village* at Newport Harbor Art Museum in California, and *The East Village Scene* show in Philadelphia in 1984. In Europe that same year, the Anna Friebe Gallery brought *The East Village* to Cologne, and the André Emmerich Gallery wanted to give its Zurich audience a glimpse *Inside the East Village*. In addition to the sheer volume of exhibitions, it is worth noting that many of them presented graffiti art as an East Village or Downtown phenomenon. Graffiti, an expression associated with hip-hop, which, along with break dancing, emceeing, and mixing, had its roots in the mostly Black neighborhoods Bronx and Harlem of the 1970s, developed an "uptown Downtown synergy" in the 1980s when graffiti artists began to mix with the Downtown club scene and show their work in galleries there. See George Nelson, *Hip Hop America* (New York: Penguin Books, 1999), 1–22.
26 Carlo McCormick, "East Village, R.I.P.," *East Village Eye*, October 1985, 23.
27 Michael Gross, "The Party Seems to be Over for Lower Manhattan Clubs," *New York Times*, October 26, 1985, 1, https://www.nytimes.com/1985/10/26/nyregion/the-party-seems-to-be-over-for-lower-manhattan-clubs.html.
28 An interview with Ela Troyano by Tessa Hughes-Freeland in issue 3 (1985) was titled "The Late Ela Troyano," hinting at the quarrel Zedd and Troyano had had over a copy of their collaboratively produced film *Totem of the Depraved*. Similarly, the masthead was the place where readers found out which contributors had just fallen out of favor. While John Smith was listed as editorial assistant in the third issue, the masthead of the sixth issue turned him into an "editorial disassociate." In issue 7 (1989), a note informs the reader that the editors "had hoped to have a piece on Jon Moritsugu for this issue but Tessa Hughes-Freeland didn't write it. Ditto Mike Wolfe on Todd Haynes." Consequently, the subsequent issue lists Hughes-Freeland and others as "contributing editors and lazy slobs."
29 Daniel Kane, *All Poets Welcome: The Lower East Side Poetry Scene in the 1960s* (Berkeley: University of California Press, 2003), 63.
30 Lucy Mulroney, *Andy Warhol, Publisher* (Chicago: University of Chicago Press, 2018), 52.

31. Tessa Hughes-Freeland, e-mail message to author, February 17, 2020. Rafik Film and Video, founded in 1974 by Rafic Azzouray, began as a postproduction facility for video and audio duplication, transfer, conversions, and editing that also lent equipment to local filmmakers. Rafik sponsored the fourth and fifth edition of the New York Film Festival Downtown (NYFFD). The shop was located in the same building that housed O-P Screen, a space that could be rented for $15 to show 16 mm films. An advertisement published in the *East Village Eye* in 1979 says, "O-P Screen will show anything, just contact Rafik a minimum of two weeks in advance." Many Downtown filmmakers took advantage of this opportunity.
32. All quotes are taken from Orion Jeriko [Nick Zedd], "The Worst Filmmaker in the World: John Spencer Interviewed by Orion Jeriko," *Underground Film Bulletin*, no. 6 (1987): 24–35.
33. Zedd received letters from Toronto and Honolulu in 1986, Quebec (1990), and Los Angeles, Zurich, Michigan, and Prague (1998).
34. Kate Eichhorn, "Copy Machines and Downtown Scenes: Deterritorializing Urban Culture in a Pre-Digital Era," *Cultural Studies* 29, no. 3 (2014): 2.
35. Eichhorn, "Copy Machines and Downtown Scenes," 5.
36. Donna Death appeared in Nick Zedd's *They Eat Scum* (1979) and *Geek Maggot Bingo* (1983); Lydia Lunch in *The Wild World of Lydia Lunch* (1983); Phoebe Legere in *Totem of the Depraved* (codirected by Ela Troyano, 1983); Richard Hell in *Geek Maggot Bingo* (1983); Rockets Redglare in *Police State* (1987), Kembra Pfahler in *War Is Menstrual Envy* (1992); and Casandra Stark in *Go to Hell* (1986).
37. Stephen Duncombe, *Notes from Underground: Zines and the Politics of Alternative Culture* (New York: Verso, 1997), 10; Lisa Gitelman, *Paper Knowledge: Toward a Media History of Documents* (Durham, NC: Duke University Press, 2014), 136–150.
38. Gwen Allen, *Artists' Magazines: An Alternative Space for Art* (Cambridge, MA: MIT Press, 2011), 91.
39. Bob Colacello, *Holy Terror: Andy Warhol Close Up* (New York: HarperCollins, 1990), 252.
40. Colacello, *Holy Terror*, 255.
41. Colacello, *Holy Terror*, 140.
42. Duncan Reekie, *Subversion: The Definitive History of Underground Cinema* (London: Wallflower Press, 2007), 139.
43. J. Hoberman and Jonathan Rosenbaum, eds., *Midnight Movies* (New York: Harper and Row, 1983), 41.
44. Stan Vanderbeek, "The Cinema Delimina: Films from the Underground," *Film Quarterly* 14, no. 4 (1961): 5–15.
45. Sheldon Renan's *An Introduction to the American Underground Film* (New York: E. P. Dutton, 1967), published two years prior to Parker Tyler's book, was the first extensive critical examination of the topic.
46. Parker Tyler, *Underground Film: A Critical History* (New York: Grove Press, 1970), 24.
47. Jonas Mekas, "Underground Film According to Parker Tyler," in *Movie Journal: The Rise of a New American Cinema, 1959–1971* (New York: Collier Books, 1972), 362–364.
48. Jan-Frederik Bandel, "Underground," in *Handbuch Literatur und Pop*, ed. Moritz Baßler and Eckhard Schumacher (Berlin: De Gruyter, 2020), 307, my translation.
49. Malcolm Le Grice, "You Killed the Underground Film or the Real Meaning of Kunst bleibt . . . bleibt . . . ," March 2, 2012, http://slypropotter.org/wilhelm-hein/le-grice.
50. Hoberman and Rosenbaum, eds., *Midnight Movies*, 40.
51. Orion Jeriko [Nick Zedd], "Editorial: Dear Tasteless Ones," *Underground Film Bulletin*, no. 7 (1988): 11–13.

52 The complete list features the mentioned films plus *Submit to Me* parts I and II by Richard Kern, *Judgement Day* by Manuel DeLanda, *The Bogus Man* by Nick Zedd, and *Last Rights* by Scott B.
53 For instance, Nick Zedd showed films at Millennium as early as 1983. In the 1990s and 2000s, screenings of his works in institutions associated with the 1960s avant-garde became more frequent, indicating that the filmmaker's attitude toward them changed from opposition to cooperation. Zedd continued to show at Millennium in 1993, 2001, and 2007, and Anthology Film Archives (AFA) hosted various screenings of his films throughout the 1990s and early 2000s, including the premier of *War Is Menstrual Envy* in 1991. In the same year, AFA presented Zedd's films as part of their *Essential Cinema Series*, followed by a program titled "Films from the Cinema of Transgression." In the recent past, AFA showed both old and new works by Bradley Eros (2012, 2016), Manuel DeLanda (2011, 2015, 2018), Richard Kern (2011), and Tessa Hughes-Freeland (2015, 2018). In 2020, the rental catalog of the Film-Maker's Coop includes films by Eros, Hughes-Freeland, Casandra Stark Mele, and Zedd—again, all filmmakers belonging to the scene from which the CoT was constructed. This information was sourced from programs and flyers found in the Nick Zedd Papers at the Fales Library and Special Collections at New York University, from Anthology Film Archive's past screening programs (http://anthologyfilmarchives.org/), and from the Film-Makers' Coop online catalog (https://film-makerscoop.com/).
54 Orion Jeriko [Nick Zedd], "Long Live the Cinema of Transgression," *Underground Film Bulletin*, no. 3 (1985): 3–4; Jeriko [Zedd], "The Cinema of Transgression Manifesto," *Underground Film Bulletin*, no. 4 (1985): 3–5.
55 Gene Suicide, "Number One with a Boley: Beyond the Myth of Nick Zedd," *Sex and Guts*, no. 2 (1997/98): 13.
56 Sargeant, *Deathtripping*, 7.
57 Sargeant, *Deathtripping*, 11.
58 Sargeant, *Deathtripping*, v.
59 Giovanni Formilan and David Stark, "Underground Testing: Name-Altering Practices as Probes in Electronic Music," *British Journal of Sociology* 71, no. 3 (2020): 573.
60 Tessa Hughes-Freeland, in discussion with the author, September 13, 2018.
61 Ela Troyano, in discussion with the author, September 7, 2018.
62 Hughes-Freeland interview.
63 Jo Andres is featured in the NYFFD programs as follows: Jo Andres, *Devil's in the Dish* (Film/Dance Performance) (1986); Film from performance piece *Lucid Possession* (with Jo Andres, C. Meyers, Rebecca Moore) (1988); *Expanded Cinema Performance* by Jo Andres (1989). She also frequently performed at other Downtown venues such as The Collective for Living Cinema, The Performing Garage, or La Mama Experimental Theatre Club.
64 C. Carr, "Art Crimes," in *On Edge: Performance at the End of the Twentieth Century* (Middletown, CT: Wesleyan University Press, 2008), 74–75.
65 Hughes-Freeland interview.
66 Carr, "Art Crimes," 74.
67 The third edition of the NYFFD lists as its sponsors the *East Village Eye*, Film/Video Arts (which is funded by the New York State Council for the Arts and The National Endowment for the Arts), Cornelius Conboy and Dennis Gattra (owners and programmers of the then already defunct 8BC), and Rafik (of Rafik Video). In comparison: the second edition in 1985 listed the *East Village Eyes*, 8BC, Chandelier (Troyano's own club) as its sponsors.

68 Sarah Schulman, "Flaming Creatures: The Other New York Film Festival," *Village Voice*, October 20, 1987.
69 Carr, "Art Crimes," 75.
70 Richard Kern, in discussion with the author, October 4, 2018.
71 Nick Zedd, "Master of Transgression," interview by Jack Sargeant, *Deathtripping: The Cinema of Transgression* (London: Creation Books, 1995), 98.
72 Nick Zedd, *Totem of the Depraved* (Los Angeles: Two Thirteen Sixty-One Publications, 1996), 51.
73 *East Village Eye*, October 1985.
74 Thomas Elsaesser, *European Cinema: Face to Face with Hollywood* (Amsterdam: Amsterdam University Press, 2005), 94–95. For his remarks on the festival as event, Elsaesser refers to Jacques Derrida's *Limited Inc.* which includes several essays originally published in 1977.
75 Elsaesser, *European Cinema*, 90–91.
76 Skadi Loist, "The Film Festival Circuit: Networks, Hierarchies, and Circulation," in *Film Festivals: History, Theory, Method, Practice*, ed. Marijke de Valck, Brendan Kredell, and Skadi Loist (London: Routledge, 2016), 49–64.
77 Loist, "The Film Festival Circuit," 59.
78 Bill Nichols, "Global Image Consumption in the Age of Late Capitalism," *East-West Film Journal* 8, no. 1 (1994): 68. However, Nichols sees the local and the global as being equally embedded in each other. Also, he argues that when local (national) cinemas enter the global festival circuit, rather than the audience discovering concealed meaning in them, new meanings are being produced.
79 Elsaesser, *European Cinema*, 96.
80 Marijke de Valck, "Fostering Art, Adding Value, Cultivating Taste: Film Festivals as Sites of Cultural Legitimization," in *Film Festivals: History, Theory, Method, Practice*, ed. Marijke de Valck, Brendan Kredell, and Skadi Loist (London: Routledge, 2016), 100–116. For an extensive discussion of European film festivals as *sites des passage*, see Marijke de Valck, *Film Festivals: From European Geopolitics to Global Cinephilia* (Amsterdam: Amsterdam University Press, 2007).
81 Hughes-Freeland, interview.
82 Troyano, interview.
83 Troyano, interview.
84 "We just decided on random reasons." Tessa Hughes-Freeland, e-mail message to author, December 7, 2018.
85 Hughes-Freeland, interview.
86 Jürgen Brüning, in discussion with the author, November 7, 2018.
87 Keith J. Sanborn, *Super-8/Berlin: The Architecture of Division* (Buffalo, NY: Hallwalls, 1983), 2.
88 Sanborn, *Super-8/Berlin*, 17.
89 Sanborn, *Super-8/Berlin*, 2.
90 The selection included a significant number of films made by filmmakers often associated with the CoT, such as Manuel DeLanda, Richard Kern, Erotic Psyche, Tommy Turner, Cassandra Stark, and M. Henry Jones, along with Tessa Hughes-Freeland and Ela Troyano themselves.
91 Torsten Alisch, "Sucking the City Pulse: Interview with Penelope Buitenhuis," in *Berlin: Images in Progress*, ed. Jürgen Brüning and Andreas Wildfang (Buffalo, NY: Hallwalls, 1989), 38.
92 Judith Fleishman, "The Shit Hits the Screen," *Say!*, November 1986.

93 "Ungewöhnliche Filme direkt aus New York," *Neue Westfälische*, March 19, 1986, 1, my translation; Anke Sterneborg, "Das ursprüngliche New York," *Der Tagesspiegel*, March 16, 1986, 64, my translation.
94 Berlin Mix, a special film screening held at the Lower East Side hip-hop club Hotel Amazon, was promoted as screening "Rare and seldom seen films from NYFFD filmmakers featured at the Quartier Latin, Berlin 1988." Given that the prefix "New York" surely helped attract German audiences to the NYFFD screenings, one can assume that this logic also works in the other direction, that evoking Berlin will attract New Yorkers.
95 "Kino in der Unterstadt," *tip* 17, no. 5 (1988): 48, my translation.
96 Karen Rosenberg, "A Cinematically Divided City," in *Berlin: Images in Progress*, ed. Jürgen Brüning and Andreas Wildfang (Buffalo, NY: Hallwalls, 1989), 15–16. Rosenberg perceives Berlin to be a "cinematically divided" city in which the 16 mm and Super 8 scenes hardly overlap. She specifies that she found the latter to be less competitive than the former, which is mostly made up of film students competing for grants, which implies that 16 or 35 mm was generally considered to be the more serious format.
97 Brüning, interview. Accounts of the screening of *Fingered* can also be found in newspaper articles by Helga Lukoschat ("Macho-Politik," *taz*, March 23, 1988, http://www.taz.de/Archiv-Suche/!1851476&s=helga%2Blukoschat&SuchRahmen=Print/) and C. C. Malzahn ("Zensur mit der Rohrenstange," *taz*, March 23, 1988, http://www.taz.de/!1851472/) and in virtually every feature on Eiszeit Kino that can be found online.

Chapter 3   Film Happens

1 Tessa Hughes-Freeland, "Shifting the Psychotic Treadmill," *East Village Eye*, February 1986, 43.
2 Karen Finley played the conservative mother in Richard Kern's family homicide story *You Killed Me First* (1985); Kembra Pfahler appeared in Kern's *Sewing Circle* (1992) and Zedd's *War Is Menstrual Envy* (1992) and made her own performance films such as *Cornella: The Story of a Burning Bush* (1985) and *Mild Seven: The Cowboy Stories* (ca. 1986); and Lydia Lunch performed in films by Vivienne Dick (*She Had Her Gun All Ready*, 1978, *Beauty Becomes the Beast*, 1979), Beth and Scott B (*Vortex*, 1982), and Nick Zedd (*The Wild World of Lydia Lunch*, 1982). She repeatedly collaborated with Kern, most notably on the making of *Right Side of My Brain* (1985) and *Fingered* (1986), for which she wrote both the screenplay and the music. Manuel DeLanda's *Raw Nerves. A Lacanian Thriller* (1979) was cowritten by Joe Coleman. He also wrote and read a poem in DeLanda's *Harmful or Fatal If Swallowed* (1982) and starred in Tommy Turner and Wojnarowicz's *Where Evil Dwells* (1985) and Jeri Cain Rossi's *Black Hearts Bleed Red* (1992).
3 Wendy Perron, "Voices of Many Voices," *SoHo Weekly News*, December 15, 1977. In the 1970s, the first reviews and studies of individual performances were published, followed by more general studies and attempts to place the notion of performance within contemporary culture and tradition. See Marvin Carlson, *Performance: A Critical Introduction* (London: Routledge, 1996).
4 Sally Banes, *Subversive Expectations: Performance Art and Paratheater in New York, 1976–85* (Ann Arbor: University of Michigan Press, 1998), 264.
5 Ronald K. Fried, "John Jesurun's 'Chang in a Void Moon,'" *Drama Review* 27, no. 2 (1983): 73.

6 John Hagan, "John Jesurun," *Artforum*, Features, October 1999, https://www.artforum.com/print/199908/john-jesurun-843.
7 Dancenoise, like many other performers of the era, moved on to more prestigious art institutions and theaters such as Lincoln Center, and a week-long presentation at the Whitney Museum in 2015 featured documentation of their performances as well as newly commissioned works by the duo. See "Dancenoise: Don't Look Back," Whitney Museum of Art, Exhibitions, July 22–26, 2015, https://whitney.org/Exhibitions/Dancenoise.
8 Banes, *Subversive Expectations*, 264.
9 Jill Dolan, "Carmelita Tropicana Chats at the Club Chandelier," *Drama Review* 29, no. 1 (1985): 31–32.
10 Dolan, "Carmelita Tropicana," 29.
11 Jacki Apple, "Performance in the Eighties: The TV Generation," in *Performance/ Media/ Art/ Culture: Selected Essays 1983–2018*, ed. Marina La Palma (Bristol, UK: Intellect, 2019), 3.
12 Banes, *Subversive Expectations*, 267.
13 Charles Tarzian, "8BC—From Farmhouse to Cabaret," *Drama Review* 29, no. 1 (1985): 109.
14 Here I specifically refer to Picabia's *Relâche* (1924) as well as to the activities at Black Mountain College in the 1950s. In both instances, artists, composers, filmmakers, and dancers got together to create live events that eluded clear categorization. As scripted live situations that are performed for an audience and mix different art forms, they both serve as historical reference points for what Kostelanetz would later call "Theatre of Mixed Means."
15 Dick Higgins, "Intermedia," in *Horizons* (Ubu Editions, 2007), 27, http://www.ubu.com/ubu/higgins_horizons.html; Richard Kostelanetz, *The Theatre of Mixed Means: An Introduction to Happenings, Kinetic Environments, and Other Mixed-Means Performances* (New York: Dial Press, 1968); Gene Youngblood, *Expanded Cinema* (New York: E. P. Dutton and Co. Inc., 1970).
16 Erika Balsom, "Live and Direct: Cinema as a Performing Art," *Artforum*, September 2014, https://www.artforum.com/print/201407/live-and-direct-cinema-as-a-performing-art-47842.
17 Gabriel Menotti, *Movie Circuits: Curatorial Approaches to Cinema Technology* (Amsterdam: Amsterdam University Press, 2019), 24.
18 Erika Balsom, *After Uniqueness: Film and Video Art in Circulation* (New York: Columbia University Press, 2017), 181.
19 Balsom, "Live and Direct."
20 This understanding was put forward most famously by Peggy Phelan in *Unmarked: The Politics of Performance* (London: Routledge, 1993).
21 Rebecca Schneider, *Performing Remains: Art and War in Times of Theatrical Reenactment* (New York: Routledge, 2011), 101f.
22 Kostelanetz, *The Theatre of Mixed Means*, 41.
23 Kostelanetz, *The Theatre of Mixed Means*, 9.
24 John Kelly, "Club Performance," in *John Kelly* (New York: 2wice books, 2001), 50.
25 For example, Chase did the camerawork and Snyder was responsible for the set design of the films *Pass the Blutwurst, Bitte* (1984) and *Diary of a Somnambulist* (1986). The former film evolves around the life of the Viennese Expressionist artist Egon Schiele; the latter is inspired by Robert Wiene's silent film *The Cabinet of Dr. Caligari* (1919). Both films were integrated into live performances by Kelly, which, for their part, exist in different variations.

26 Anthony Chase, phone interview with the author, June 20, 2019.
27 Sophie Cavoulacos, Kate Zembrano, and Sean Yetter, "*The City Stars*: Performing Gender Downtown," MoMA, Art and Artists, Magazine, July 8, 2019, https://www.moma.org/magazine/articles/117?fbclid=IwAR3UXS01uyyP-IOVK6-PxozjSHJM2qunaVlgCFooDIl00wv3Z0eKsxIJN-g.
28 Dagmar Onassis's full name refers to her mother's birth name, Maria Anna Cecilia Sofia Kalogeropoulos.
29 The film continued to be screened on its own, most recently at MoMA in 2018 in a series that accompanied the exhibition *Club 57: Film, Performance, and Art in the East Village, 1978–1983*.
30 John Kelly, "The Birth of Dagmar Onassis," in *John Kelly* (New York: 2wice books, 2001), 45.
31 John Kelly, "In Praise of Drag," in *John Kelly* (New York: 2wice books, 2001), 55.
32 Judith Butler, *Bodies That Matter: On the Discursive Limits of "Sex"* (New York: Routledge, 1993), 129.
33 C. Carr, "Silence = Life," in *On Edge: Performance at the End of the Century* (Middletown, CT: Wesleyan University Press, 2008), 351.
34 The mentioned performers were particularly active in the orbit of the Pyramid Club, where they were regular contributors (as drag performers or hosts of events) and also acted as facilitators and supporters. Butterick, for instance, was owner and manager of the Pyramid Club and fundamentally encouraged its queer and experimental programing that allowed a community to emerge in and through the club.
35 Gerald Rabkin, "Theatre of the Ridiculous: An Introduction," *Performing Arts Journal* 3, no. 1 (1978): 41.
36 Kelly I. Aliano, *Theatre of the Ridiculous: A Critical History* (Jefferson, NC: McFarland and Company, 2019), 6.
37 Jack Smith designed posters for the Ridiculous Theatrical Company productions, such as *Big Hotel*, written and directed by Charles Ludlam, and created costumes for Vaccaro's Playhouse of the Ridiculous. His influence on Ludlam and Vaccaro is strongly emphasized in all scholarly works on the Ridiculous Theatre cited here (Aliano's *Theatre of the Ridiculous* and Rabkin's "Theatre of the Ridiculous: An Introduction").
38 Marc Siegel, "Ridiculous Screenplays," in *Andy Warhol's Ridiculous Screenplays*, ed. Ronald Tavel (Silverton, OR: Fast Books, 2015), xxi.
39 For instance, at the Wigstock Benefit at the Pyramid Club in 1987, John Kelly performed as Dagmar Onassis, singing a Joni Mitchell song. See "John Kelly as Dagmar Onassis as Joni Mitchell at the Wigstock Benefit in 1987," May 13, 1987, video, 4:02, September 7, 2011, https://www.youtube.com/watch?v=iWGspFxRnJA.
40 "Palladium, Michael Musto's *Downtown* Party, Card, 1986," Gallery 98, Ephemera, Palladium, https://gallery98.org/2018/palladium-michael-mustos-downtown-party-card-1986/. This invitation for Palladium's publication party for Michael Musto's *Downtown*, held on May 28, 1986, advertises a midnight show with Gabriel Rotello's Downtown Follies, featuring John Kelly, Dagmar Onassis, and Helen Wheels, which was emceed by Gary Dee as Joan Rivers.
41 Joe E. Jeffreys, "Madame Dagmar Onassis Speaks (and Sings)!," *Outweek*, March 27, 1991, 54–56.
42 Sybille Krämer and Doris Kolesch, "Stimmen im Konzert der Disziplinen," in *Stimme*, ed. Sybille Krämer and Doris Kolesch (Frankfurt, Germany: Suhrkamp, 2006), 7–15.

43 Krämer and Kolesch, "Stimmen im Konzert der Disziplinen," 12, my translation.
44 Roland Barthes, *A Lover's Discourse: Fragments*, trans. Richard Howard (New York: Hill and Wang, 1978) 34–36.
45 Doris Kolesch, "Die Spur der Stimme: Überlegungen zu einer performativen Ästhetik," in *Medien/Stimmen*, ed. Cornelia Epping-Jäger and Erika Linz (Cologne, Germany: DuMont, 2003), 257, my translation.
46 Sigrid Weigel, "Die Stimme als Medium des Nachlebens: Pathosformel, Nachhall, Phantom," in *Stimme*, ed. Sybille Krämer and Doris Kolesch (Frankfurt, Germany: Suhrkamp, 2006), 16–39.
47 Ingeborg Bachmann, quoted in Weigel, "Die Stimme als Medium des Nachlebens," 25.
48 Anthony Chase, e-mail message to author, June 4, 2019.
49 "'Me Minus You' By Nick Zedd, Phoebe LeGere, and Jessica Jason [Script], 1985," Guide to the Nick Zedd Papers, 1963–2016, MSS.311, Series I: Writing, Subseries A: Zedd A–Z, box 2, folder 27, Fales Library and Special Collections, New York University, https://findingaids.library.nyu.edu/fales/mss_311/contents/aspace_ref1/#aspace_ref12.
50 On flyers and in the *Underground Film Bulletin*, it was usually described as an Expanded Cinema Performance. A performance/film weekend at Hallwalls in Buffalo, New York, held September 27–29, 1985, announced "An Ordeal with Nick Zedd" for Friday, September 27 ("Nick Zedd's Theatre of Shame presents SHE, a performance written in collaboration with Lydia Lunch, featuring Nick Zedd. Zedd will also screen films including *The Wild World of Lydia Lunch*... and *They Eat Scum*") and "Nick Zedd: Theater of Shame" for Saturday, September 28 ("Nick Zedd's Theatre of Shame presents ME MINUS YOU, a performance featuring Nick Zedd, Phoebe Legere and Eric Pryor, and including *Thrust in Me*, [Richard Kern and Nick Zedd]. Followed by Zedd's *Monster Movie, aka Geek Maggot Bingo*"). In an interview with Nicholas Zurbrugg, Zedd mentions the terms "performance thing" and "live movie" (Nicholas Zurbrugg, "Nick Zedd," in *Art, Performance, Media: 31 Interviews* [Minneapolis: University of Minnesota Press, 2004], 383).
51 James Fenwick, Kieran Foster, and David Eldridge, "Introduction," in *Shadow Cinema: The Historical Production Contexts of Unmade Films*, ed. James Fenwick, Kieran Foster, and David Eldridge (New York: Bloomsbury Academic, 2021), 1–14.
52 "At the time, in 1985, I was really broke and I couldn't afford to buy film and shoot anything, so I thought I'll write this thing and perform it live—it'll be like a live movie" (Zurbrugg, "Nick Zedd," 383).
53 The Nick Zedd Papers at New York University's Fales Library include two video-tape recordings of *Me Minus You* performances. However, as most audiovisual materials from this collection have not yet been preserved, they are not available to researchers.
54 Jonathan Gray, *Show Sold Separately: Promos, Spoilers, and Other Media Paratexts* (New York: New York University Press, 2010), 4; Amelia Jones, "'Presence' in Absentia: Experiencing Performance as Documentation," *Art Journal* 56, no. 4 (1997): 11.
55 Jones, "'Prescence' in Absentia," 11.
56 Gray, *Show Sold Separately*, 6.
57 Gray, *Show Sold Separately*, 7.
58 Jack Smith, "Jack Smith Film Enterprises, Inc.," in *Wait for Me at the Bottom of the Pool: The Writings of Jack Smith*, ed. J. Hoberman and Edward Leffingwell (London: Serpent's Tail, 1997), 149.

59 Uzi Parnes, "Jack Smith: Legendary Filmmaker, Theatrical Genius, and Exotic Art Consultant," in *European Media Art Festival [EMAF]* (1994): 166, http://uziny.com/Uzi_Parnes_on_Jack_Smith-94.pdf.

60 Smith deployed a similar procedure in his live appearances, which "were commonly accompanied by slideshows and silent film rushes, while the artist played sound effects and LPs from his collection. Known for their trailing duration and provisional rehearsal-like nature, these events saw relatively small audiences, though the marquee-esque flyers that announce them promise entertainment on a spectacular scale" (*Jack Smith: Art Crust of Spiritual Oasis* [New York: Artists Space, 2018], 3, https://texts.artistsspace.org/5az3hjnw).

61 Fried, "John Jesurun's 'Chang in a Void Moon,'" 73.

62 Fried, "John Jesurun's 'Chang in a Void Moon,'" 74.

63 "'Me Minus You' [Script], 1985."

64 The Dream Syndicate, "John Coltrane Stereo Blues," track 7 on *Medicine Show*, A&M, 1984.

65 Zedd also assumed his drag character on private nights out: "One night, after I got made up in drag, a bunch of us went to a girl named Tessa's apartment, high on dope, vodka and mushrooms." Nick Zedd, *Totem of the Depraved* (Los Angeles: Two Thirteen Sixty-One Publications, 1996), 5.

66 "'Me Minus You' [Flyers], c1985," Guide to the Nick Zedd Papers, 1963–2016, MSS.311, Series II: Projects, Subseries B: Distribution, box 6, folder 63, Fales Library and Special Collections, New York University, https://findingaids.library.nyu.edu/fales/mss_311/contents/aspace_ref2/#aspace_ref17.

67 Zurbrugg, "Nick Zedd," 384.

68 Nick Zedd, untitled report on *Me Minus You*, in *Underground Film Bulletin*, no. 3 (1985): 23.

69 Schneider, *Performing Remains*, 100.

70 C. Carr, "Loisaida Talking Pictures," in *On Edge: Performance at the End of the Twentieth Century* (Middletown, CT: Wesleyan University Press, 2008), 79.

71 Death stared in Zedd's *They Eat Scum* (1979) and *Geek Maggot Bingo* (1983). The trained composer Legere worked as resident composer for New York multidisciplinary company The Wooster Group and had a career as a singer and musician but was also involved in the filmmaking scene, variously as codirector, performer, and composer. Parnes was a photographer, filmmaker, and writer, who began collaborating with Ela and Alina Troyano in the 1980s. Jack Smith, who had been making films, performing, and taking photographs since the 1950s, met Troyano and Parnes through John Zorn and became a friend, mentor, and collaborator. Smith starred in other films made by the younger generation of Super 8 filmmakers. He played, for instance, the role of Dr. Shrinkelstein in Beth and Scott B's *The Trap Door* (1980). Shortly after the making of *Bubble People*, Troyano and Parnes founded and ran Club Chandelier, a small, short-lived bar and performance space located on the East Village's Avenue C, where said friends and collaborators regularly gathered and performed.

72 Tessa Hughes-Freeland, "Interview with Ela Troyano," in *Underground Film Bulletin*, no. 3 (1985): 48.

73 Carr, "Loisaida Talking Pictures," 82.

74 "I wanted to give the actors a script, but I wanted them to choose where they played the scenes and which props they used so they could move them from one scene to another." Ela Troyano interviewed by Tessa Hughes-Freeland in *Underground Film Bulletin*, no. 3 (1985): 48.

75 "It [*Bubble People*] was my first film and it was not like I had really thought it through. And so I thought, let's have a solo and a duo. I was using the same kinds of scores that I had used with John Zorn when he wanted to do an experiment. For example, when he wanted to work with three projectionists, he would give us a score and have us use the projectors for whatever we were using to project as musical instruments. So he would say, have a phrase, and then repeat it. Two of you repeat the phrase together, a duo. Three do it, and then improvise on the one phrase and then add to it. So, it was just writing it down [for *Bubble People*]. First, we're gonna have a trio, then a duo. Then a solo. Then a group." Ela Troyano in discussion with the author, October 2, 2019.

76 John Zorn, "The Game Pieces," in *Audio Culture: Readings in Modern Music*, ed. Christoph Cox and Daniel Warner (New York: Bloomsbury, 2017), 275.

77 Ela Troyano, e-mail message to author, July 29, 2019.

78 Ela Troyano, in discussion with the author, October 2, 2019.

79 Dominic Johnson, *Glorious Catastrophe: Jack Smith, Performance and Visual Culture* (Manchester, UK: Manchester University Press, 2012), 40, 43.

80 José Esteban Muñoz, *Cruising Utopia: The Then and There of Queer Futurity* (New York: New York University Press, 2019), 173.

81 Michael Moon, "Flaming Closets," *October* 51 (1989): 50.

82 In a press release for *Hamlet in the Rented Island*, dated 1971 and addressed to Anthology Film Archives, he writes about the Reptilian Acting Technique, that it "rests on the premise that everybody already is a fine actor . . . and that it's the fault of the theatre that nothing of this can survive on the stage because of the way that the drama is stamped out of everything on the stage, which has turned the actor into a Jelly—a thing that can only memorize lines." Jack Smith, "ACTAVISTIC, ACTION PACKED; ACTION ACTING OF PFA: *HAMLET* and the 1001 Psychologic Jingoleanisms of Prehistoric Landlordism of Rima-Puu," in *Wait for Me at the Bottom of the Pool*, 166.

83 Troyano, interview, October 2, 2019.

84 Troyano, interview, September 7, 2018.

85 Lydia Lunch acted, for example, in Vivienne Dick's *Guérillère Talks* (1978), *She Had Her Gun All Ready* (1978), *Beauty Becomes the Beast* (1979), *Liberty's Booty* (1980), and *Like Dawn to Dusk* (1983); in Beth and Scott B's *Black Box* (1978), *The Offenders* (1980), and *Vortex* (1982); in Nick Zedd's *The Wild World of Lydia Lunch* (1983) and *School of Shame* (1984); in Richard Kern's *The Right Side of My Brain* (1984), *Submit to Me* (1985), *Fingered* (1986), and *Submit to Me Now* (1987).

86 Callie Angell, *Andy Warhol Screen Tests: The Films of Andy Warhol Catalogue Raisonné, Volume 1* (New York: Abrams, 2006), 14; Jonathan Flatley, "Collecting and Collectivity," *October* 132 (2010): 92.

87 Flatley, "Collecting and Collectivity," 92. See also Jonathan Flatley, "Allegories of Boredom," in *A Minimal Future? Art as Object 1958–1968*, ed. Ann Goldstein (Cambridge, MA: MIT Press, 2004), 51–76.

88 Zedd, *Totem of the Depraved*, 33–34.

89 Troyano, interview, October 2, 2019.

90 Troyano, interview, October 2, 2019.

91 Homay King, "Stroboscopic: Warhol and the Exploding Plastic Inevitable," *Criticism* 56, no. 3 (2014): 469.

92 Philip Auslander, *Liveness: Performance in a Mediatized Culture* (London: Routledge, 1999), 20.

93 King, "Stroboscopic," 470.

94 Embracing (technical) mistakes and making them part of the work was common practice for Jack Smith as well. Uzi Parnes quotes P. Adams Sitney about the making of Smith's film *Scotch Tape* (1959–1962), which was shot on the set of Ken Jacobs's *Star Spangled to Death* (1957–1959): "*Scotch Tape* ... appears to have been constructed in the camera without much subsequent editing, if any ... He [Jacobs] had shot several rolls of film before he realized that the tape had gotten caught in the camera. Rather than let this accident ruin his film, Smith capitalized upon it in his title" (Parnes, "Jack Smith: Legendary Filmmaker, Theatrical Genius, and Exotic Art Consultant," 163).

95 Erhard Schüttpelz, "Akademie der Dilettanten (Back to D.)," in *Akademie*, ed. Stephan Dillemuth (Cologne, Germany: Permanent Press, 1995), 40–57.

96 Ela Troyano interviewed by Tessa Hughes Freeland, in *Underground Film Bulletin*, no. 3 (1985): 51.

97 Carr, "Loisaida Talking Pictures," 78, 82, 79.

98 Balsom, *After Uniqueness*, 178.

99 See for instance Auslander, *Liveness*; Philipp Auslander, "The Performativity of Performance Documentation," *Performance Art Journal* 28, no. 3 (2006): 1–10; Mechtild Widrich, "The Informative Public of Performance. A Study of Viennese Actionism, 1965–1970," *Drama Review* 57, no. 1 (2013): 137–151.

100 André Lepecki, "The Body as Archive: Will to Re-Enact and the Afterlives of Dances," *Dance Research Journal* 42, no. 2 (2010): 31.

101 Paul Clarke, Simon Jones, Nick Kaye, and Johanna Linsley, "Introduction: Inside and Outside the Archive," in *Artists in the Archive: Creative and Curatorial Engagements with Documents of Art and Performance*, ed. Paul Clarke, Simon Jones, Nick Kaye, and Johanna Linsley (London: Routledge, 2018), 15.

102 Jonas Mekas, "Movie Journal," *Village Voice*, November 18, 1965, 21.

103 The script for *Rehearsal for the Destruction of Atlantis* is featured in the revised edition of Bonnie Marranca and Gautam Dasgupta's book *The Theatre of the Ridiculous* (Baltimore: John Hopkins University Press, 1998).

104 Muñoz, *Cruising Utopia*, 169.

105 Jack Smith, "Capitalism of Lotusland," in *Wait for Me at the Bottom of the Pool*, 11; Jack Smith, "What's Underground About Marshmallows," in *Wait for Me at the Bottom of the Pool*, 140.

106 "Recycling Atlantis," New York University Steinhardt School of Culture, Education, and Human Development, Department of Art and Art Professions, 80WSE Gallery, November 12–14, 2014, https://steinhardt.nyu.edu/80wse/gallery/2014/10/recyclingatlantis.

107 *Jack Smith: Art Crust of Spiritual Oasis*, 8. For a comprehensive consideration of New York's loft performance scene, see *Rituals of Rented Island: Object Theater, Loft Performance, and the New Psychodrama: Manhattan 1970–1980*, ed. Jay Sanders and J. Hoberman (New York: Whitney Museum of American Art, 2013).

108 J. Hoberman, "'Like Canyons and Rivers': Performance for Its Own Sake," in Sanders and Hoberman, *Rituals of Rented Island*, 12.

109 John Matturri, "Jack Smith: Notes on Some Homeless Objects," *Criticism* 56, no. 2 (2014): 283–284.

Chapter 4   Afterlife Formats

1 The press release can be found on the KW Institute for Contemporary Art website (Program, Archive, 2012, *You Killed Me First*, February 19–April 2, 2012, https://www.kw-berlin.de/en/you-killed-me-first/). The tape's synopsis reads as follows:

"Compilation of films made by avant-garde filmmakers and artists based in the New York City's Lower East Side between 1979 to 1993. In 1984 the manifesto for the 'Cinema of Transgression' was announced, a movement looking to transform values by breaking all taboos of cinematic expression, conservative religion, politics, and aesthetics." The tape includes, in this order, *Nymphomania* (1993) by Tessa Hughes-Freeland and Holly Adams, *Baby Doll* (1982) by Tessa Hughes-Freeland, *Police State* (1987) by Nick Zedd, *The Evil Cameraman* (1990) by Richard Kern, *Stigmata* (1991) by Beth B, *Black Hearts Bleed Red* (1992) by Jeri Cain Rossi, *Soul City* (1979) by M. Henry Jones, *Where Evil Dwells* (1985) by Tommy Turner and David Wojnarowicz, *Cornella: The Story of a Burning Bush* (1985) by Kembra Pfahler, and *Mommy, Mommy, Where's My Brain?* (1986) by Jon Moritsugu.

2 Julia Knight and Peter Thomas, *Reaching Audiences: Distribution and Promotion of Alternative Moving Image* (Bristol, UK: Intellect, 2011), 107. The quote is taken from British Film Institute, "Publicising and Distributing Film and Television," February 23, 1982, 3, British Film Institute Archive, Library, box 32, Distribution Division 1980–87.

3 The films are *Shithaus* by John Spencer, *Worm Movie* by Lung Leg, *A Suicide* by Richard Klemann, *The Bogus Man* and *Go To Hell* by Nick Zedd (codirected by David Rutsala), *Mutable Fire* by Erotic Psyche, *Simonland* by Tommy Turner, *You Killed Me First* and *King of Sex* by Richard Kern, *N——Night* by Manuel Wolfe, and *Judgement Day* and *Ism Ism* by Manuel DeLanda. Other sources date the release of the VHS to 1986. However, the fourth issue of the *Underground Film Bulletin* (1985) already includes an ad for ordering the tape.

4 Brian Larkin, *Signal and Noise: Media, Infrastructure, and Urban Culture in Nigeria* (Durham, NC: Duke University Press, 2008), 5.

5 Axel Volmar, Marek Jancovic, and Alexandra Schneider, "Format Matters: An Introduction to Format Studies," in *Format Matters: Standards, Practices, and Politics in Media Cultures*, ed. Axel Volmar, Marek Jancovic, and Alexandra Schneider (Lüneburg, Germany: Meson Press, 2020), 10, 11.

6 Benoît Turquety, *Medium, Format, Configuration: The Displacements of Film* (Lüneburg, Germany: Meson Press, 2019), 51.

7 Michael Z. Newman argues that in the very first phase of its history, the era of the development of broadcasting, "video was another word for television," denoting the same notion of liveness and immediacy and thus holding the same cultural value. It was only in the second phase, when television was already established as the dominant medium, that videotape and related new technologies marked video as distinct from television and as both an alternative and a solution to some of television's problems, namely its economic and ideological influence over its audience. See Michael Z. Newman, *Video Revolutions: On the History of a Medium* (New York: Columbia University Press, 2014) 2–4, 21.

8 Christina Bartz, "Video. Vom Alternativfernsehen zum Massenmedium," in *Formationen der Mediennutzung III: Dispositive Ordnungen im Umbau*, ed. Irmela Schneider and Cornelia Epping-Jäger (Bielefeld, Germany: Transcript Publishing, 2008), 135, my translation. Although Bartz writes from a German perspective, the same is true for the United States, since its consumer and distribution market evolved in a similar way.

9 Tobias Haupts, *Die Videothek: Zur Geschichte und medialen Praxis einer kulturellen Instituion* (Bielefeld, Germany: Transcript Publishing, 2014), 80.

10 Monday/Wednesday/Friday Video Club, http://www.brickhaus.com/amoore/MWFdoc1.html.

11 Joshua M. Greenberg, *From Betamax to Blockbuster: Video Stores and the Invention of Movies on Video* (Cambridge, MA: MIT Press, 2008), 65, 66.
12 Greenberg, *From Betamax to Blockbuster*, 42.
13 However, the re-creation of the cinema space in the home did indeed become a popular practice. For an in-depth analysis of the home theater, see Barbara Klinger, *Beyond the Multiplex: Cinema, New Technologies, and the Home* (Berkeley: University of California Press, 2006).
14 Raymond Bellour, "The Pensive Spectator," trans. Lynne Kirby, *Wide Angle* 9, no. 1 (1987): 6–10; Vinzenz Hediger, "'You Haven't Seen It Until You've Seen It Twice': Film Spectatorship and the Discipline of Repeat Viewing," *Cinéma and Cie*, no. 5 (2004): 36.
15 Uma Dinsmore-Tuli, "The Pleasures of 'Home Cinema,' or Watching Movies on Telly: An Audience Study of Cinephiliac VCR Use," *Screen* 41, no. 3 (2000): 327.
16 Magazines for videophiles and video hobbyists included advice on how to care for videotapes noting that they were best stored vertically, like a book. See Greenberg, *From Betamax to Blockbuster*, 44.
17 Roland Barthes, *Die Vorbereitung des Romans, Vorlesung am Collège de France 1978–1979 und 1979–1980*, ed. Éric Marty (Frankfurt, Germany: Suhrkamp, 2008), 290, my translation; Anke Kramer and Annegret Pelz, eds., *Album: Organisationsform narrativer Kohärenz* (Göttingen, Germany: Wallstein, 2013), 12.
18 Petra McGillen, "Kompilieren," in *Historisches Wörterbuch des Mediengebrauchs*, ed. Heiko Christians, Nikolaus Wegmann, and Matthias Bickenbach (Cologne, Germany: Böhlau, 2014), 355, my translation.
19 McGillen, "Kompilieren," 357, 358.
20 Duncan Reekie, *Subversion: The Definitive History of Underground Cinema* (London: Wallflower Press, 2007), 133.
21 Reekie, *Subversion*, 140.
22 Mark McKenna, "Whose Canon Is It Anyway? Subcultural Capital, Cultural Distinction and Value in High Art and Low Culture," in *Cult Media: Re-Packaged, Re-Released, and Restored*, ed. Jonathan Wroot and Andy Willis (London: Palgrave Macmillan, 2017), 45.
23 "Letter to the British Film Institute," Guide to the Nick Zedd Papers, 1963–2016, MSS.311, Series III: Correspondence, Subseries A: Professional, box 9, folder 12, Fales Library and Special Collections, New York University, https://findingaids.library.nyu.edu/fales/mss_311/contents/aspace_ref3/#aspace_ref21.
24 "He [Zedd] asked everyone for permission to use their films. He sold it to us as a promotion for the Cinema of Transgression." Richard Kern, e-mail message to author, March 25, 2020.
25 "When he [Nick Zedd] put out that VHS tape . . . , some people perceived that as the core group of films. But then he did these screenings on the moniker of Cinema of Transgression where he would basically show whatever he wanted to show." Tessa Hughes-Freeland, in discussion with the author, September 13, 2018.
26 Conceived in 1979 by a group of filmmakers, actors, writers, musicians, and artists, EZTV's first space opened in 1982 and housed a forty-seat video theater, an art gallery dedicated to new media art, and a media lab. It soon expanded to include a larger theater, another gallery space, a production studio, and video editing rooms. See "EZTV: Hacking the Timeline v3.0: Digilantism and the LA Digital Art Movement (1985–2005)," 18th Street Arts Center, Past Events and Exhibitions, April 14–June 27, 2014, https://18thstreet.org/eztv-hacking-timeline/.
27 Greenberg, *From Betamax to Blockbuster*, 52; Haupts, *Die Videothek*, 291.

28 "Penetration Films [Distribution Materials], various," Guide to the Nick Zedd Papers, 1963–2016, MSS.311, Series II: Projects, Subseries B: Distribution, box 7, folder 3, Fales Library and Special Collections, New York University, https://findingaids.library.nyu.edu/fales/mss_311/contents/aspace_ref2/#aspace_ref17; "[Penetration Films], various," Guide to the Nick Zedd Papers, 1963–2016, MSS.311, Series III: Correspondence, Subseries A: Professional, box 9, folder 22, Fales Library and Special Collections, New York University, https://findingaids.library.nyu.edu/fales/mss_311/contents/aspace_ref3/#aspace_ref21.
29 Haupts, *Die Videothek*, 35.
30 Kern, e-mail.
31 Kern, e-mail.
32 The New American Cinema Group, "First Statement of the New American Cinema," in *Film Manifestos and Global Cinema Cultures. A Critical Anthology*, ed. Scott MacKenzie (Berkeley: University of California Press, 2014), 58–60. Originally published in *Film Culture* 22–23 (1961): 131–133.
33 Erika Balsom, *After Uniqueness: A History of Film and Video Art in Circulation* (New York: Columbia University Press, 2017), 42.
34 Balsom, *After Uniqueness*, 136–137.
35 Balsom, *After Uniqueness*, 54ff.
36 Knight and Thomas, *Reaching Audiences*, 101–102.
37 Ulrike Rosenbach, "Video als Medium der Emanzipation," in *Videokunst in Deutschland 1963–1982: Videobänder, Installationen, Objekte, Performances*, ed. Wulf Herzogenrath (Stuttgart, Germany: Gerd Hatje, 1982), 101–102, my translation.
38 Balsom, *After Uniqueness*, 13.
39 Kern, e-mail.
40 *Film Threat* began as a low-circulation film zine in 1985 and later developed into a distributor who made exclusive U. S. deals with Kern as well as his New York peers Casandra Stark, Lydia Lunch, and Nick Zedd.
41 "Artware Production," Discogs, Label, https://www.discogs.com/label/9398-Artware-Production.
42 Photos of Artware's catalog 4 (1989) were posted to a listing on eBay but are no longer visible online at https://www.ebay.com/itm/Artware-Kata-4-1989-Alternative-Art-amp-Music-Catalog-John-Wayne-Gacy-/143433086566?nma=true&si=q%252FCxRb2LiofehyGVNFkYxVR4pII%253D&orig_cvip=true&nordt=true&rt=nc&_trksid=p2047675.l2557.
43 Hamm-Fürhölter wrote about the CoT for the Frankfurt-based *Filmhaus 68/69* (1988). See "Nick Zedd International Press Pack," "Cinema of Transgression Parts 1 and 2" by Cricket Delembard for *Draculina* Numbers 13–14 [Zines], 1992, Guide to the Nick Zedd Papers, 1963–2016, MSS.311, Series II: Projects, Subseries D: Ads, Reviews, and Literature, box 8, folder 37, Fales Library and Special Collections, New York University, https://findingaids.library.nyu.edu/fales/mss_311/contents/aspace_ref2/#aspace_ref19.
44 Flyer for Nick Zedd's Germany tour in "Tour '90: Nick Zedd Underground Filmmaker [Flyers] 1990," Guide to the Nick Zedd Papers, 1963–2016, MSS.311, Series II: Projects, Subseries B: Distribution, box 7, folder 23, Fales Library and Special Collections, New York University, https://findingaids.library.nyu.edu/fales/mss_311/contents/aspace_ref2/#aspace_ref17.
45 Johannes Schönherr, *Trashfilm Roadshows: Off the Beaten Track with Subversive Movies* (Manchester, UK: Headpress Books, 2002).

46 Joan Hawkins, "Burning Down the House: Community Access TV and the Downtown Art Shows," *Flow*, November 13, 2007, https://www.flowjournal.org/2007/11/burning-down-the-house-community-access-tv-and-the-Downtown-art-shows-1/.

47 In 1972, this was realized on a national level when the Federal Communications Commissions (FCC) issued the Cable Television Report and Order, which stated that any cable television system operating in the top 100 television markets had to provide access channels, which were divided into four classifications: public, educational, governmental, and leased access. Although the Supreme Court later ruled that the FCC could not require operators to provide access channels, they continued to develop throughout the country. See Barry T. Janes, "History and Structure of Public Access Television," *Journal of Film and Video* 39, no. 3 (1987): 14–23.

48 The number of cable systems grew from 70 with 14,000 subscribers to 7,471 with 4.3 million subscribers between 1950 and 1986. See Janes, "History and Structure of Public Access Television," 15.

49 In 1976, just before cable came to Downtown Manhattan, a group of artists and arts organizations formed a nonprofit called Cable Soho, which included Anthology Film Archives and the performance venues the Kitchen and Franklin Furnace. Renamed Artist's Television Network one year later, they created a television station for arts programming, renting tapes from individual artists, commissioning work, and producing original shows. They did this, however, on Manhattan Cable Television's own channel, Channel 10. See Leah Churner, "Un-TV: Public Access Cable Television in Manhattan; An Oral History," *Moving Image Source*, February 10, 2011, www.movingimagesource.us/articles/un-tv-20110210.

50 Churner, "Un-TV."

51 Deirdre Boyle, "Subject to Change: Guerrilla Television Revisited," *Art Journal* 45, no. 3 (1985): 228–232.

52 David Little, "Colab Takes a Piece, History Takes It Back: Collectivity and New York Alternative Spaces," *Art Journal* 66, no. 1 (2007): 64.

53 Reports of prices vary from $35 to $60 for an hour of black-and-white studio time, plus an additional $20 for tape recording. Other often more professional production facilities included Downtown Community TV, Young Filmmakers, Electronic Arts Intermix, and Community Film Workshop. See Churner, "Un-TV."

54 Benjamin Olin, "TV Party: A Cocktail Party That Could Also Be a Political Party," in *Downtown Film and TV Culture 1975–2001*, ed. Joan Hawkins (Bristol, UK: Intellect, 2015), 198, 199.

55 Olin, "TV Party," 200.

56 Ann Magnuson, "It Takes an East Village," in *Club 57: Performance and Art in the East Village, 1978–1982*, ed. Ron Magliozzi and Sophie Cavoulacos (New York: Museum of Modern Art, 2017), 157.

57 Original collage for Club 57 calendar, March 1980, Collection Ann Magnuson. Printed in *Club 57: Performance and Art in the East Village, 1978–1982*, ed. Ron Magliozzi and Sophie Cavoulacos (New York: Museum of Modern Art, 2017), 156.

58 https://www.dictionary.com/browse/nostomania.

59 Newman, *Video Revolutions*, 11.

60 Lynn Spigel, "Installing the Television Set: Popular Discourses on Television and Domestic Space, 1948–1955," in *Private Screenings: Television and the Female Consumer*, ed. Lynn Spigel and Denise Mann (Minneapolis: University of Minnesota Press, 1992), 4.

61 Spigel, "Installing the Television Set," 7, 8.

62 Spigel, "Installing the Television Set," 9.
63 C. Carr, "Bad Company at the Love Club," in *On Edge: Performance at the End of the Twentieth Century* (Middletown, CT: Wesleyan University Press, 2008), 96.
64 Carr, "Bad Company at the Love Club"; Michael Azerrad, "Notes from the Underground: Bad Music Video," *Optic Music* (1986): 32–33; Karen Finley and Michael Overn, e-mail messages to author, July 22–26, 2020.
65 Carr, "Bad Company at the Love Club," 95.
66 Newman, *Video Revolutions*, 10.
67 This is according to information I received after having contacted MMN's Programming Department via e-mail. When typing *The Adventures of Electra Elf* into the search engine on MMN's current website, no results appear. An interview with Nick Zedd on Vice.com gives different information, stating the following: "Manhattan Neighborhood Network originally aired it after school. The network quickly reconsidered and switched the show to a 1 A.M. slot, but it remained an enthusiastic supporter." Avi Davis, "Why Cinema of Transgression Director Nick Zedd Stayed Underground," *Vice*, June 6, 2014, https://www.vice.com/en_us/article/dpwd7v/a-new-breed-of-asshole-0000327-v21n5.
68 "Mission, Vision and Values," Manhattan Neighborhood Network, About, https://www.mnn.org/about/mission-vision-and-values.
69 Nick Zedd and David Sjöberg, "The Case of Electra Elf: Towards New Possibilities of Underground Counterculture in the Twenty-First Century," in *Downtown Film and TV Culture 1975–2001*, ed. Joan Hawkins (Bristol, UK: Intellect, 2015), 217.
70 Newman, *Video Revolutions*, 2.
71 808sANDadlibs, "Adventures of Electra Elf and Fluffer s01e02 Maggot on a Hot Tin Roof (2004)," Reddit, r/ObscureMedia, March 1, 2022, https://www.reddit.com/r/ObscureMedia/comments/t4lems/comment/hyz6qpu/.
72 "The Adventures of Electra Elf: The Complete Series," Amazon, Movies and TV, Featured Categories, DVD, Special Interests, Click image to open expanded view, https://www.amazon.com/Adventures-Electra-Elf-Complete/dp/B0034KVTOO.
73 Reverend Jen, "New York Magazine," Diary of an Art Star, April 12, 2010, https://reverendjen.wordpress.com/2010/04/12/new-york-magazine/.
74 Alex Vadukul, "Big Hair and Bad Luck: The Hard Times of the Troll Museum," *New York Times*, January 18, 2019, https://www.nytimes.com/2019/01/18/nyregion/big-hair-and-bad-luck-the-hard-times-of-the-troll-museum.html.
75 Davis, "Why Cinema of Transgression Director Nick Zedd Stayed Underground."
76 Davis, "Why Cinema of Transgression Director Nick Zedd Stayed Underground."
77 "Nick Zedd (1958–2022)," *Artforum*, News, February 28, 2022, https://www.artforum.com/news/nick-zedd-1958-2022-88031.
78 Klinger, *Beyond the Multiplex*, 19.
79 Kenneth Goldsmith, *Duchamp Is My Lawyer: The Polemics, Pragmatics, and Poetics of UbuWeb* (New York: Columbia University Press, 2020), 3.
80 Abigail De Kosnik, *Rogue Archives: Digital Cultural Memory and Media Fandom* (Cambridge, MA: MIT Press, 2016), 2, 18.
81 Goldsmith, *Duchamp Is My Lawyer*, 5.
82 Goldsmith, *Duchamp Is My Lawyer*, 10–11.
83 Goldsmith, *Duchamp Is My Lawyer*, 12.
84 See Laura Katharina Mücke, Olga Moskatova, and Chris Tedjasukmana, "Editorial: Messy Images–Unordnungen digital vernetzter Bilder," *Montage AV* 31, no. 1 (2022): 4–17. For a critical discussion of these metaphors within a media scholarly discourse, see Ghislain Thibault, "Streaming: A Media Hydrography of Televisual

Flows," *VIEW* 4, no. 7 (2015): 110–119, and Mathias Denecke, "Flows and Streams of Data: Notes on Metaphors in Digital Cultures," in *Explorations in Digital Cultures*, ed. Marcus Burkhardt, Mary Shnayien, and Katja Grashöfe (Lüneburg, Germany: Meson Press, 2020), 1–18, https://doi.org/10.25969/mediarep/14851.
85 Goldsmith, *Duchamp Is My Lawyer*, 78.
86 Goldsmith, *Duchamp Is My Lawyer*, 82–83. Operating out of various locations and under different names, Kim's was a video and music retail store in the East Village between the mid-1980s and 2014. It was notorious among film students and cinephiles, not least for its extensive collection and knowledgeable staff (including Nick Zedd). In 2005, the store made headlines after being raided by police for selling pirated movies. It reopened in 2022 under the name Kim's Video Underground. See Anna Rahmanan, "NYC's Iconic Kim's Video Is Reopening Inside the Alamo This Month," *Time Out*, March 22, 2022, https://www.timeout.com/newyork/news/nycs-iconic-kims-video-is-reopening-inside-the-alamo-this-month-032222.
87 Larkin, *Signal and Noise*, 218–219.
88 Lucas Hilderbrand, *Inherent Vice: Bootleg Histories of Videotape and Copyright* (Durham, NC: Duke University Press, 2009), 6.
89 Hilderbrand, *Inherent Vice*, 163.
90 Jesse Hultberg, YouTube, @jessehultberg, https://www.youtube.com/@jessehultberg.
91 In his biography, it is listed as follows: "1988: *Beautiful People*, starring Jesse Hultberg, approx. 30 minutes (soundtrack unfinished)." The David Wojnarowicz Papers at Fales Library include black and white as well as color Super 8 footage and outtakes of various lengths, dated 1988–1989: "Originals contains completed film works plus original source material by David Wojnarowicz. Access copies may not be available for all material," Guide to the David Wojnarowicz Papers, MSS.092, Series X: Video and Film, Subseries B: Film—Originals, Fales Library and Special Collections, New York University, https://findingaids.library.nyu.edu/fales/mss_092/contents/aspace_ref1643/#aspace_ref1840.
92 David Wojnariwicz, *Heroin*, 1981, https://mubi.com/en/us/films/heroin.
93 Tarleton Gillespie, "The Politics of 'Platforms,'" *New Media and Society* 12, no. 3 (2010): 347–364.
94 Thomas Poell, David B. Nieborg, and Brooke Erin Duffy, *Platforms and Cultural Production* (Cambridge, UK: Polity Press, 2022), 6.
95 De Kosnik, *Rogue Archives*, 3.
96 Andreas Bernard, *Theory of the Hashtag* (Cambridge, UK: Polity Press, 2019), 3.
97 Bernard, *Theory of the Hashtag*, 422.

Coda

1 Especially in the context of teaching. In a seminar at the University of Mainz (winter semester 2020–2021), I wanted to reflect on the practice of film history with students using the example of the historiography of the Cinema of Transgression. Given that none of the students were familiar with the Cinema of Transgression, however, a sense of dissatisfaction grew over the course of the term because I could not provide a clear definition of it. And even though many reacted with irritation to the polemics of the manifesto and the violence in the films, the greater majority was fascinated by the idea of a taboo-breaking film movement.
2 Donna J. Haraway, "A Game of Cat's Cradle: Science Studies, Feminist Theory, Cultural Studies," *Configurations* 2, no. 1 (1994): 60, 62.

Bibliography

Acker, Kathy. "Getting the Alphabet Right." Undated annotated typescript. Viewed in the exhibition *Kathy Acker: Get Rid of Meaning* at Badischer Kunstverein, Karlsruhe, Germany, October 5–December 2, 2018.

Acland, Charles. *Screen Traffic: Movies, Multiplexes, and Global Culture*. Durham, NC: Duke University Press, 2003.

Acland, Charles, and Haidee Wasson. "Introduction: Utility and Cinema." In *Useful Cinema*, edited by Charles Acland and Haidee Wasson, 1–14. Durham, NC: Duke University Press, 2011.

Adler, Melissa. *Cruising the Library: Perversities in the Organization of Knowledge*. New York: Fordham University Press, 2017.

Aliano, Kelly I. *Theatre of the Ridiculous: A Critical History*. Jefferson, NC: McFarland and Company, 2019.

Alisch, Torsten. "Sucking the City Pulse: Interview with Penelope Buitenhuis." In *Berlin: Images in Progress*, edited by Jürgen Brüning and Andreas Wildfang, 35–38. Buffalo, NY: Hallwalls, 1989.

Allen, Gwen. *Artist's Magazines: An Alternative Space for Art*. Cambridge, MA: MIT Press, 2011.

Alsous, Zaina. "'Spill' Maps a Future in Which Black Women Inherit the Universe," *Bitch Media*, October 13, 2017. https://www.bitchmedia.org/article/spill-scenes-black-feminist-fugitivity/alexis-pauline-gumbs.

Altman, Lawrence K. "Rare Cancer Seen in 41 Homosexuals." *New York Times*, July 3, 1981. https://www.nytimes.com/1981/07/03/us/rare-cancer-seen-in-41-homosexuals.html.

Angell, Callie. *Andy Warhol Screen Tests: The Films of Andy Warhol Catalogue Raisonné, Volume 1*. New York: Abrams, 2006.

Apple, Jacki. "Performance in the Eighties: The TV Generation." In *Performance/ Media/ Art/ Culture: Selected Essays 1983–2018*, edited by Marina La Palma, 3–11. Bristol, UK: Intellect, 2019.

Auslander, Philipp. *Liveness: Performance in a Mediatized Culture*. London: Routledge, 1999.

Auslander, Philipp. "The Performativity of Performance Documentation." *Performance Art Journal* 28, no. 3 (2006): 1–10.
Austin, J. L. *How to Do Things with Words: The William James Lectures Delivered at Harvard University in 1955*. Oxford: Oxford University Press, 1962.
Azerrad, Michael. "Notes from the Underground: Bad Music Video." *Optic Music* (1986): 32–33.
Baer, Nicholas, Maggie Hennefeld, Laura Horak, and Gunnar Iversen. "Introduction: Envisioning the Unwatchable." In *Unwatchable*, edited by Nicholas Baer, Maggie Hennefeld, Laura Horak, and Gunnar Iversen, 1–29. New Brunswick, NJ: Rutgers University Press, 2019.
Balsom, Erika. *After Uniqueness: Film and Video Art in Circulation*. New York: Columbia University Press, 2017.
Balsom, Erika. "Live and Direct: Cinema as a Performing Art." *Artforum*, September 2014. https://www.artforum.com/print/201407/live-and-direct-cinema-as-a-performing-art-47842.
Bandel, Jan-Frederik. "Underground." In *Handbuch Literatur und Pop*, edited by Moritz Baßler and Eckhard Schumacher, 304–325. Berlin: De Gruyter, 2020.
Banes, Sally. *Subversive Expectations: Performance Art and Paratheater in New York, 1976–85*. Ann Arbor: University of Michigan Press, 1998.
Barthes, Roland. *A Lover's Discourse: Fragments*, translated by Richard Howard. New York: Hill and Wang, 1978.
Barthes, Roland. *Die Vorbereitung des Romans, Vorlesung am Collège de France 1978–1979 und 1979–1980*, edited by Éric Marty. Frankfurt, Germany: Suhrkamp, 2008.
Bartz, Christina. "Video. Vom Alternativfernsehen zum Massenmedium." In *Formationen der Mediennutzung III*, edited by Irmela Schneider and Cornelia Epping-Jäger, 133–146. Bielefeld, Germany: Transcript Publishing, 2008.
Bataille, Georges. "Formless." In *Visions of Excess: Selected Writings, 1927–1939*, edited by Allan Stoekl, 31. Minneapolis: University of Minnesota Press, 1985.
Bellour, Raymond. "The Pensive Spectator," translated by Lynne Kirby. *Wide Angle* 9, no. 1 (1987): 6–10.
Benedetti, Mark. "Beneath New York: The Formations and Effects of Canons in American Underground Film Movements." PhD diss., Indiana University, 2013.
Benedetti, Mark. "Canonization and No Wave Cinema History." In *Downtown Film and TV Culture 1975–2001*, edited by Joan Hawkins, 265–281. Bristol, UK: Intellect, 2015.
Bernard, Andreas. *Theory of the Hashtag*. Cambridge, UK: Polity Press, 2019.
Blerk, Ernie. N.t. *ZAT Magazine*, no. 5 (1985): 20–22.
Bois, Yve-Alain. "The Use Value of 'Formless.'" In *Formless: A User's Guide*, edited by Yve-Alain Bois and Rosalind E. Krauss, 13–40. New York: Zone Books, 1997.
Boyle, Deirdre. "Subject to Change: Guerrilla Television Revisited." *Art Journal* 45, no. 3 (1985): 228–232.
Brandstetter, Gabriele. "YES! Das Manifest als künstlerische Praxis." In *"Clean the Air": Künstlermanifeste seit den 1960er Jahren*, edited by Burcu Dogramaci and Katja Schneider, 17–25. Bielefeld, Germany: Transcript Publishing, 2017.
Bruce, Bryan. "Pissing on the Cinema of Transgression." *CineAction!*, no. 3 (1986): 21–27.
Buscombe, Edward. "Generic Overspill: A Dirty Western." In *More Dirty Looks: Gender, Pornography and Power*, 2nd ed., edited by Pamela Church Gibson, 27–30. London: BFI Publishing, 2004.
Butler, Judith. *Bodies That Matter: On the Discursive Limits of "Sex."* London: Routledge, 1993.

Butler, Judith. *Excitable Speech: A Politics of the Performative*. London: Routledge, 1997.
Bydler, Charlotte. "The Global Art World, INC.: On the Globalization of Contemporary Art." In *The Biennial Reader: An Anthology on Large-Scale Perennial Exhibitions of Contemporary Art*, edited by Elena Filipovic, Marieke van Hal, and Solveig Øvstebø, 378–405. Ostfildern, Germany: Hatje Cantz, 2010.
Carlson, Marvin. *Performance: A Critical Introduction*. London: Routledge, 1996.
Carr, C. *On Edge: Performance at the End of the Twentieth Century*, rev. ed. Middletown, CT: Wesleyan University Press, 2008.
Cavoulacos, Sophie, Kate Zembrano, and Sean Yetter. "*The City Stars*: Performing Gender Downtown." MoMA, Art and Artists, Magazine, July 8, 2019, https://www.moma.org/magazine/articles/117?fbclid=IwAR3UXS01uyyP-IOVK6-PxozjSHJM2qunaVlgCFooDIloowv3ZoeKsxIJN-g.
Church, David. *Grindhouse Nostalgia: Memory, Home Video and Exploitation Film Fandom*. Edinburgh: Edinburgh University Press, 2015.
Churner, Leah. "Un-TV: Public Access Cable Television in Manhattan; An Oral History." *Moving Image Source*, February 10, 2011. www.movingimagesource.us/articles/un-tv-20110210.
Clarke, Paul, Simon Jones, Nick Kaye, and Johanna Linsley. "Introduction: Inside and Outside the Archive." In *Artists in the Archive: Creative and Curatorial Engagements with Documents of Art and Performance*, edited by Paul Clarke, Simon Jones, Nick Kaye, and Johanna Linsley, 11–23. London/New York: Routledge, 2018.
Colacello, Bob. *Holy Terror: Andy Warhol Close Up*. New York: HarperCollins, 1990.
Crimp, Douglas, and Adam Rolston, eds. *AIDS Demo Graphics*. Seattle: Bay Press, 1990.
Danto, Arthur C. *The Philosophical Disenfranchisement of Art*. New York: Columbia University Press, 1986, 2004.
Davis, Avi. "Why Cinema of Transgression Director Nick Zedd Stayed Underground." *Vice*, June 6, 2014. https://www.vice.com/en_us/article/dpwd7v/a-new-breed-of-asshole-0000327-v21n5.
De Kosnik, Abigail. *Rogue Archives: Digital Cultural Memory and Media Fandom*. Cambridge, MA: MIT Press, 2016.
Delembard, Cricket. "The Cinema of Transgression: Where Are They Now? A Recollection." In *Captured: A Film/Video History of the Lower East Side*, edited by Clayton Patterson, 265–272. New York: Seven Stories Press, 2005.
Deleuze, Gilles and Félix Guattari. *Rhizom*. Berlin: Merve, 1977.
Denecke, Mathias. "Flows and Streams of Data: Notes on Metaphors in Digital Cultures." In *Explorations in Digital Cultures*, edited by Marcus Burkhardt, Mary Shnayien, and Katja Grashöfe, 1–18. Lüneburg, Germany: Meson Press, 2020. https://doi.org/10.25969/mediarep/14851.
De Rosa, Miriam, and Vinzenz Hediger. "Post-what? Post-when? A Conversation on the 'Posts' of Post-media and Post-cinema." *Cinéma and Cie* 16, no. 26/27 (2016): 9–20.
Derrida, Jacques. "Archive Fever: A Freudian Impression." *Diacritics* 25, no. 2 (1995): 9–63.
Derrida, Jacques. "Archive Fever: A Seminar by Jacques Derrida, University of the Witwatersrand, August 1998. Transcribed by Verne Harris." In *Refiguring the Archive*, edited by Carolyn Hamilton, Verne Harris, Jane Raylor, Michele Pickover, Graeme Reid, and Razia Saleh, 39–80. Dordrecht/Boston/London: Kluwer Academic Publishers, 2002.
Derrida, Jaques. *Limited Inc*. Evanston, IL: Northwestern University Press, 1988.
De Valck, Marijke. "Fostering Art, Adding Value, Cultivating Taste: Film Festivals as Sites of Cultural Legitimization." In *Film Festivals: History, Theory, Method,*

Practice, edited by Marijke de Valck, Brendan Kredell, and Skadi Loist, 100–116. London: Routledge, 2016.

Dinsmore-Tuli, Uma. "The Pleasures of 'Home Cinema,' or Watching Movies on Telly: An Audience Study of Cinephiliac VCR Use." *Screen* 41, no. 3 (2000): 315–327.

Dolan, Jill. "Carmelita Tropicana Chats at the Club Chandelier." *The Drama Review* 29, no. 1 (1985): 29–32.

Douglas, Mary. *Purity and Danger: An Analysis of Concepts of Pollution and Taboo*. Vol. 2 of *Collected Works*. Routledge and Kegan Paul, 1966; London: Routledge, 2003.

Dreschke, Anja, Ilham Huynh, Raphaela Knipp, and David Sittler. "Einleitung." In *Reenactments. Medienpraktiken zwischen Wiederholung und kreativer Aneignung*, edited by Anja Dreschke, Ilham Huynh, Raphaela Knipp, and David Sittler, 9–23. Bielefeld, Germany: Transcript Publishing, 2016.

Duffy, Brooke Erin, and Jeremy Packer. "Wifesaver: Tupperware and the Unfortunate Spoils of Containment." In *Re-Understanding Media: Feminist Extensions of Marshall McLuhan*, edited by Sarah Sharma and Rianka Sing, 98–118. Durham, NC: Duke University Press, 2022.

Duncombe, Stephen. *Notes from Underground: Zines and the Politics of Alternative Culture*. New York: Verso, 1997.

Eichhorn, Kate. "Copy Machines and Downtown Scenes: Deterritorializing Urban Culture in a Pre-Digital Era." *Cultural Studies* 29, no. 3 (2014): 1–16.

Elsaesser, Thomas. *European Cinema: Face to Face with Hollywood*. Amsterdam: Amsterdam University Press, 2005.

Fenwick, James, Kieran Foster, and David Eldridge. "Introduction." In *Shadow Cinema: The Historical Production Contexts of Unmade Films*, edited by James Fenwick, Kieran Foster, and David Eldridge, 1–14. New York: Bloomsbury Academic, 2021.

Filipovic, Elena. "The Global White Cube." In *The Manifesta Decade: Debates on Contemporary Art Exhibitions and Biennials in Post-Wall Europe*, edited by Barbara Vanderlinden and Elena Filipovic, 65–84. Cambridge, MA: MIT Press, 2006.

Fischer-Lichte, Erika. *Performativität: Eine Einführung*. Bielefeld, Germany: Transcript Publishing, 2012.

Flatley, Jonathan "Allegories of Boredom." In *A Minimal Future? Art as Object 1958–1968*, edited by Ann Goldstein, 51–76. Cambridge, MA: MIT Press, 2004.

Flatley, Jonathan. "Collecting and Collectivity." *October* 132 (2010): 78–98.

Fleishman, Judith. "The Shit Hits the Screen." *Say!*, November 1986.

Formilan, Giovanni, and David Stark. "Underground Testing: Name-Altering Practices as Probes in Electronic Music." *British Journal of Sociology* 71, no. 3 (2020): 572–589.

Foster, Hal. *Bad New Days: Art, Criticism, Emergency*. London: Verso, 2015.

Foucault, Michel. *Discipline and Punish: The Birth of the Prison*. Portland: Peregrine Press, 1979.

Foucault, Michel. "Of Other Spaces: Utopias and Heterotopias," translated by Jay Miskowiec. *Diacritics* 16, no. 1 (1986): 22–27.

Foucault, Michel. "A Preface to Transgression." In *Language, Counter-Memory, Practice: Selected Essays and Interviews*, edited and translated by Donald F. Bouchard, 29–52. Ithaca, NY: Cornell University Press, 1977.

Fox, Dan. "A Better View." *Frieze*, December 19, 2017. https://www.frieze.com/article/better-view.

Fried, Ronald K. "John Jesurun's 'Chang in a Void Moon.'" *Drama Review* 27, no. 2 (1983): 73–77.

Gaudreault, André, and Philippe Marion. *The End of Cinema? A Medium in Crisis in the Digital Age*, translated by Timothy Barnard. New York: Columbia University Press, 2015.

Gillespie, Tarleton. "The Politics of 'Platforms.'" *New Media and Society* 12, no. 3 (2010): 347–364.

Gitelman, Lisa. *Paper Knowledge: Toward a Media History of Documents*. Durham, NC: Duke University Press, 2014.

Goldsmith, Kenneth. *Duchamp Is My Lawyer: The Polemics, Pragmatics, and Poetics of UbuWeb*. New York: Columbia University Press, 2020.

Gray, Jonathan. *Show Sold Separately: Promos, Spoilers, and Other Media Paratexts*. New York: New York University Press, 2010.

Greenberg, Joshua M. *From Betamax to Blockbuster: Video Stores and the Invention of Movies on Video*. Cambridge, MA: MIT Press, 2008.

Grønstad, Asbjørn. "The Two Unwatchables." In *Unwatchable*, edited by Nicholas Baer, Maggie Hennefeld, Laura Horak, and Gunnar Iversen, 151–154. New Brunswick, NJ: Rutgers University Press, 2019.

Gross, Michael. "The Party Seems to Be Over for Lower Manhattan Clubs." *New York Times*, October 26, 1985. https://www.nytimes.com/1985/10/26/nyregion/the-party-seems-to-be-over-for-lower-manhattan-clubs.html.

Guins, Raiford. *Game After: A Cultural Study of Video Game Afterlife*. Cambridge, MA: MIT Press, 2014.

Gumbs, Alexis Pauline. *Spills: Scenes of Black Feminist Fugitivity*. Durham, NC: Duke University Press, 2016.

Hagan, John. "John Jesurun." *Artforum*, October 1999. https://www.artforum.com/print/199908/john-jesurun-843.

Halberstam, Jack. *The Queer Art of Failure*. Durham, NC: Duke University Press, 2011.

Haraway, Donna J. "A Game of Cat's Cradle: Science Studies, Feminist Theory, Cultural Studies." *Configurations* 2, no. 1 (1994): 59–71.

Harris, Verne. "Genres of the Trace: Memory, Archives and Trouble." *Archives and Manuscripts* 40, no. 3 (2012): 147–155.

Haslett, Tobi. "Modern Love: Gary Indiana Has Told the Story of His Life with Many of the Legendary Parts Cut Out." *n+1* 26 (2016). https://www.nplusonemag.com/issue-26/reviews/modern-love/.

Haupts, Tobias. *Die Videothek*. Bielefeld, Germany: Transcript Publishing, 2014.

Hawkins, Joan. "Burning Down the House: Community Access TV and the Downtown Art Shows." *Flow*, November 13, 2007. https://www.flowjournal.org/2007/11/burning-down-the-house-community-access-tv-and-the-Downtown-art-shows-1/.

Hawkins, Joan. "Downtown Cinema Revisited." In *Downtown Film and TV Culture 1975–2001*, edited by Joan Hawkins, xi–xxix. Bristol, UK: Intellect, 2015.

Hediger, Vinzenz. "'You Haven't Seen It Until You've Seen It Twice': Film Spectatorship and the Discipline of Repeat Viewing." *Cinéma and Cie*, no. 5 (2004): 24–39.

Higgins, Dick. "Intermedia." 1965. In *Horizons*, 21–31. Ubu Editions, 2007. http://www.ubu.com/ubu/higgins_horizons.html.

Hilderbrand, Lucas. *Inherent Vice: Bootleg Histories of Videotape and Copyright*. Durham, NC: Duke University Press, 2009.

Hilderbrand, Lucas, Alexandra Juhasz, Debra Levine, and Ricardo Montez. "Downtown's Queer Asides." In *Downtown Film and TV Culture 1975–2001*, edited by Joan Hawkins, 243–258. Bristol, UK: Intellect, 2015.

Hoberman, J. "'Like Canyons and Rivers': Performance for Its Own Sake." In *Rituals of Rented Island: Object Theater, Loft Performance, and the New Psychodrama-Manhattan*, edited by Jay Sanders, 9–25. New York: Whitney Museum of American Art, 2013.

Hoberman, J., and Jonathan Rosenbaum, eds. *Midnight Movies*. New York: Harper and Row, 1983.

Horn, Daniel. "After Anger." *Frieze*, April 6, 2012. https://www.frieze.com/article/after-anger.

Hughes-Freeland, Tessa. "Interview with Ela Troyano." *Underground Film Bulletin*, no. 3 (1985): 47–58.

Hughes-Freeland, Tessa. "Shifting the Psychotic Treadmill." *East Village Eye*, February 1986.

Hüser, Rembert. "Agent im Kreis." In *Handbuch Filmanalyse*, edited by Malte Hagener and Volker Pantenburg, 1–16. Wiesbaden, Germany: Springer VS, 2020. https://link.springer.com/referenceworkentry/10.1007/978-3-658-13352-8_18-1.

Irwin, Jon. *Scenes*. Beverly Hills: Sage, 1977.

Jack Smith: Art Crust of Spiritual Oasis. New York City: Artists Space, 2018. https://texts.artistsspace.org/5az3hjnw.

James, David E. *To Free the Cinema: Jonas Mekas and the New York Underground*. Princeton, NJ: Princeton University Press, 1992.

Janes, Barry T. "History and Structure of Public Access Television." *Journal of Film and Video* 39, no. 3 (1987): 14–23.

Jeffreys, Joe E. "Madame Dagmar Onassis Speaks (and Sings)!" *Outweek*, March 27, 1991.

Jeriko, Orion [Nick Zedd]. "The Cinema of Transgression Manifesto." *Underground Film Bulletin*, no. 4 (1985): 3–5.

Jeriko, Orion [Nick Zedd]. "Editorial: Dear Tasteless Ones." *Underground Film Bulletin*, no. 7 (1988): 11–13.

Jeriko, Orion [Nick Zedd]. "Long Live the Cinema of Transgression." *Underground Film Bulletin*, no. 3 (1985): 3–4.

Jeriko, Orion [Nick Zedd]. "The Worst Filmmaker in the World: John Spencer Interviewed by Orion Jeriko." *Underground Film Bulletin*, no. 6 (1987): 24–35.

Johnson, Dominic. *Glorious Catastrophe: Jack Smith, Performance and Visual Culture*. Manchester, UK: Manchester University Press, 2012.

Jones, Amelia. "'Presence' in Absentia: Experiencing Performance as Documentation." *Art Journal* 56, no. 4 (1997): 11–18.

Jones, Caroline A. "Biennial Culture: A Longer History." In *The Biennial Reader: An Anthology on Large-Scale Perennial Exhibitions of Contemporary Art*, edited by Elena Filipovic, Marieke van Hal, and Solveig Øvstebø, 66–87. Ostfildern, Germany: Hatje Cantz, 2010.

Kane, Daniel. *All Poets Welcome: The Lower East Side Poetry Scene in the 1960s*. Berkeley: University of California Press, 2003.

Kelly, John. *John Kelly*. New York: 2wice books, 2001.

King, Homay. "Stroboscopic: Warhol and the Exploding Plastic Inevitable." *Criticism* 56, no. 3 (2014): 457–480.

Klinger, Barbara. *Beyond the Multiplex: Cinema, New Technologies, and the Home*. Berkeley: University of California Press, 2006.

Klinger, Barbara. "Cinema's Shadow: Reconsidering Non-theatrical Exhibition." In *Going to the Movies: Hollywood and the Social Experience of Cinema*, edited by Richard Maltby, Melvyn Stokes, and Robert C. Allen, 35–36. Exeter, UK: University of Exeter Press, 2005.

Knight, Julia, and Peter Thomas. *Reaching Audiences: Distribution and Promotion of Alternative Moving Image*. Bristol, UK: Intellect, 2011.
Kolesch, Doris. "Die Spur der Stimme: Überlegungen zu einer performativen Ästhetik." In *Medien/Stimmen*, edited by Cornelia Epping-Jäger and Erika Linz, 267–281. Cologne, Germany: DuMont, 2003.
Kostelanetz, Richard. *The Theatre of Mixed Means: An Introduction to Happenings, Kinetic Environments, and Other Mixed-Means Performances*. New York: Dial Press, 1968.
Kramer, Anke, and Annegret Pelz, eds. *Album: Organisationsform narrativer Kohärenz*. Göttingen, Germany: Wallstein, 2013.
Krämer, Sybille, and Doris Kolesch. "Stimmen im Konzert der Disziplinen." In *Stimme*, edited by Sybille Krämer and Doris Kolesch, 7–15. Frankfurt, Germany: Suhrkamp, 2006.
Kuhn, Nicola. "Berlins SoHo—nur so lala." *Der Tagesspiegel*, Kultur, March 12, 2000. https://www.tagesspiegel.de/kultur/berlins-soho-nur-so-lala/128886.html.
Larkin, Brian. *Signal and Noise: Media, Infrastructure, and Urban Culture in Nigeria*. Durham, NC: Duke University Press, 2008.
Law, John. *After Method: Mess in Social Science Research*. London/New York: Routledge, 2004.
Lawrence, Tim. *Life and Death on the New York Dance Floor, 1980–1983*. Durham, NC: Duke University Press, 2016.
Le Grice, Malcolm. "You Killed the Underground Film or the Real Meaning of Kunst bleibt . . . bleibt . . ." March 2, 2012. http://slypropotter.org/wilhelm-hein/le-grice.
Lepecki, André. "The Body as Archive: Will to Re-Enact and the Afterlives of Dances," *Dance Research Journal* 42, no. 2 (2010): 28–48.
Leslie, Esther. *Liquid Crystals: The Science and Art of a Fluid Form*. London: Reaktion Books, 2016.
Lind, Maria. "The Collaborative Turn." In *Taking the Matter into Common Hands: On Contemporary Art and Collaborative Practices*, edited by Johanna Billing, Maria Lind, and Lars Nilsson, 15–31. London: Black Dog Publishing, 2007.
Little, David. "Colab Takes a Piece, History Takes It Back: Collectivity and New York Alternative Spaces." *Art Journal* 66, no. 1 (2007): 60–74.
Loist, Skadi. "The Film Festival Circuit: Networks, Hierarchies, and Circulation." In *Film Festivals: History, Theory, Method, Practice*, edited by Marijke de Valck, Brendan Kredell, and Skadi Loist, 49–64. London: Routledge, 2016.
Love, Heather. "Queer Messes." *WSQ: Women's Studies Quarterly* 44, no. 3–4 (2016): 345–349.
Loveless, Natalie S. "Reading with Knots: On Jane Gallop's Anecdotal Theory." *S: Journal of the Jan van Eyck Circle for Lacanian Ideology Critique* 4 (2011): 24–36.
Lyon, Janet. *Manifestoes: Provocations of the Modern*. Ithaca, NY: Cornell University Press, 1999.
MacKenzie, Scott, ed. *Film Manifestos and Global Cinema Cultures. A Critical Anthology*. Berkeley: University of California Press, 2014.
Magnuson, Ann. "Club 57." *Artforum* 38, no. 2 (1999). https://www.artforum.com/print/199908/club-57-840.
Magnuson, Ann. "It Takes an East Village." In *Club 57: Performance and Art in the East Village, 1978–1982*, edited by Ron Magliozzi and Sophie Cavoulacos, 152–159. New York: Museum of Modern Art, 2017.
Manoff, Marlene. "Theories of the Archive from Across the Disciplines." *Libraries and the Academy* 4, no. 1 (2004): 9–24.

Marchessault, Janine. "Film Scenes: Paris, New York, Toronto." *Public* 22, no. 23 (2001): 59–75.
Marranca, Bonnie, and Gautam Dasgupta. *The Theatre of the Ridiculous*. Baltimore: John Hopkins University Press, 1998.
Matturri, John. "Jack Smith: Notes on Some Homeless Objects." *Criticism* 56, no. 2 (2014): 279–294.
Mbembe, Achille. "The Power of the Archive and Its Limits." In *Refiguring the Archive*, edited by Carolyn Hamilton, Verne Harris, Jane Raylor, Michele Pickover, Graeme Reid, and Razia Saleh, 19–26. Dordrecht/Boston/London: Kluwer Academic Publishers, 2002.
McCormick, Carlo. "East Village, R.I.P." *East Village Eye*, October 1985.
McGill, Douglas C. "Art Boom Slows in the East Village." *New York Times*, July 25, 1987. https://www.nytimes.com/1987/07/25/arts/art-boom-slows-in-the-east-village.html.
McGillen, Petra. "Kompilieren." In *Historisches Wörterbuch des Mediengebrauchs*, edited by Heiko Christians, Nikolaus Wegmann, and Matthias Bickenbach, 352–368. Cologne, Germany: Böhlau, 2014.
McKenna, Mark. "Whose Canon Is It Anyway? Subcultural Capital, Cultural Distinction and Value in High Art and Low Culture." In *Cult Media: Re-Packaged, Re-Released, and Restored*, edited by Jonathan Wroot and Andy Willis, 31–47. London: Palgrave Macmillan, 2017.
Mekas, Jonas. "Movie Journal." *Village Voice*, November 18, 1965.
Mekas, Jonas. "Underground Film According to Parker Tyler." In *Movie Journal: The Rise of a New American Cinema, 1959–1971*, 362–364. New York: Collier Books, 1972.
Mele, Christopher. "Forging the Link Between Culture and Real Estate: Urban Policy and Real Estate Development." In *The Gentrification Debates*, edited by Japonica Brown-Saracino, 127–132. New York: Routledge, 2010.
Mellencamp, Patricia. *Indiscretions: Avant-Garde Film, Video and Feminism*. Bloomington: Indiana University Press, 1990.
Mellencamp, Patricia. "Receivable Texts: U.S. Avant-Garde Cinema, 1960–1980." *Wide Angle* 7, no. 1–2 (1985): 74–91.
Menotti, Gabriel. *Movie Circuits: Curatorial Approaches to Cinema Technology*. Amsterdam: Amsterdam University Press, 2019.
Moon, Michael. "Flaming Closets." *October* 51 (1989): 19–54.
Mulroney, Lucy. *Andy Warhol, Publisher*. Chicago: University of Chicago Press, 2018.
Mücke, Laura Katharina, Olga Moskatova, and Chris Tedjasukmana. "Editorial: Messy Images–Unordnungen digital vernetzter Bilder." *Montage AV* 31, no. 1 (2022): 4–17. https://montage-av.de/31-1-2022/.
Muñoz, José Esteban. *Cruising Utopia: The Then and There of Queer Futurity*. New York: New York University Press, 2019.
Muñoz, José Esteban. "Ephemera as Evidence: Introductory Notes to Queer Acts." *Women and Performance: A Journal of Feminist Theory* 8, no. 2 (1996): 5–16.
Nelson, George. *Hip Hop America*. New York: Viking Penguin, 1998.
Neue Westfälische. "Ungewöhnliche Filme direkt aus New York." March 19, 1986.
New American Cinema Group. "The First Statement of the New American Cinema Group." In *Film Manifestos and Global Cinema Cultures. A Critical Anthology*, edited by Scott MacKenzie, 58–60. Berkeley: University of California Press, 2014. Originally published in *Film Culture* 22–23 (1961): 131–133.
Newman, Michael Z. *Video Revolutions: On the History of a Medium*. New York: Columbia University Press, 2014.

New York Magazine. "AIDS in New York: A Biography." May 26, 2006. http://nymag.com/news/features/17158/.

New York Times. "Keith Haring Paints Mural on Berlin Wall." October 24, 1986. https://www.nytimes.com/1986/10/24/arts/keith-haring-paints-mural-on-berlin-wall.html.

Nichols, Bill. "Global Image Consumption in the Age of Late Capitalism." *East-West Film Journal* 8, no. 1 (1994): 68–85.

Olin, Benjamin. "TV Party: A Cocktail Party That Could Also Be a Political Party." In *Downtown Film and TV Culture 1975–2001*, edited by Joan Hawkins, 193–209. Bristol, UK: Intellect, 2015.

Parnes, Uzi. "Jack Smith: Legendary Filmmaker, Theatrical Genius, and Exotic Art Consultant." In *European Media Art Festival [EMAF]* (1994): 163–171. http://uziny.com/Uzi_Parnes_on_Jack_Smith-94.pdf.

Penley, Constance, and Janet Bergstrom. "The Avant-Garde: Histories and Theories." *Screen* 19, no. 3 (1978): 113–119.

Perron, Wendy. "Voices of Many Voices." *SoHo Weekly News*, December 15, 1977.

Phelan, Peggy. *Unmarked: The Politics of Performance*. London/New York: Routledge, 1993.

Poell, Thomas, David B. Nieborg, and Brooke Erin Duffy. *Platforms and Cultural Production*. Cambridge, UK: Polity Press, 2022.

Rabinovitz, Lauren. *Points of Resistance: Women, Power and Politics in the New York Avant-garde Cinema, 1943–71*, 2nd ed. Urbana: University of Illinois Press, 2003.

Rabkin, Gerald. "Theatre of the Ridiculous: An Introduction." *Performing Arts Journal* 3, no. 1 (1978): 40–42.

Rahmanan, Anna. "NYC's Iconic Kim's Video Is Reopening Inside the Alamo This Month." *Time Out*, March 22, 2022. https://www.timeout.com/newyork/news/nycs-iconic-kims-video-is-reopening-inside-the-alamo-this-month-032222.

Reekie, Duncan. *Subversion: The Definitive History of Underground Cinema*. London: Wallflower Press, 2007.

Renan, Sheldon. *An Introduction to the American Underground*. New York: E. P. Dutton, 1967.

Reverend Jen. "New York Magazine." Diary of an Art Star. April 12, 2010. https://reverendjen.wordpress.com/2010/04/12/new-york-magazine/.

Rosenbach, Ulrike. "Video als Medium der Emanzipation." In *Videokunst in Deutschland 1963–1982. Videobänder, Installationen, Objekte, Performances*, edited by Wulf Herzogenrath, 99–102. Stuttgart, Germany: Gerd Hatje, 1982.

Rosenberg, Karen. "A Cinematically Divided City." In *Berlin: Images in Progress*, edited by Jürgen Brüning and Andreas Wildfang, 15–16. Buffalo, NY: Hallwalls, 1989.

Sailing, Jasmine. "Nick Zedd Interview." *Cyber-Psycho's A.O.D.*, no. 3 (1993): 32

Sanborn, Keith J. *Super-8/Berlin: The Architecture of Division*. Buffalo, NY: Hallwalls, 1983.

Sargeant, Jack. *Deathtripping: The Cinema of Transgression*. London: Creation Books, 1995.

Schaefer, Eric. *"Bold! Daring! Shocking! True!": A History of Exploitation Films, 1919–1959*. Durham, NC: Duke University Press, 1999.

Schaffer, Johanna. "Formlos wie Spucke." In *Radikal ambivalent: Engagement und Verantwortung in den Künsten heute*, edited by Rachel Mader, 209–222. Zurich: Diaphanes, 2014.

Schneider, Rebecca. *Performing Remains: Art and War in Times of Theatrical Reenactment*. London/New York: Routledge, 2011.

Schönherr, Johannes. *Trashfilm Roadshows: Off the Beaten Track with Subversive Movies*. Manchester, UK: Headpress Books, 2002.

Schulman, Sarah. "Flaming Creatures: The Other New York Film Festival." *Village Voice*, October 20, 1987.

Schulman, Sarah. *Gentrification of the Mind: Witness to a Lost Imagination.* Berkeley: University of California Press, 2012.

Schüttpelz, Erhard, "Akademie der Dilettanten (Back to D.)." In *Akademie*, edited by Stephan Dillemuth, 40–57. Cologne, Germany: Permanent Press, 1995.

Siegel, Marc. "Ridiculous Screenplays." In *Andy Warhol's Ridiculous Screenplays*, edited by Ronald Tavel, ix–xxii. Silverton, OR: Fast Books, 2015.

Smith, Harris. "No New Cinema: Punk and No Wave Underground Film 1976–1984." In *Captured: A Film/Video History of the Lower East Side*, edited by Clayton Patterson, 173–178. New York: Seven Stories Press, 2005.

Smith, Jack. *Wait for Me at the Bottom of the Pool: The Writings of Jack Smith.* Edited by J. Hoberman and Edward Leffingwell. New York/London: High Risk, 1997.

Spigel, Lynn. "Installing the Television Set: Popular Discourses on Television and Domestic Space, 1948–1955." In *Private Screenings: Television and the Female Consumer*, edited by Lynn Spigel and Denise Mann, 3–38. Minneapolis: University of Minnesota Press, 1992.

Spunt, Barry. *Heroin, Acting, and Comedy in New York City.* New York: Palgrave Macmillan, 2017.

Stark Mele, Casandra. "Why I Left the 'Cinema of Transgression' Behind, Or Why It Left Me." In *Captured: A Film/Video History of the Lower East Side*, edited by Clayton Patterson, 277–279. New York: Seven Stories Press, 2005.

Sterneborg, Anke. "Das ursprüngliche New York." *Der Tagesspiegel*, March 16, 1986.

Stevenson, Jack. "Grindhouse and Beyond." In *From the Arthouse to the Grindhouse: Highbrow and Lowbrow Transgression in Cinema's First Century*, edited by John Clide and Robert G. Weiner, 129–152. Lanham, MD: Scarecrow Press, 2010.

Straw, Will, "Scenes and Sensibilities." *Public* 22, no. 23 (2001): 245–257.

Suárez, Juan A. *Bike Boys, Drag Queens and Superstars: Avant-Garde, Mass Culture, and Gay Identities in the 1960s Underground Cinema.* Bloomington: Indiana University Press, 1996.

Suicide, Gene. "Number One with a Boley: Beyond the Myth of Nick Zedd." *Sex and Guts*, no. 2 (1997/98): 13.

Tarzian, Charles. "8BC—From Farmhouse to Cabaret." *Drama Review* 29, no. 1 (1985): 108–112.

Taubin, Amy. "The Other Cinema." *SoHo Weekly News*, June 7, 1979.

Taylor, Marvin J., ed. *The Downtown Book: The New York Art Scene 1974–1984.* Princeton, NJ: Princeton University Press, 2006.

Taylor, Marvin J. "I'll Be Your Mirror, Reflect What You Are: Postmodern Documentation and the Downtown New York Scene from 1975 to the Present." *RBM: A Journal of Rare Books, Manuscripts, and Cultural Heritage* 3, no. 1 (2002): 32–51.

Thibault, Ghislain. "Streaming: A Media Hydrography of Televisual Flows." *VIEW* 4, no. 7 (2015): 110–119.

Tip, "Kino in der Unterstadt," 17, no. 5 (1988): 48.

Treichler, Paula A. "AIDS, Homophobia, and Biomedical Discourse. An Epidemic of Signification." *October* 43 (1987): 31–70.

Turquety, Benoît. *Medium, Format, Configuration: The Displacements of Film.* Lüneburg, Germany: Meson Press, 2019.

Tyler, Parker. *Underground Film: A Critical History.* New York: Grove Press, 1970.

Vadukul, Alex. "Big Hair and Bad Luck: The Hard Times of the Troll Museum." *New York Times*, January 18, 2019. https://www.nytimes.com/2019/01/18/nyregion/big-hair-and-bad-luck-the-hard-times-of-the-troll-museum.html.

Vanderbeek, Stan. "The Cinema Delimina: Films from the Underground." *Film Quarterly* 14, no. 4 (1961): 5–15.
Volmar, Axel, Marek Jancovic, and Alexandra Schneider. "Format Matters: An Introduction to Format Studies." In *Format Matters: Standards, Practices, and Politics in Media Cultures*, edited by Axel Volmar, Marek Jancovic, and Alexandra Schneider, 7–22. Lüneburg, Germany: Meson Press, 2020.
Wasson, Haidee. *Museum Movies: The Museum of Modern Art and the Birth of Art Cinema*. Berkeley: University of California Press, 2005.
Watney, Simon. *Policing Desire: Pornography, AIDS, and the Media*, 3rd ed. Minneapolis: University of Minnesota Press, 1997.
Weigel, Sigrid. "Die Stimme als Medium des Nachlebens: Pathosformel, Nachhall, Phantom." In *Stimme*, edited by Sybille Krämer and Doris Kolesch, 16–39. Frankfurt, Germany: Suhrkamp, 2006.
Weltzien, Friedrich. "Von Cozens bis Kerner. Der Fleck als Transformator ästhetischer Erfahrung." In *Ästhetische Erfahrung: Gegenstände, Konzepte, Geschichtlichkeit*, edited by Sonderforschungsbereich 626: Ästhetische Erfahrung im Zeichen der Entgrenzung der Künste. Berlin: Free University of Berlin, 2006. https://www.geschkult.fu-berlin.de/e/sfb626/veroeffentlichungen/online/aesth_erfahrung/aufsaetze/weltzien.pdf.
Widrich, Mechtild. "The Informative Public of Performance. A Study of Viennese Actionism, 1965–1970." *The Drama Review* 57, no. 1 (2013): 137–151.
Williams, Linda. "Film Bodies: Gender, Genre, and Excess." *Film Quarterly* 44, no. 4 (1991): 2–13.
Wojnarowicz, David. "Losing the Form in Darkness." In *David Wojnarowicz: Tongues of Flame*, edited by Barry Blinderman, 65–74. Normal: Illinois State University, 1990.
Wojnarowicz, David. "Sidewalk Begging." *East Village Eye*, October 1985.
Woo, Benjamin, Jamie Rennie, and Stuart R. Poyntz. "Scene Thinking." *Cultural Studies* 29, no. 3 (2014): 285–297.
Yokobosky, Matthew. "No Wave Cinema, 1978–87—Not a Part of Any Wave: No Wave." In *Captured: A Film/Video History of the Lower East Side*, edited by Clayton Patterson, 179–184. New York: Seven Stories Press, 2005.
Youngblood, Gene. *Expanded Cinema*. New York: P. Dutton and Co. Inc., 1970.
Zedd, Nick. "Nick Zedd." In *Captured: A Film/Video History of the Lower East Side*, edited by Clayton Patterson, 273–274. New York: Seven Stories Press, 2005.
Zedd, Nick. *Totem of the Depraved*. Los Angeles: Two Thirteen Sixty-One Publications, 1996.
Zedd, Nick. Untitled report on *Me Minus You*. *Underground Film Bulletin*, no. 3 (1985): 20–26.
Zedd, Nick, and David Sjöberg. "The Case of Electra Elf: Towards New Possibilities of Underground Counterculture in the Twenty-First Century." In *Downtown Film and TV Culture 1975–2001*, edited by Joan Hawkins, 211–220. Bristol, UK: Intellect, 2015.
Zorn, John. "The Game Pieces." In *Audio Culture, Revised Edition: Readings in Modern Music*, edited by Christoph Cox and Daniel Warner, 196–200. New York: Bloomsbury, 2017.
Zukin, Sharon. "The Creation of a 'Loft Lifestyle.'" In *The Gentrification Debates*, edited by Japonica Brown-Saracino, 175–184. London: Routledge, 2010.
Zurbrugg, Nicholas. "Interview with Nick Zedd." In *Art, Performance, Media. 31 Interviews*, edited by Nicholas Zurbrugg, 381–390. Minneapolis: University of Minnesota Press, 2004.

Index

ABC No Rio, 32
Abdoh, Reza, 27, 140n24
Abnormal: The Sinema of Nick Zedd (DVD compilation), 122
Acker, Kathy, 35, 42
Acland, Charles, 15
Adler, Melissa, 38
Adventures of Electra Elf, The (Zedd, 2005–2008), 19, 114, 119–121, 122, 160n67
agency, shared, 5
AIDS Coalition to Unleash Power (ACT UP), 10
AIDS/HIV crisis, 3–4, 9, 10–11, 35, 126; "bad old days" of New York City and, 24; impact on Western art world, 12
All Color News (Colab, 1977–1978), 115
Allen, Gwen, 51
Alphabet City, 42
Altenhaus, Adrienne, 61
Amazon, CoT DVDs sold on, 122
American Film, 32, 55
André Emmerich Gallery (Zurich), 145n25
Andres, Jo, 59–60, 81, 147n63
Angell, Callie, 92–93
Anger, Kenneth, 27, 34, 54, 101, 107, 140n24
Anna Friebe Gallery (Cologne, Germany), 145n25
Anthology Film Archives, 45, 139n6, 147n53, 159n49
Apple, Jacki, 70

Archive Fever (Derrida), 39
archives/archivization, 34–40, 99
Artaud, Antonin, 49
Artforum, 115
art history, 16
Artist's Television Network, 159n49
art market, 47
art museums, 15
Artware (Wiesbaden, Germany), 112, 114, 158n42
A.S.S. Magazine, 120, 121
Astor Film-Maker's Cinematheque, 97
audiences, active involvement of, 84
automatic writing, 6
Avalanche magazine, 51
avant-garde, 13, 32; break with "old" avant-garde, 54; of 1950s, 71; UbuWeb and historiography of, 124
Azzouray, Rafic, 146n31

B, Beth, 43, 92, 124, 149n2, 153n71, 154n85
B, Scott, 92, 147n52, 149n2, 153n71, 154n85
Baby Doll (Hughes-Freeland, 1982), 156n1
Bad Music Videos, at Limelight (1986), 117, 118
Balsom, Erika, 16–17, 71, 72, 110
Bandel, Jan-Frederik, 53
Banes, Sally, 70
Barthes, Roland, 80, 106
Bartz, Christina, 104–105, 156n8
Basquiat, Jean-Michel, 9–10, 115

Bataille, Georges, 6, 7, 8, 136n23; concept of transgression and, 9; texts reprinted in *Underground Film Bulletin*, 49
BDSM scenes, 8
Beautiful People (Wojnarowicz, ca. 1988), 125, 161n91
Beauty Becomes the Beast (Dick, 1979), 149n2, 154n85
Bellour, Raymond, 105
Benedetti, Mark, 44
Berlin, 24, 25, 27; Eiszeit Kino, 65, 66, 67; film festivals in, 63; Kino Arsenal, 64; Super 8 and 16 mm scenes separated in, 149n96
Berlin Biennale of Contemporary Art, 26
Berlin Wall, 10, 25
Bernstein, Richard, 51
Betamax tapes, 103, 110
BeuysBlock (Zorn), 96
"Beyond the Myth of Nick Zedd" (interview, 1997), 55
Biesenbach, Klaus, 26, 140n19
Big Hotel (Ridiculous Theatre), 151n37
Bitch magazine, 6
Black, White, and in Color (Spillers), 6
Black/African American communities, 63
Black Box (Beth and Scott B, 1978), 154n85
Black feminism, 6
Black Hearts Bleed Red (Rossi, 1992), 149n2
Black Mountain College, 150n14
Blank Generation, The (Poe, 1976), 44
Bleecker St. Cinema, 32, 53
Bleu du Ciel, Le (Bataille, 1957), 8
Blondie (band), 115
Bloody Stump (Wolfe, 1985), 66
B movies, 60, 79, 93, 103, 121
body spectacle, 8
Bogus Man, The (Zedd, 1980), 7–8, 88, 93, 124, 125, 147n52, 156n3
Bold, Alf, 64
BOMB magazine, 115
Boo-Hooray, 127
Bosio, Angélique, 2, 3
Bradfield, Polly, 96
Brakhage, Stan, 53, 111
Brand, Axel, 65
Breton, André, 6
British Film Institute (BFI), 33–34, 101, 107–108, 124
Bruce, Bryan, 33, 39

Brüning, Jürgen, 35, 64, 65, 112
Bubble People (Troyano, 1982), 8, 18, 88–100; camerawork in, 93–94; script based on Cukor's *Let's Make Love,* 89; Troyano's collaboration with Zorn and, 89, 154n75
Bufferin (Warhol, 1966), 94
Buitenhuis, Penelope, 65
Bunny Atlanta (Lady Bunny), 82
Buñuel, Luis, 8, 53
Bush Tetras, 44
Butler, Judith, 78
Butterick, Brian, 79, 126
Butthole Surfers, 61
Bydler, Charlotte, 26

cabaret entertainment, 69, 70, 116
Cabinet of Dr. Caligari, The (Wiene, 1919), 150n25
Cable Soho, 159n49
Café Iguana, 44
Callas, Maria, 75, 77, 78, 87
Canyon Cinema (San Francisco), 110
"Capitalism of Lotusland" (Smith, 1978), 97–98
Captured: A Film/Video History of the Lower East Side (Patterson, ed., 2005), 2
Carr, C., 41, 59–60, 61, 78, 95, 117, 119
CBGB, 43, 44
censorship, 3, 23, 111
Chang in a Void Moon (Jesurun), 68, 69, 84
Charas New Assembly Theater, 60
Charles Theater, 53
Chase, Anthony, 18, 35, 68, 73; on clubs as "rowdy spaces," 75; collaborations with Kelly, 74, 81, 150n25
Chelsea Girls (Warhol, 1966), 54
Chien andalou, Un (Buñuel and Dalí, 1929), 8
Christmas on Earth (Rubin, 1963), 54
CineAction! (Canadian magazine), 33, 39
Cinema 16 film society, 43
"Cinema Delimina, The" (Vanderbeek, 1961), 52
Cinema of Transgression (BFI VHS compilation, 2000), 33, 124, 142n54
Cinema of Transgression (CoT), 4, 14, 45; "afterlife formats" of, 104; BFI videotape release of, 33, 101–102, *102*; birth as a movement, 10, 17; "body spectacle" of, 8; containment and, 7; genealogy of underground filmmaking and, 107;

historiography of, 23, 34, 56, 161n1; interdisciplinarity and, 15, 16; on the Internet and social media, 122–128; lack of scholarly research on, 2; as male-dominated underground movement, 3; marketed and promoted by Zedd, 33; as neo-underground movement, 54; as shape-shifting phenomenon, 121; spillover of, 17, 114, 119, 129–130
"Cinema of Transgression, The: Where Are They Now?" (Delembard), 3
Cinema of Transgression, Vol. I, The (Zedd, videocassette compilation, 1985), 19, 31, 122, 127
"Cinema of Transgression Manifesto" (Zedd, 1985), 1, 9, 18, 56, 67, 108; birth of a movement and, 28–34; historiography of CoT and, 23, 27–28; KW exhibition (2012) and, 156n1; *Underground Film Bulletin* (UFB) and, 113
Clarke, Shirley, 32
Climbing: The East Village (Hal Bromm Gallery, 1984), 47–48
Club 8BC, 41, 44, 48, 60, 71, 147n67
Club 57 (St. Mark's Place), 10, 29, 44, 58, 116–117, 119
Club 57: Film, Performance, and Art in the East Village, 1978–1983 (MoMA exhibition, 2017), 24, 116
Club Chandelier, 44, 58, 70, 96, 116, 147n67, 153n71
club culture, 15, 41
Cobra (Zorn, 1984), 89
Cocktails with Jack (Parnes, 1983), 96
Colacello, Bob, 51
Coleman, Joe, 27, 42, 56, 68
Collaborative Projects, Inc. (Colab), 105, 115
Collective for Living Cinema, 32, 44, 61, 64, 82
Color of Pomegranates, The (Parajanov, 1969), 127
Community Film Workshop, 159n53
Conboy, Cornelius, 71, 147n67
Connoisseur Video (BFI), 101
conservatism, political, 9
constructivism, 13
Consume and Die/Generation Z (Zedd and Zyklon Beatles), 127
containment, 7, 10, 14, 28, 106; centrality to history of Cinema of Transgression, 28; dialectical relationship with spilling, 4, 14, 17, 48, 57, 103, 113, 128; "Downtown" label and, 67, 113; festival format and, 64; formatting practices and, 104; geographical boundaries of scenes and, 14; video distribution and, 113
Cooper, Dennis, 35
copy machines, zine circulation and, 50
Cornella: The Story of a Burning Bush (Pfahler, 1985), 149n2, 156n1
Cortez, Diego, 47
Cramps, the, 115
cross-dressing, 79
Crystal, Coco, 115
Cukor, George, 89
cultural studies, 16
Cyber-Psycho's A.O.D., 31

Dadaism, 30, 33, 71
DAF (band), 65
Dagmar Onassis Story, The (Kelly and Chase, 1984), 18, 73–81, 97; *Dagmar Poisoned the Pizza* as alternative title, 77; set design for, 74–75, 74; video documentation of, 74
Dailymotion, 122
dance, 3, 71
Dancenoise, 11, 70, 81, 150n7
Danceteria, 24, 44, 58, 96, 116
Danto, Arthur C., 22
Darinka, 44, 48
Davidovich, Jaime, 115
David Wojnarowicz Photography and Film 1978–1992 (KW exhibition, 2019), 27
Death, Donna, 51, 88, 146n36, 153n71
Deathtrip Films, 112, 139n6
Deathtripping: The Cinema of Transgression (Sargeant, 1995), 2, 55
Deathtrip Vol. 1 and *Vol. 2* (Kern compilations, 1993), 112
Dee Dee Lux character, 8, 136n24
Deepwell, Katy, 142n46
De Kosnik, Abigail, 39, 123, 127
DeLanda, Manuel, 30, 139n6, 141n27, 156n3; Anthology Film Archives and, 147n53; drawings by, 56; films shown in Germany, 148n90; NYFFD and, 62; private archive of, 35; at School of Visual Arts, 42; Zedd's CoT manifesto and, 54, 108
Delembard, Cricket, 3

178 • Index

Deleuze, Gilles, 96, 138n54
De Rosa, Miriam, 15
Derrida, Jacques, 37, 39, 62, 142n57, 148n74
Desperate Teenage Love Dolls (Markey, 1984), 46
de Valck, Marijke, 63
Devil's in the Dish (Andres, 1986), 147n63
Diary of a Somnambulist (Kelly, 1986), 150n25
Dick, Vivienne, 44, 92, 149n2, 154n85
digital media, 15, 19, 104
dilettantism, productive, 13–14
Dinsmore-Tuli, Uma, 105–106
Direct Art Ltd., 30
Dirty (Hughes-Freeland and Lee, 1993), 8
disciplinarity, 12
disorder, 5, 6, 7, 9
distribution, 16, 19, 111
"disturbation," art of, 22
DIY aesthetic, 1, 21, 51, 130
DNA (band), 115
Documenta exhibition (Kassel, Germany), 9, 26
Downtown Collection, Fales Library (New York University), 12, 24, 34–40, 99; *Underground Film Bulletin* (UFB) in, 49; Wojnarowicz papers at, 161n91; Zedd materials in, 36–39, 50, 123
Downtown Community TV, 159n53
Downtown Show, The (Grey Art Gallery exhibition, 2006), 24
drag scene, 44, 70, 78
Drawing Center, 96
drugs, 3, 46, 130
Duchamp, Marcel, 53
Duffy, Brooke Erin, 7
Dumbfucker (zine), 110
Duncombe, Stephen, 51
durational works, 71
DVD bonus material, 17, 83
DVDs, 112, 122

East Village, 10, 22, 66, 128; art galleries, 47; Berlin compared to, 27; club culture in, 41, 44–46; as internationally recognized scene, 18; making and breaking of scene in, 42–48. *See also* Lower East Side; New York Downtown scenes
East Village, The (Anna Friebe Gallery, Cologne, Germany, 1984), 145n25
East Village Artists (Virginia Museum of Fine Art, 1984), 145n25
East Village Scene show (Philadelphia, 1984), 145n25
East Village USA (New Museum exhibition, 2004–2005), 24, 139n11, 141n27
East Village USA Film Festival, 141n27
eBay, CoT DVDs sold on, 122
Eichelberger, James Roy, 79
Eichhorn, Kate, 14, 50
80WSE gallery (New York University), 97–98
Electra Elf: The Beginning (Zedd, 2005), 120
Electronic Arts Intermix (EAI), 111, 159n53
Elf Panties: The Movie (Zedd, 2001), 120
Elsaesser, Thomas, 148n74
End of Cinema?, The: A Medium in Crisis in the Digital Age (Gaudreault and Marion, 2015), 14
Eros, Bradley, 30, 65, 141n27; Anthology Film Archives and, 147n53; named in Zedd's CoT manifesto, 108; private archive of, 35
Erotic Psyche, 62, 65, 148n90, 156n3. *See also* Mare, Aline
Erotisme, L' (Bataille, 1957), 136n23
Essa Distribution (Husum, Germany), 112
ETC/Metro Access (cable TV), 115
event, festival as, 62, 148n74
Evil Cameraman, The (Kern, 1986–1990), 8, 156n1
EVOL (Sonic Youth album, 1986), 51
Exotic Dreams (Parnes, 1982–1989), 96
Expanded Cinema Performance (Andres, 1989), 147n63
Expérience intérieure, L' (Bataille, 1943), 136n23
Exploding Plastic Inevitable (Warhol), 3, 94
exploitation genre, 8, 111
Expressionism, German, 74
EYE (*East Village Eye*), 32, 46, 48, 55, 67, 147n67
EZTV, 108, 109, 157n26

Facebook, 122
Factory (Warhol), 13
fan fiction, 17
fan forums, 15
fashion shows, 12

Fear of Disclosure: Psycho-Social Implications of HIV Revelation (Wojnarowicz and Zwickler, 1989), 11–12
Fehlfarben (band), 65
feminists, 16, 63, 142n46; Black feminists, 6; feminist theater, 88; Zedd's films protested by, 113
festival programs, 16
film: death of cinema, 14; entanglement with other media, 15–16; "expanded cinema," 71–72; liveness of, 72, 83; performance in spill-over connection to, 71, 73, 95, 99–100; performative nature of, 72. *See also* Super 8 films/filmmaking
film, 16 mm, 22, 52; *Bubble People* in, 88, 95; cameras, 66, 92, 94; divide with Super 8 filmmakers, 66; as format of choice among 1960s avant-garde filmmakers, 110; transferred to video, 103; of Zedd, 82
film, experimental, 8, 52, 79, 100, 107, 121; institutionalized avant-garde and, 2; as part of emergent counter-culture, 107
film and media studies, 5, 14, 15, 16–17, 130
Film Comment, 32, 55, 58
film festivals, 58, 63
Filmhaus (Cologne, Germany), 65
Filminstitut (Düsseldorf, Germany), 65
Film Journal, 43
Film-Maker's Cinematheque, 43
Film-Maker's Cooperative, 43, 147n53
film posters, 16, 127
Film Society of Lincoln Center, 58
Film Threat Video (Los Angeles), 112, 158n40
Film Threat zine, 50, 158n40
Fingered (Kern, 1986), 28, 51, 66–67, 109, 154n85
Finley, Karen, 11, 35, 149n2; *Bad Music Videos* at Limelight (1986) hosted by, 117, *118*, 119; live performance and, 68
Fisher, Ellen, 62
Flaming Creatures (Smith, 1963), 53–54, 83, 111
fluidity, 5, 7, 17
Fluxus, 13
Foreman, Richard, 89
forgetting, 39–40
Foster, Hal, 12
Foucault, Michel, 9, 12, 35
Fox, Dan, 24
Frank, Robert, 32
Franklin Furnace, 159n49

From Betamax to Blockbuster: Video Stores and the Invention of Movies on Video (Greenberg), 105
Fun Gallery, 48
Futurism, 33

Galietti, Ivan, 66, 88
galleries, 23, 24, 46, 47, 69, 144n12; archives of, 35; in Berlin, 25, 26; East Village, 47, 48; gentrification and, 10; graffiti art in, 145n25; limited-edition model of commercial galleries, 111; performance in, 69
Gamba, Gia, 93
Game Pieces (Zorn), 89
Gattra, Dennis, 147n67
Gaudreault, André, 14
gay and lesbian communities, 63
Geek Maggot Bingo (Zedd, 1983), 61, 82, 93, 146n36, 153n71; DVD copies of, 127; *Electra Elf* compared with, 121
gender, 7, 71, 78
genres, 8, 37
gentrification, 18, 26, 35, 144n5
Gentrification of the Mind, The: Witness to a Lost Imagination (Schulman), 10
Goldsmith, Kenneth, 123, 124–125
Goodbye 42nd Street (Kern, 1983), 43, 61
Goosebumps teen horror novels (Stine), 21
Go to Hell (Zedd and Rutsala, 1986), 146n36, 156n3
graffiti art, 9, 10, 12, 47, 145n25
Gray, Jonathan, 17, 82, 83
Greater New York (MoMA PS1 exhibition, 2015–2016), 24
Greenberg, Joshua M., 105
Guattari, Félix, 138n54
Guérillère Talks (Dick, 1978), 154n85
Gumbs, Alexis Pauline, 6

Hagan, John, 69–70
Halberstam, Jack, 23
Hal Bromm Gallery, 47
Hamm-Fürhölter, Uwe, 112, 158n43
Haneke, Michael, 8
happenings, 12, 59, 81, 125
Haring, Keith, 9–10
Harmful or Fatal If Swallowed (DeLanda, 1982), 149n2
Harris, Verne, 39
Haslett, Toby, 35, 36

Hathaway, Hattie (drag persona of Butterick), 79, 126
Haupts, Tobias, 104–105
Hawkins, Joan, 45
Haxan Films (France), 112
Hediger, Vinzenz, 15
Hell, Richard, 35, 44, 46, 51, 146n36
Heroin (Wojnarowicz, ca. 1981), 125, 126
Heroin Addict (zine), 110
heterosexuality, 11, 87
Hilderbrand, Lucas, 24, 125
History of the Avant-Garde, A (BFI home video series), 33, 101, *102*, 124
HIV. See AIDS/HIV crisis
Hoberman, J., 53–54, 108, 109
Hohauser, William, 114–115
Hollywood cinema, 53, 56, 79, 98, 103, 110
"Hommage à Maria Callas" (Bachmann), 81
homosexuality, 11
horror genre, 93, 111
Hotel Amazon, 149n94
Hughes, Fred, 51
Hughes, Holly, 44, 70
Hughes-Freeland, Tessa, 8, 18, 31, 32, 46, 141n27; analog films transferred to video, 105; Anthology Film Archives and, 147n53; on *The Dagmar Onassis Story*, 73; films shown in Germany, 148n90; as founder/curator of NYFFD, 58, 60, 63; private archive of, 35; Pyramid Club and, 44; UbuWeb and, 124; *Underground Film Bulletin* (UFB) and, 49
Hujar, Peter, 140n24
Hultberg, Jesse, 125–126
Hüser, Rembert, 15, 16

I, a Man (Warhol, 1967), 94
If I Can't Dance You Can Keep Your Revolution (Crystal, 1977), 115
Ilic, Dragan, 62
Inauguration of the Pleasure Dome (Anger, 1954), 54
indisciplinarity, 12–14, 45, 100
Inner Tube (Tschinkel, 1974–1984), 115
Inside the East Village (André Emmerich Gallery, Zurich, 1984), 145n25
Instagram, 122
Institute for Art and Urban Resources (IAUR), 26
interdisciplinarity, 5, 13

intermediality, 5
Internal Digging (KW exhibition, 2007), 27
Interview (*INTER/View*) magazine, 51, 52, 115
Introduction to the American Underground Film, An (Renan, 1967), 146n45
Iobst, Anne, 11, 70
Irwin, John, 41
Ism Ism (DeLanda), 156n3

Jack Smith: Normal Love (MoMA PS1 exhibition, 2012), 27
Jacobs, Ken, 155n94
James Chance and the Contortions, 44
Jason, Jessica, 82
Jeriko, Orion (alter ego of Nick Zedd), 29, 30, 48, 54, 103
Jesurun, John, 68, 69, 84
Johnson, Dominic, 90
Jonas, Joan, 111
Jones, Amelia, 82–83
Jones, Caroline A., 26
Jones, M. Henry, 42, 124, 148n90, 156n1
Judgement Day (DeLanda, 1983), 147n52, 156n3

Kane, Daniel, 49
Kelly, John, 18, 35, 68, 81, 86; *Bad Music Videos* and, 117; as performer in *The Dagmar Onassis Story*, 75–78; Pyramid Club and, 73–74, 151n39; "traditional drag craft" of, 78
Kenneth Anger (MoMA PS1 exhibition, 2009), 27
Kern, Richard, 8, 11, 92, 141n27, 156n3; Anthology Film Archives and, 147n53; films shown in Germany, 148n90; on KW exhibition (2012), 24, 27; photographs by, 56; private archive of, 35; UbuWeb and, 123; *Underground Film Bulletin* (UFB) and, 49; as "underground invisible," 30; on unique allure of New York City, 43; video distribution and, 111–112, 139n6; Zedd's CoT manifesto and, 54, 108
Kern, Richard, films of: *The Evil Cameraman* (1986–1990), 8, 156n1; *Fingered* (1986), 28, 51, 66–67, 109, 149n2, 154n85; *Goodbye 42nd Street* (1983), 43, 61; *King of Sex* (1986), 156n3; *The Manhattan Love Suicides* (1985), 112; *Nazi* (1991), 112;

The Right Side of My Brain (1985), 110, 149n2, 154n85; *Sewing Circle* (1992), 149n2; *Submit to Me* (1986), 8, 51, 61, 147n52, 154n85; *Submit to Me Now* (1987), 51, 61–62, 147n52, 154n85; *Thrust in Me* (with Zedd, 1985), 62; *You Killed Me First* (1985), 51, 149n2, 156n3; *Zombie Hunger 1* and *2* (1984), 61
Kim's Video and Music, 124–125, 161n86
King of Sex (Kern, 1986), 156n3
Kino im KOMM (Nuremberg, Germany), 112–113
Kino Lichtwerk (Bielefeld, Germany), 65
Kiss Me Goodbye (Zedd, 1987), 31
Kitchen, The, 32, 75, 144n12, 159n49
Klemann, Richard, 30, 62, 108, 156n3
Klemm, Donna, 112
Kolesch, Doris, 80
Kommunales Kino (Hanover, Germany), 65
Kostelanetz, Richard, 72–73, 150n14
Krämer, Sybille, 80
Kuchar, George, 54, 55–56
Kuchar, Mike, 55–56
KW Institute for Contemporary Art (Berlin), 2, 3, 21, 25–26, 27, 33

La Bruce, Bruce, 39
La Mama Experimental Theatre Club, 75, 144n12
Lankton, Greer, 8, 62, 136n24
Larkin, Brian, 125
Law, John, 4–5
Lawrence, Tim, 12, 22
Lee, Annabel, 8
Legere, Phoebe, 51, 68, 146n36; in *Bubble People*, 88, 90, 93; in *Me Minus You*, 82, 85, 152n50; in *Totem of the Depraved*, 94–95
Le Grice, Malcolm, 53
Lepecki, André, 96
Leslie, Alfred, 32
Let's Make Love (Cukor, 1960), 89, 96
Liberty's Booty (Dick, 1980), 154n85
Lichtenstein, Roy, 48
Life and Death on the New York Dance Floor, 1980–1983 (Lawrence, 2016), 12
Like Dawn to Dusk (Dick, 1983), 154n85
Limbo Lounge, 44, 48, 77; Celluloid Cantina series, 58; New York Film Festival Downtown at, 96; NYFFD and, 57–58, 60

Limelight club, 117, *118*
Lincoln Center, 150n7
lip-synching, 70, 78, 80
LIVE FILM! JACK SMITH! Five Flaming Days in a Rented World festival (HAU and Arsenal, Berlin, 2009), 96
Live! Show, The (Davidovich, 1979–1984), 115
Llik Your Idols (Bosio documentary, 2007), 2, 3
Loisada, 42
Loisada Lusts (Troyano and Parnes, 1985), 65
"Loisaida Talking Pictures" (Carr, 1985), 95
Loist, Skadi, 63
London Film-Makers' Co-op (LFMC), 53, 110
London Video Arts (LVA), 111
"Long Live the Cinema of Transgression" (Zedd, 1985), 29–30, 32, 55
Lord of the Cockrings (Zedd, 2002), 120, 122
"Losing the Form in Darkness" (Wojnarowicz), 12
Love, Heather, 16
Love Club, 117
Lower East Side, 1, 22, 28; attractive image of, 41; gentrification of, 4
Lower East Side Troll Museum, 121
Lucid Possession (Andres, Meyers, Moore, 1988), 147n63
Ludlam, Charles, 79, 151n37
Lunch, Lydia, 11, 44, 51, 86; acting roles, 154n85; *Bad Music Videos* and, 117; live performance and, 68; performances in films, 146n36, 149n2; recognizable persona of, 92; *Underground Film Bulletin* (UFB) and, 49
Lung Leg (Elizabeth Carr), 51, 52, 56, 62, 112, 156n3
Lyon, Janet, 30, 31

MacKenzie, Scott, 32
Magnetic Fields, The [*Les Champs Magnétiques*] (Breton and Soupault, 1919), 6
Magnuson, Ann, 24, 119
Malaria (band), 65
Mal Seh'n (Frankfurt, Germany), 65
Manhattan Cable Television, 159n49
Manhattan Love Suicides, The (Kern, 1985), 112
Manhattan Neighborhood Network (MNN), 114, 119–120, 160n67
manifesto form, 32, 142n46

Marchessault, Janine, 41
Mare, Aline, 30, 65, 108. *See also* Erotic Psyche
Mario Banana I and *II* (Warhol, 1964), 86
Marion, Philippe, 14
Maschmann, Anette, 65
Matturri, John, 98–99
Max's Kansas City, 29, 43, 44, 52
Mbembe, Achille, 35, 37
McCormick, Carlo, 46, 48, 117, *118*, 119
McGillen, Petra, 106
Mead, Taylor, 121
Mekas, Jonas, 32, 53, 54, 55, 111
Mele, Christopher, 47
Mellencamp, Patricia, 3, 33
Me Minus You (Zedd, 1985), 18, 68, 81–88, 93; as "expanded cinema" performance, 82, 152n50; as film made by other means, 82, 152n52
memory, 39–40
Menotti, Gabriel, 72
merchandise, 17
"messy methods," 4
Midnight Movies (Hoberman and Rosenbaum, 1983), 54
Mild Seven: The Cowboy Stories (Pfahler, ca. 1986), 149n2
Millennium Film Workshop Inc., 32, 43, 44, 45, 54
Miller, Reverend Jen, 120, 121
Mitchell, Eric, 65
MoMA (Museum of Modern Art), 25, 26, 75; *Club 57* exhibition (2017), 24, 116; film and video library, 139n6; PS1 Contemporary Art Center, 25, 26, 27, 32, 47
Mommy, Mommy, Where's My Brain? (Moritsugu, 1986), 156n1
Mona Lisa (Kelly and Chase, 1983), 74
Montez, María, 79, 87
morality, 1, 3, 4, 9, 28, 30, 32, 55
Moran, Brian, 60, 61
Moritsugu, Jon, 62, 124, 145n28, 156n1
MP4s, 125
MPI Home Video, 109
Mubi streaming site, 126
Mudd Club, 43, 47, 116
Mueller, Cookie, 46
Mühl, Otto, 49
Mulroney, Lucy, 49
multidisciplinarity, 5

multimediality, 5
Muñoz, José Esteban, 37, 38, 97
music, 44, 71, 96
Music Video Distribution (MVD), 112
Mutable Fire (Erotic Psyche, 1984), 156n3
M/W/F Video Club, 105

Nares, James, 115
Nazi (Kern, 1991), 112
New American Cinema, 32, 54, 110
New American Filmmakers series (Whitney Museum), 43
New Cinema, 43, 44
Newman, Michael Z., 116, 156n7
New York, New Music 1980–1986 (Museum of the City of New York exhibition), 24
New York Downtown scenes (1970s and 1980s), 3, 9; bleak state of New York City and, 22; club scene, 73; collaborative practice in, 13; cultural climate and, 9–10; definition of "scene," 14; indisciplinary nature of, 18; marginalization within, 64; TV formats and culture in, 114–121, *118*. *See also* East Village; Lower East Side
New York Film Festival, 58
New York Film Festival Downtown. *See* NYFFD
New York Film-Makers' Cooperative, 110, 111
New York Times, 10, 48
New York University, bohemia destroyed by, 35–36
Nichols, Bill, 63
"Nick Zedd" (Zedd), 2
Nietzsche, Friedrich, 9
N——Night (Wolfe), 156n3
nightclubs, 3, 23, 29, 144n12
Noé, Gaspar, 8
Nomi, Klaus, 115
Norman, Michael, 79
nostalgia, 14, 116
Notion of Expenditure, The (Bataille, 1933), 136n23
No Wave Cinema, 2, 43
No Wave music, 44, 115
NYFFD (New York Film Festival Downtown), 18, 48, 57–67, 77, 96, 113; flyers for, *58*; founders of, 58, 59; German tour, 65–67, 149n94; initiation of (1984), 42,

44; Rafik Film and Video store and, 146n31; sponsors of, 60, 147n67
Nymphomania (Hughes-Freeland and Adams, 1993), 156n1

O'Brien, Glenn, 115
Offenders, The (Beth and Scott B, 1980), 154n85
Olin, Benjamin, 115–116
opera, 75–76, 77, 81
O-P Screen, 29, 146n31
"Other Cinema, The" (Taubin, 1979), 29
Overn, Michael, 35, 117, 119

Packer, Jeremy, 7
painting, 11, 71
Parajanov, Sergei, 127
paratexts, 17, 82, 83
Parente, Leticia, 111
Paris, Texas (Wenders, 1984), 57
Parnes, Uzi, 44, 65, 88, 96–97, 153n71, 155n94
Pass the Blutwurst, Bitte (Kelly, 1984), 150n25
Patterson, Clayton, 2
Penetration Films, 109, 139n6
Peppermint Lounge, 44, 116
performance, 3, 11, 15, 44; cross-dressing, 79; embodiment of multiple identities, 80; film in spill-over connection to, 71, 73, 95, 99–100; "mixed means," 72–73; recognized as art form in itself, 69; spilling beyond art into everyday life, 70–71; in *You Killed Me First* exhibition, 21
performativity, 78, 81, 83, 144n3
Performing Garage, The, 144n12
Pfahler, Kembra, 51, 105, 139n6, 141n27; live performance and, 68; performances by, 56; in Zedd films, 92, 146n36
Pfeffer, Susanne, 21, 140n24
Phelan, Peggy, 72
philosophy, 16
photography, 11
Picabia, Francis, 150n14
"Pissing on the Cinema of Transgression" (Bruce, 1986), 33, 39
Place, Pat, 44
Place to Beware, A (Schmidlapp, 1982–1988), 59
Plaster Foundation, The, 98
Poe, Amos, 44, 115
Police State (Zedd, 1987), 31, 146n36, 156n1

Pompeii: New York Pt. I: Pier Caresses (Galietti, 1982), 66
Ponzos Masterwork (Spencer), 50
pornography, 8, 103, 109, 111
post-punk music, 3, 9, 65, 115
primitivism, 54, 55
private collections, 15
provocation, 9, 21
Pryor, Eric (aka Rick Strange), 82, 84, 87, 152n50
PUS (Spencer), 50
Pyramid Club, 44, 64, 69–70, 82; *The Dagmar Onassis Story* performed at, 73–81; events structured by party atmosphere, 116; flyer for, 45; indisciplinarity and, 45; *Me Minus You* performed at, 87

Queer Art of Failure, The (Halberstam, 2011), 23
"Queer Messes" (Love), 16
queer scholars, 16

Rabinovitz, Lauren, 32
Rabkin, Gerald, 79
Radium Films (Sweden), 112
Rafik (film/video/audiotape store), 50, 146n31, 147n67
randomness, 5, 88
Raw Nerves. A Lacanian Thriller (DeLanda, 1979), 149n2
Ray, Man, 53, 101, 107
Reagan, Ronald, 4, 9
real estate development, 47
Recycling Atlantis (Parnes/Troyano/Tropicana, 2014), 97, 99
Reekie, Duncan, 2, 52, 107
reformatting, 19, 124–125
Rehearsal for the Destruction of Atlantis (Smith, 1965), 97, 155n103
Relâche (Picabia, 1924), 150n14
Renan, Sheldon, 146n45
rent strikes, 49
Reza Abdoh (MoMA PS1, 2018, and KW exhibition, 2019), 27
rhizome, analogy of, 138n54
Rhoda in Potatoland (Foreman, 1976), 89
Rice, Bill, 61, 86
Richardson, James, 93
Richter, Hans, 34, 101, 107

Ridiculous Theatre, 79, 151n37
Right Side of My Brain, The (Kern, 1985), 110, 149n2, 154n85
Rivera, René (aka Mario Montez), 79, 86, 87
Rockets Redglare, 44, 51, 146n36
Rolling Stone magazine, 51
Rosenbach, Ulrike, 111
Rosenbaum, Jonathan, 53–54
Rosenberg, Karen, 149n96
Rosler, Martha, 111
Rossi, Jeri Cain, 124, 149n2, 156n1
Rubin, Barbara, 54

Sanborn, Keith, 64, 65
Sargeant, Jack, 2, 3, 55–56, 107
Scemama, Marion, 126
scene, concept of, 9, 14
Schaffer, Johanna, 6
Schiele, Egon, 150n25
Schmidlapp, David, 59
Schneider, Rebecca, 72, 88
Schönherr, Johannes, 112–113
School of Shame (Zedd, 1984), 154n85
School of Visual Arts (SVA), 42
Schulman, Sarah, 10
Schüttpelz, Erhard, 13–14, 95
Schweigen von Marcel Duchamp überbewertet, Das [The silence of Marcel Duchamp is overrated] (Beuys, 1964), 96
science fantasy genre, 8
Scotch Tape (Smith, 1959–1962), 155n94
Screen Tests (Warhol, 1964–1966), 92–93
Secret of Rented Island, The (Smith, 1976), 89, 91
Sewing Circle (Kern, 1992), 149n2
sex, 3, 9, 130
Sex and Guts zine, 50, 55
Sexton, Lucy, 11, 70
sexuality, 2, 9, 53, 55
Shamberg, Michael, 115
SHE (Zedd and Lunch), 61, 86, 87, 152n50
She Had Her Gun All Ready (Dick, 1978), 149n2, 154n85
Shithaus (Spencer), 50, 156n3
Siegel, Marc, 79
Silence of Marcel Duchamp, The (Troyano/Parnes/Zorn), 96
Simonland (Turner), 156n3
singularity, 7
Sink or Swim (Fun Gallery, 1984), 48

Sitney, P. Adams, 42–43, 155n94
Smith, Jack, 27, 35, 53, 54, 55, 100, 153n71; on actors and acting technique, 91, 154n82; in *Bubble People*, 88, 90; failure in artistic practices of, 90–91; on "live film," 83; loft performance tradition and, 98; rehearsal-like live performances of, 153n60; Ridiculous Theatre and, 151n37; Zorn and, 89
Smith, John, 145n28
Smith, Kiki, 62
Smith, Patti, 44
Snyder, Huck, 74, 150n25
Sohozat (comic and zine shop), 50
Soiree Piquante, 44
Somma, Andy, 59, 117
Sonic Youth, 51
Soul City (Jones, 1979), 156n1
soundtracks, 17, 96
Soupault, Philippe, 6
Spacely, John, 51
special effects, 22
Spencer, John, 50, 156n3
Spillers, Hortense, 6
spilling, notion of, 8, 12, 17, 80; concept of scene and, 14; dialectic of spilling and containment, 4, 14, 17, 48, 57, 103, 113, 128; film–performance relationship and, 19, 73, 81, 86, 100; "generic overspill," 8; interdisciplinarity and, 99–100; labels and, 42, 130; methodology and, 4–7; reformatting and, 124; television and, 116; transgression and, 9; video and, 103, 113
Spill: Scenes of Black Feminist Fugitivity (Gumbs, 2016), 6
splatter genre, 8
Sprinkle, Annie, 56, 121
squatting, 49
Stark Mele, Casandra, 2–3, 49, 51; films shown in Germany, 148n90; NYFFD and, 62; poems by, 56; in Zedd films, 146n36
Star Spangled to Death (Jacobs, 1957–1959), 155n94
Stein, Chris, 115
Stigmata (Beth B, 1991), 156n1
Stine, R. L., 21
striptease, 70
structuralism, 32
Studio Museum in Harlem, 75, 76, 77

Index • 185

Submit to Me (Kern, 1986), 8, 51, 61, 147n52, 154n85
Submit to Me Now (Kern, 1987), 51, 61–62, 147n52, 154n85
Subversion: The Definitive History of Underground Cinema (Reekie, 2007), 2
Suicide, A (Klemann, 1978), 156n3
Super 8 films/filmmaking, 3, 4, 22, 74; in Germany, 65; of Kern, 43; post-punk, 32; video and, 44, 103, 110–111, 122; of Wojnarowicz, 125–126, 161n91; of Zedd, 3, 85, 86
Surrealism, 6, 13, 24
Sussler, Betsy, 115

taboos, breaking of, 8, 9, 54, 55
Talking Heads, 44
Taubin, Amy, 29, 30, 42
Tavel, Ronald, 79
Taylor, Marvin J., 12, 37
technical mistakes, embrace of, 94–95, 155n94
Teenage Jesus and the Jerks, 44
television, 15, 17, 103, 114; circulation of CoT films on, 19; democratic potential of, 119; nostalgic club events and, 116–117, *118*, *119*; "post-television" culture, 119; public access cable television, 19, 104, 105, 114–115, 159nn47–48; video in relation to, 104, 156n7
Television (band), 44
Television-Nostomania! (Club 57 event), 116–117, *118*
theater, experimental, 3
Theatre of Mixed Means, 150n14
They Eat Scum (Zedd, 1979), 3, 29, 30, 86, 146n36, 153n71; on cable television, 115; DVD copies sold online, 122, 127; *Electra Elf* compared with, 121
Thirlwell, JG, 35, 117
37 Räume [37 Rooms] (KW exhibition, 1992), 26
3 Teens Kill 4 (post-punk band), 9, 125, 126
Thrust in Me (Zedd and Kern, 1985), 62, 85–86, 152n50
Thus Spake Zarathustra (Zedd, 2001), 120
Tödliche Doris, Die, 65
Totem of the Depraved (Troyano and Zedd, 1983), 8, 91–95, *92*, 145n28, 146n36
Town Called Tempest, A (Kuchar, 1963), 54
trailers, 17

transdisciplinarity, 5
transgression, 9, 28, 29, 129; articulated in *Underground Film Bulletin*, 55; transformation through, 30
Trap Door, The (Beth and Scott B, 1980), 153n71
Tropicana, Carmelita (Alina Troyano), 64, 70, 88, 97, 98
Troyano, Ela, 8, 18, 31, 39, 97, 100, 139n6; Club Chandelier and, 147n67, 153n71; on club culture in 1980s, 44–45; collaboration with Zorn, 89, 96, 154n75; film happenings of, 81; films shown in Germany, 148n90; as founder/curator of NYFFD, 58, 60, 63; interviewed in *Underground Film Bulletin*, 145n28; private archive of, 35; WOW Café Theatre and, 64
Trump Tower, 10
Tschinkel, Paul, 115
Turner, Amy, 61
Turner, Tommy, 30, 44, 61, 82, 139n6, 156n3; films shown in Germany, 148n90; in *Me Minus You*, 82; named in Zedd's CoT manifesto, 108
TV Party (ETC/Metro Access, 1978–1982), 115–116, 120
TVTV, 115
Twitter, 127
Tyler, Parker, 52, 53, 54, 55, 146n45

UbuWeb, 34, 123–125, 139n6
underground cinema, 2, 16, 18, 55
Underground Film: A Critical History (Tyler, 1969), 52–53
"Underground Film After Parker Tyler" (Mekas, 1969), 53
Underground Film Bulletin (UFB), 2, 10, 18, 19, 42; audience of, 50; borderline status of, 48–49; Cinema of Transgression and, 56, 113; collage of text and image in, 28, 49; community-building potential of, 49; films on tape advertised in, 108–110; *Interview* magazine compared with, 52; at juncture between artists' magazine and subcultural fanzine, 51; "The Late Ela Troyano" (1985), 145n28; *Me Minus You* performance recounted in, 82, 87; "The Most Hated Filmmaker in the World: John Spencer" (1987), 50; "Ten Greatest

Underground Film Bulletin (UFB) (cont.)
Underground Films of All Time by Orion Jeriko" (1987), 54, 56; transgression aesthetic and, 55; Zedd's writings in, 29–30
"unwatchable films," 8

Vaccaro, John, 79, 151n37
Valium Addict (zine), 110
Van Cook, Marguerite, 121
Vanderbeek, Stan, 52
VCR (videocassette recorder), 105
VHS tapes, 4, 16, 103, 110, 157n25; circulation of CoT films on, 19; expansion of CoT into transatlantic network, 113; mail-order distribution of, 23, 109–110, 111, 122
Vice magazine, 121, 122
video, 11, 15, 103, 105; home theater experience and, 105–106, 157n13; participatory potential of, 119; reconfiguration in 1970s, 104–106; storage and display of videotapes, 106, 157n16; television in relation to, 104, 156n7; women artists and, 111, 114
Village Voice, 32, 41, 43, 55; film critics of, 54, 108; Mekas's "Movie Journal" column, 53
Vimeo, 122
violence, 2, 8, 22, 61, 130, 161n1; of police, 3; of the state, 64; as transgression, 9, 129–130
visual art, 44
Vole Show (public access TV program), 114–115
Voluptuous Horror of Karen Black, 92
Von Trier, Lars, 8
Vortex (Beth and Scott B, 1982), 149n2, 154n85

Warhol, Andy, 3, 10; Factory of, 13; films of, 52, 54, 55, 79, 86, 121; *Interview* magazine and, 51, 52; short portrait films of, 92–93; "stroboscopic" jump cuts of, 94
War Is Menstrual Envy (Zedd, 1990–1992), 8, 92, 127, 146n36, 147n53, 149n2
Wasson, Haidee, 27
Waters, John, 55, 56, 127
Weigel, Sigrid, 81
Weirdo Video, 19, 103, 109, 139n6
Weltzien, Friedrich, 5
Wenders, Wim, 57

Werkstattkino (Munich), 65
What's Underground About Marshmallows (Smith, 1981), 97
Where Evil Dwells (Turner and Wojnarowicz, 1985), 149n2, 156n1
White Rabbit (Somma), 59
Whitney Museum, 43, 150n7
"Why I Left the Cinema of Transgression Behind, or Why It Left Me" (Stark Mele, 2005), 2
Wiene, Robert, 150n25
Wild World of Lydia Lunch, The (Zedd, 1983), 31, 86, 87, 146n36, 149n2, 154n85
Williams, Linda, 8
Wiseblood (JG Thirlwell), 117
Wojnarowicz, David, 11, 12–13, 139n6; as busboy at Peppermint Lounge, 44; as cult star, 61, 62; death of (1992), 140n24; KW exhibition (2019), 27; personal papers in Downtown Collection, 35, 38; "Sidewalk Begging" column in *EYE*, 46; Super 8 film projects of, 125–126, 161n91
Wolfe, Michael, 66, 156n3
Wooster Group, 153n71
Worm Movie (Lung Leg, 1985), 51, 156n3
WOW Café Theatre, 64

Xerox aesthetic, 28, 51, 101
Xerox art, 12

Yo, Yana, 65
Yokosbosky, Matthew, 2
You Killed Me First (Kern, 1985), 51, 149n2, 156n3
You Killed Me First: The Cinema of Transgression (exhibition, KW Institute for Contemporary Art, Berlin, 2012), 1, 3, 11, *21*, 67, 99, 101; description of, 20–21; exhibition brochure as zine, 28, *29*; framing of CoT as deviant countercultural movement, 23–24; Kern's visit to, 24, 27; as reenactment, 25; significance of title, 21–22; Zedd manifesto as introduction to exhibition, 34
Young Filmmakers, 159n53
YouTube, 122, 126

ZAT magazine, 33
Zedd, Nick, 1, 141n27; accused of misogyny, 39; autobiography of, 30, 32; BFI

compilation of CoT and, 107–108; birth name (James Harding), 36, 56; Cinema of Transgression launched by (1985), 10, 17, 18; death of (2022), 122; drag alter ego Nichole, 82, 85, 86, 153n65; "expanded cinema" and, 83–84; foray into television, 119; German tour (1990), 112–113; indisciplinary practice of, 37; at Kim's Video and Music, 161n86; "Long Live the Cinema of Transgression," 29–30, 32, 55; Mekas compared with, 55; "Nick Zedd," 2; notion of live film in work of, 81; NYFFD and, 60–61; personal material in Downtown Collection, 36–37, 38–39, 50; self-promotion of, 3; video distribution and, 111, 139n6; Weirdo Video business of, 103; on working with Troyano, 93. *See also* "Cinema of Transgression Manifesto"; Jeriko, Orion; *Underground Film Bulletin* (UFB)

Zedd, Nick, films of: *The Bogus Man* (1980), 7–8, 88, 93, 124, 125, 147n52, 156n3; *Geek Maggot Bingo* (1983), 62, 82, 93, 121, 146n36, 153n71; *Go to Hell* (with Rutsala, 1986), 146n36, 156n3; *Kiss Me Goodbye* (1987), 31; *Police State* (1987), 31, 146n36, 156n1; *School of Shame* (1984), 154n85; *Thrust in Me* (with Kern, 1985), 62, 85–86, 152n50; *Totem of the Depraved* (with Troyano, 1983), 8, 91–95, *92*, 145n28, 146n36; *War Is Menstrual Envy* (1990–1992), 8, 92, 127, 146n36, 147n53, 149n2; *The Wild World of Lydia Lunch* (1983), 31, 86, 87, 146n36, 149n2, 154n85. See also *Me Minus You*; *They Eat Scum*

Zedd, Nick, video work of: *The Adventures of Electra Elf* (2005–2008), 19, 114, 119–121, 122, 160n67; *Electra Elf: The Beginning* (2005), 120; *Elf Panties: The Movie* (2001), 120; *Lord of the Cockrings* (2002), 120, 122; *Thus Spake Zarathustra* (2001), 120

zines, 15, 16; collage style in, 49; of Kern, 35, 110, 142n58; punk, 51, 101

Zorn, John, 89, 96, 153n71

Zurbrugg, Nicholas, 152n50

Zwickler, Phil, 11

Zyklon Beatles (noise punk band), 127

About the Author

MARIE SOPHIE BECKMANN is a postdoctoral researcher and lecturer at the Institute for Art and Visual Culture at Carl von Ossietzky Universität of Oldenburg, Germany. In addition to her academic practice in film and media studies, she has worked as an independent curator in the fields of contemporary audiovisual art and performance.